THE SLAMMER

The Crisis in Canada's Prison System

ALSO BY KEVIN MARRON

Ritual Abuse
Witches, Pagans and Magic in the New Age
Apprenticed in Crime
Fatal Mistakes

THE SLAMMER

The Crisis in Canada's Prison System

Kevin Marron

Doubleday Canada Limited

Canadian Cataloguing in Publication Data

Marron, Kevin
   The slammer: the crisis in canada's prison system

Includes bibliographical references and index.
Hardcover ISBN 0-385-25534-9; paperback 0-385-25616-7

1. Prisons — Canada. 2. Prisoners — Canada —
Social conditions. I. Title.

HV9507.M37 1996   365'.971   C95-932394-5

Jacket design by Avril Orloff
Text design by Heidy Lawrance Associates
Printed and bound in the USA

Published in Canada by
Doubleday Canada Limited
105 Bond Street
Toronto, Ontario
M5B 1Y3

The vilest deeds like poison weeds,
Bloom well in prison-air;
It is only what is good in man
That wastes and withers there.

Oscar Wilde, *The Ballad of Reading Gaol*

CONTENTS

ACKNOWLEDGEMENTS

I would like to thank the prisoners and staff of the Correctional Service of Canada for the help and cooperation that I received while working on this book. It would be impossible to name all the individuals who provided me with valuable information and insight during the course of my cross-country tour of prisons and other correctional facilities. I will mention only that John Vandoremalen, director of public relations for the correctional service, took great trouble to set up my initial contacts, and kept me supplied with reams of reports and background information. Almost everywhere I went, I was treated with courtesy, shown whatever I asked to see and permitted to speak freely with prisoners and staff. I received similar cooperation from staff and members of the National Parole Board. I would particularly like to thank Carol Sparling, Ontario regional communications and training coordinator, for the time she spent educating me about parole board activities and arranging for me to attend hearings.

Psychiatrist Neil Conacher was one of many professionals working in the prison system who provided me with research material and expert opinions. Graham Stewart of the John Howard Society of Ontario, Clare Culhane, Ruth Morris, Dave Gustafson and Jim Campbell were among the many community prison activists who assisted me. Some ex-offenders whom I will not name provided me with very valuable insights. Bob Boucher of the Public Service Alliance of Canada and many representatives of the Union of Solicitor General Employees were also most helpful.

A short-term project and travel grant from the Canada Council assisted greatly in financing my research. I would like to point out that it is particularly difficult to do research of this nature in Canada because the size of the country makes travel and phone calls prohibitively expensive. In this respect, as in many others, the Canada Council plays a vital role in helping to offset the disadvantages faced by writers and other artists attempting to survive in the Canadian marketplace.

I would like to thank Glenys Elliott for the wonderful hospitality that she extended to me while I was doing my research in Kingston, as well as for the help that she gave me in making contact with various people in the prison system. Nairn Galvin provided me with a valuable perspective on issues relating to women in the prison system. Many other friends helped me in numerous ways, especially my partner Susan Goodman who read early drafts of my manuscripts, making many insightful suggestions and identifying boring parts by falling asleep.

My agent Dean Cooke was, as always, energetic and resourceful in supporting this project. I would like to thank Malcolm Lester for suggesting the title for the book. Editor Jennifer Glossop did deft and meticulous work on the manuscript, in addition to providing creative suggestions about how to organize my material. It was again a pleasure to work with people at Doubleday and I would like to thank everyone involved in producing this book, especially John Pearce, Alison Maclean, Kathryn Exner and Maggie Reeves.

INTRODUCTION

The problems of crime and punishment have been of interest and concern to me throughout my career as a journalist and author. As a newspaper reporter, covering courts on a regular basis, I watched hundreds of offenders led away to jail. Most of the cases I covered involved serious crimes, many of them ugly and vicious. An almost palpable feeling of relief would sometimes run through the courtroom as one of these dangerous individuals received an apparently well-deserved punishment. It was more common, however, for onlookers to express uneasiness and scepticism, as they questioned how soon the offenders would be released on parole and whether the prison sentence would rehabilitate them or deter others.

One seldom, if ever, heard about what happened to the prisoners after they were escorted out of the courtroom, and I often wondered about it. Even though I felt quite familiar with the workings of most aspects of the criminal justice system, my hazy knowledge of the prison system was based entirely on hearsay and myth. It scarcely comforted me to learn that few of the judges imposing the sentences knew much more about prisons than I did.

In researching previous books on youth crime and on the victims' group CAVEAT, I interviewed young people whose only ambition was to go to adult jail, and I talked to crime victims who believed that the prison system was failing to protect society. This book is the product of my attempt to look beyond the myth, the hearsay and false expectations that cloud our view of the prison system and to find out for myself what happens behind prison walls.

This book is based on my personal observations as well as interviews with hundreds of offenders and staff at federal prisons, treatment centres and parole offices in eight provinces. During the two years that I worked on the book, I also attended parole hearings and met with victims of crime. I canvassed the views of critics of the prison system and examined every report, study or survey that I could find.

I decided to focus on the federal prison system, which deals with the more serious and potentially dangerous offenders sentenced to prison terms of two years or more. Federal prisons house the convicts whom society has most reason to fear, and it is the system that we most rely on to keep everyone safe. It would be too confusing, for readers and for myself, if I also discussed the issues and problems involved in the various provincial prison systems, which handle accused people incarcerated while awaiting trial and offenders sentenced to less than two years.

In considering federal prisons and prisoners, I felt it important to examine the National Parole Board and the process by which offenders are released into the community. I also looked at what happens after offenders are released, how they are supervised, what problems they encounter in the community and what help they receive.

When I interviewed prisoners and ex-offenders, I promised that I would not use their names. I did this because I wanted to have frank and open discussions with a large number of prisoners, including sex offenders and others in vulnerable positions within the jails. To use prisoners' names, I would have had to secure written releases. The bureaucratic process involved in obtaining releases would probably have scared away many informants and may well have made staff members less cooperative in facilitating the interviews, most of which did in fact take place without the presence of any staff. Where I identify prisoners only by their first names in this book, these are invariably pseudonyms. In some cases I also changed details, such as the prisoner's province of origin, in order to avoid publishing information that would identify them. When I do not have to conceal the identity of the person interviewed, I use his or her full name.

Some prison staff gave me sensitive information or made forthright statements that could have a detrimental impact on their careers if they were identified. In such circumstances, I have chosen not to name the source of the quote or piece of information, as I did not want to make anyone pay for being frank with me or give the more mealy-mouthed reason to congratulate themselves.

Like any closed world, the prison system tends to use a lot of acronyms and initials. I try to avoid these where possible, but I have made some exceptions. The Correctional Service of Canada is the current name for the service that handles prisoners in federal prisons and supervises them in the community while they are on parole or other forms of early release. It is commonly known by the initials CSC, and I sometimes use this abbreviation in order to avoid continually repeating such a cumbersome title. I also sometimes use initials for the Special Handling Units, known as SHUs, the prisons within the prison system for those who commit serious offences while they are in jail.

According to official definitions, all federal correctional facilities are called "penitentiaries," and the word "jail" denotes a provincially run detention centre for prisoners awaiting trial. But prisoners and staff commonly refer to all prisons, including federal penitentiaries, as jails, and I have adopted that common usage. For the sake of variety and, sometimes, because it seemed appropriate in the context, I use all these words as well as the official euphemisms "institution" and "correctional facility."

Officially, prisoners are called "inmates," but they often object to that word and prefer "prisoners," "offenders" or the more old-fashioned word "convict," often shortened to "con." Again, I will use all these words at different times.

After doing a lot of groundwork by cultivating contacts and writing lengthy letters of introduction to senior officials, I found that the Correctional Service of Canada was very cooperative in giving me access to its institutions and staff. Once I got inside the prisons, I encountered many individuals who were most willing to help because they strongly believed that the public should be better informed about prison life. As an outsider, I was usually able to talk on an even footing with administrators, prisoners and guards. Together, they helped me put together a composite picture of Canada's federal correctional system.

I had a unique opportunity to explore a bizarrely distorted looking-glass world that exists on the other side of the law. It was sometimes shocking and always unsettling, a world where horror is routine and cruelty commonplace. I offer no apologies for including some disturbing details and occasionally recording the obscenities that punctuated the speech of prisoners and guards alike. I hope that this book will convey some of the tension and energy of the aberrant culture of prisons, as well as their complex and perplexing realities.

1

LOSING FAITH
IN PRISONS

For those seeking simple solutions to the confusing problems of modern society, there is much to be said for the idea of sweeping criminals off the streets, locking them up and letting them rot in jail. But it does not seem to occur to people who glibly air such views that in an age of blue boxes we do not even treat our garbage like that.

This is a book about society's rejects and the prisons that house Canada's most serious criminals. It is the story of a system that punishes and sometimes destroys, but also seeks to reclaim the humanity of those whom the rest of us fear and despise. This is an account of the compassion, as well as the horror and turmoil that I found behind prison walls. It is a story about people struggling to keep the hope of positive change alive in a chaotic, degrading and dangerous environment.

The very architecture of Canada's oldest penitentiary appears to embody the confusion and contradictions of our prison system, with its ambitious ideals of justice and rehabilitation, together with the brutal realities of punishment and repression. The stately limestone columns at the main gate of Kingston Penitentiary resemble the entrance to a library, a museum or a place of worship. But this pleasing portico is set in an ugly and forbidding prison wall, overlooked by armed guards in watchtowers. It is a scene calculated to inspire awe and trepidation, a reminder that prisons were built to embody the power and majesty of the law, as well as its naked force.

A similar contrast awaits the few people allowed to pass through the gate or forced to live behind the walls. One finds oneself in a tranquil grass-covered courtyard containing huge, classically styled buildings with monotonous rows of barred windows that seem to give the lie to their graceful form. Gleaming after a recent restoration, the buildings look like starkly beautiful temples — dedicated to reason and justice, perhaps, or to some ancient god of retribution.

Inside, there is a cacophony of sound: a constant clashing of metal doors, men running and pacing on metal walk-ways, banging on bars, raising their voices in anger and bravado or shouting to make themselves heard over ghetto-blasters and television sets blaring away in cells. The musty, stale air is charged with the tension and pent-up energy of hundreds of prisoners, many of whom are confined with another inmate in antiquated, windowless cells no bigger than the bathroom of an average home.

The main prison building is arranged in the form of a cross around a central atrium, with a domed roof. The layout resembles that of a cathedral, but the gloomy echoing dome does not feel like a place where anyone's prayers would be answered.

Many Canadians have lost faith in the prison system. It is supposed to deter people from committing crimes, rehabilitate criminals and protect the public by keeping dangerous offenders off the streets. But Canada has been steadily building more and more prisons over the years to accommodate the ever-increasing number of citizens who have apparently not been deterred. People have lost confidence in the system's ability to fulfil its promises because of crimes committed by ex-offenders who have obviously not been rehabilitated and have not been kept off the streets.

Canada's federal penitentiaries have been failing to achieve their goals ever since the gates of Kingston Penitentiary closed on its first inmates. The penitentiary was conceived as a rational and humane way of dealing with violent or troublesome criminals. Until then, offenders were executed, whipped or exposed to public abuse and ridicule, but these brutal punishments did not reduce crime. The new regime was supposed to reform inmates by disciplining them through hard labour and a meticulously regulated timetable, while giving them plenty of opportunity for solitary reflection and repentance. The prison's forbidding, but awe-inspiring, appearance and harsh conditions were designed to deter others from committing crimes.

It had been in operation only fourteen years, when an inquiry exposed corrupt management and excessive punishments, concluding that the "reformation of convicts was unknown," because the unfair way in which prisoners were treated obliterated any feelings of guilt they might have had for their own crimes and "thoroughly brutalized all their feelings."

This inquiry was the first in a series of official commissions and inquiries over the next 140 years that criticized the Kingston prison and the federal correctional system that eventually grew out of it. Canada's prison service has always struggled to do several things at once, often at odds with itself and seldom satisfying anybody else. While successive governments called for measures to rehabilitate prisoners, inquiries repeatedly concluded that attempts at rehabilitation were undermined by a lack of resources and the punitive attitudes of staff. A royal commission in 1936 found that prison programs made inmates "lazy, shiftless and unreliable."

A parliamentary subcommittee report in 1977 concluded, "Society has spent millions of dollars over the years to create and maintain the proven failure of prisons. Incarceration has failed in its two essential purposes — correcting the offender and providing permanent protection to society."

Similar conclusions were reached in a 1988 report by a House of Commons standing committee on justice, which stated, "It is now generally recognized that imprisonment has not been effective in rehabilitating or reforming offenders, has not been shown to be a strong deterrent, and has achieved only temporary public protection and uneven retribution."

Nevertheless, Canadians are afraid of violent crime — perhaps more so now than ever before — and still look to the prison system for protection. Canada sends more of its citizens to jail than most other countries in the world, with only the United States, Russia and Hungary reporting higher rates of incarceration. What's more, our prison population is rising rapidly, and many members of the public are vociferously demanding that more criminals be locked up for longer periods of time.

Although crime and punishment have always been emotive, politically charged issues, only recently have they climbed to the top of the public agenda. Protection from crime has now become a concern for people from all sectors of society, whereas it used to be an issue espoused primarily by conservatives. Increased awareness of sexual abuse and domestic violence has focussed attention on the shortcomings of the justice system, as well as the risks to which women and children are exposed.

Although many women and children may be more at risk of sexual assault and violence in their own homes than on the streets, public anxieties have focussed on the dangers posed by muggers, predatory rapists, pedophiles and serial killers. These fears have been fuelled by extensive media coverage of high-profile murders of children and young women, particularly the trial of Paul Bernardo, who was assisted by his wife, Karla Homolka, as he abducted, tortured, sexually assaulted and killed two teenagers.

Victims' families often channel their anguish into campaigns for tougher laws, and their fury strikes a chord with a huge segment of the population. As a result, crime has become a prime focus for public fears and insecurities. There is enormous public pressure on courts to impose longer prison sentences, on parole boards not to release violent offenders and on politicians to enact tougher laws.

This pressure does not result, however, in effective and coherent policies to combat crime. Our justice system is fragmented, and no one appears able or willing to take a long-term view. The courts have no responsibility for the operation of prisons, and prison administrators have no influence on the courts. Politicians find it easier to enact laws than to provide funding for prison programs or crime prevention strategies. Parole boards, made up of citizens appointed by the government, have every reason to be cautious, when they may be held responsible for releasing a criminal who proves to be dangerous.

But where is our headlong flight from violent crime leading? Can prisons really provide us with the protection that we crave?

I was searching for answers to these questions when I visited prisons and investigated the inner workings of the federal prison service. I was looking for insight into whether rehabilitative programs can work, in spite of the popular perception that they do not. I wanted to examine the process by which prisoners are allowed to return to society before their sentences end. By talking to prisoners and staff, attending parole hearings and exploring all aspects of prison operations, I was hoping to understand a hidden and mysterious world and in so doing, shed light on issues that are a constant subject of public debate.

It soon became obvious to me that the federal prison system is already bursting at the seams, as it struggles to cope with the ever-increasing demands placed upon it. I saw problems festering and tensions building. I found that the prison environment was plagued by the very problems from which society expects the prison system to provide protection. Violence, sexual abuse, extortion, intimidation and drug trafficking are all perhaps more common behind bars than on the street. And, far from solving these problems, prison staff often seem to be fighting a losing battle to keep them in check.

In asking whether prisons protect society from crime, I realized that it was also important to consider the possibility that relying too much on prisons might make us less safe. During my visits to penitentiaries in every region of Canada, I continually posed the question, "Are we creating more problems than we are solving by sending more people to prison?" Few of the answers that I received were reassuring, and I began to wonder whether the prison system is even protecting us from itself.

We expect a lot from prisons and it may be that our high expectations are actually making prisons less effective. Employees who are given too much to do often end up doing less. They may feel forced to take shortcuts and make compromises. They are also far more likely to make mistakes.

The costs of prisons must give everyone cause for some concern, especially when one considers the example of the United States, where prison populations have quadrupled during the past twenty years and some jurisdictions spend more on jailing citizens than educating them. Canada spends more than $7 billion on its criminal justice system, of which about $2 billion is allocated to correctional services. Just over half this money is spent on provincial systems, which run detention centres for accused people awaiting trial and prisons for offenders serving sentences of less than two years. Besides handling about 20,000 prisoners, the provincial correctional systems supervise close to 100,000 offenders on parole, probation or community service orders. Each provinces also provide correctional services for young offenders from twelve to eighteen years old.

These provincial services are beyond the scope of this book, since I decided to focus on the federal system, which deals with the more serious offenders and the problems that pose the greatest risk to society. It is important to bear in mind, however, that many federal offenders have already "graduated" from provincial or youth justice systems, many of which are also beset with problems like overcrowding, violence and drug abuse. It is also worth remembering that much of the money that Canada spends on correctional services is devoted to keeping relatively minor offenders in provincial prisons and that some is wasted on duplication of services that are administered by thirteen different jurisdictions.

Federal prisons are run by the Correctional Service of Canada (CSC), under the leadership of the commissioner of the CSC, who reports to the federal solicitor general. The CSC national headquarters in Ottawa sets policies and provides administrative services, while five regional headquarters are responsible for the day-to-day operation of more than 40 prisons and other services or facilities, which include psychiatric centres, halfway houses for prisoners on community release programs and parole offices, responsible for supervising offenders in the community. The National Parole Board, a separate body, which also reports to the solicitor general, is responsible for making decisions about the early release of prisoners on community supervision programs.

Until recently, there were nearly as many federal prison employees as there were prisoners. Cutbacks and increases in the inmate population have changed this ratio somewhat, but there are still at least 9,000 people working with about 14,000 prisoners in institutions. The remainder of the correctional service's 10,600 work force is made up of administrators at the national and regional headquarters and about 1,100 parole officers, who supervise approximately 10,000 offenders on parole or some other form of community release.

Only 13 per cent of CSC's resources is devoted to supervising and assisting offenders on parole, in spite of the fact that the ultimate goal of the prison system is to return offenders safely to the community. Penitentiaries absorb most of CSC's budget. The average direct cost of maintaining an inmate in a federal prison in 1992–93 was $48,000, but the auditor general of Canada estimated in his 1994 report that this figure rose to nearly $80,000 when capital costs and other administrative expenses were considered.

Penitentiaries are expensive to run because each institution is a self-contained community, responsible for looking after all the daily needs of a population that is not allowed to leave. Basic needs for food, clothing and health services have to be met. Recreational facilities and programs must also be provided. These may seem like luxuries to those who believe that prisons should be hell on earth, but they are necessities from any perspective that includes a humanitarian concern for basic human rights, a belief in rehabilitation and a pragmatic interest in keeping prisoners relatively healthy and less prone to let off steam in riots.

Work must be provided to keep prisoners busy and to teach skills and attitudes that could assist in reintegrating into the community after their release. The correctional service is also committed to educational programming to bring prisoners up to a high-school graduation academic level and to a variety of rehabilitative programs designed to address the problems that contribute to criminal behaviour.

The most expensive prisons to run are the maximum security institutions, which have rigorous security measures, not only at the gates and along the perimeter walls or fences, but also inside the buildings where inmates' movements are strictly controlled and weapons are available to guards. Medium security prisons also have perimeter fences and strict controls on the gates, but there is more freedom of movement and less supervision inside. In minimum security institutions, prisoners are not allowed to leave, but there are no fences to stop them.

The inmate population of Canada's federal penitentiaries includes professional killers, dangerous psychopaths, sexual sadists, recalcitrant pedophiles and many other types of violent or extremely disturbed offenders. Some of these are scary individuals who pose serious problems for staff and other prisoners alike. But most of the offenders sentenced to penitentiary terms do not belong in this category. Between 35 and 40 per cent of the inmate population is made up of non-violent drug or property offenders, while another 20 per cent or more is comprised of offenders serving sentences for robbery, a crime that involves using force or threat of force, but does not necessarily include an act of violence.

The overwhelming majority of federal penitentiary inmates are males from 20 to 40 years old. There are fewer than 400 women out of a total population of 15,000. About 40 per cent of the women are also serving time for non-violent offences, and a large proportion of those who committed crimes of violence did so in domestic situations where they were victims of abuse. A hugely disproportionate number of prisoners are of aboriginal descent, especially in the Prairies, where Natives represent about 5 per cent of the general population, but 32 per cent of the federal inmate population. This discrepancy is a sad comment on Canadian social justice and must give us pause to think about what other, less easily measured, forms of prejudice or unfairness exist in our justice and social systems.

What we ask prisons to do sometimes seems contradictory. Harsh punishments can make prisoners more bitter and more dangerous, yet fewer people are likely to be deterred by prison programs that teach offenders new skills and boost their self-esteem. Keeping dangerous criminals off the streets for a long time may protect the public, but it could result in more violent and anti-social ex-offenders when they eventually return to society.

Whether we like it or not, an overwhelming majority of prisoners do return to the community. For that reason alone, what happens in our prisons is of concern to everyone. People who believe that no punishment is too harsh have an interest in ensuring that offenders do not come back more angry or unstable than before. It is not only "bleeding-hearts" who must worry about prison conditions when jails can easily become incubators for contagious diseases that bars and steel fences will not contain.

Prisons are closed, mysterious places where few law-abiding

citizens ever set foot. Modern penitentiaries are not designed, like Kingston, as grimly imposing public buildings. They are usually nondescript, low-profile structures that could easily be mistaken for factories and warehouses, if it were not for the fact that they are surrounded by steel fences and overlooked by security towers. Like landfill sites, prisons are often located in remote rural areas. But they can never be so far away that they do not have an impact on the community. Everything in contemporary society is interconnected and prisons do not stand apart.

This was the experience of people living in the Miramichi region of northeastern New Brunswick, who were promised that they would never be bothered by the inmates of a maximum security prison buried deep in the bush. Nicknamed "Alcatraz North" when it was opened in 1987, the Atlantic Institution at Renous was located at an old munitions depot. It seemed like the perfect site for a prison. The most dangerous and explosive offenders could be contained in a secure setting, as far as possible from other human habitation.

Public fears about violent crime were escalating. The popular sentiment — then, as now — favoured locking criminals up and forgetting about them. A new prison in the Miramichi region seemed like a particularly good idea politically, as the federal government was contemplating closing the Canadian Forces Base in Chatham, the principal town in the region. The new jobs to be created by the prison would serve as an economic consolation prize.

The government that decided to build the maximum security institution at Renous overlooked one crucial factor. There were not really that many dangerous offenders in Atlantic Canada and the 240-cell jail remained half-empty for several years.

Then one of the relatively few truly dangerous inmates at Renous escaped. Convicted murderer Alan Legere got away from two guards while he was attending a hospital in Moncton in 1989. Before he was recaptured, Legere terrorized northeastern New

Brunswick for seven months, brutally murdering three women and a Roman Catholic priest. He became known as "the Madman of the Miramichi."

The Atlantic Institution is a large, metal-clad, brick and concrete building situated on an expanse of cleared land close to the Renous River, a tributary of the Miramichi. It is protected by two rows of security fencing, topped with coils of razor wire and equipped with electronic movement detectors. Staff at the prison assured me that the institution's security is impeccable and that people in the community had got an unfortunate impression, as a result of Legere's escape while on an escorted medical pass. I was told that the public relations problems were further compounded in 1992, when Valmond LeBouthillier, who had been freed on parole from the institution after serving nineteen years of a life sentence for second degree murder, stabbed and sexually assaulted a woman in Chatham.

When the institution was opened, politicians promised the community "a win-win situation," in which more than 200 new jobs would be created in a totally secure prison from which no one would escape. The community was also led to believe that inmates at Renous would not get out on parole, since maximum security prisoners are generally not considered for parole until they have been transferred to a lower security institution and proved that they can function in that less controlled environment. The medium and minimum security prisons in New Brunswick were in the Moncton area, more than 150 kilometres to the south. Politicians argued that paroled offenders were unlikely to return to the Miramichi region after their release.

Legere and LeBouthillier had proven that such assurances were illusory. Now there is every prospect that more prisoners will be released from the institution, as a result of changing circumstances and new policies. The extra cells, which had been empty for years because there were not enough maximum security prisoners, are now filled with prisoners who are considered to be of a lower risk to the community. In fact, because of over-crowding in the prison system as a whole, some of the prisoners are being doubled up in cells. The institution has a capacity for 240 beds, but it now houses 275 inmates. These extra inmates are not as dangerous as the maximum security inmates for which the prison was built, but people in the community are worried because most of the inmates now have shorter sentences and are more likely to be released on parole.

We continue to believe that we can solve the problem of crime by locking up more and more criminals in some remote and secure location. Then we are constantly taken by surprise when the same criminals return, like pieces of debris blowing off a garbage dump that has grown too full and no longer seems quite as far from town as it once did.

When prisons are used as dumping grounds for problems that society cannot handle, it is almost inevitable that they will become places of decay and contamination. If we throw all serious offenders into the same isolated and overcrowded jails, it is only to be expected that many will eventually return to the community more dangerous and less able to cope with the pressures of ordinary life. We can respond by sending more and more people to prison for longer periods in an attempt to bury our problems even deeper. Or we can try to shed light on these problems by examining how the prison system works, what it can realistically be expected to achieve, and what can be salvaged from its failures.

Part One

PRISONS IN CRISIS

Prison life with its endless privations and restrictions makes one rebellious. The most terrible thing about it is not that it breaks one's heart — hearts are made to be broken — but that it turns one's heart to stone.

Oscar Wilde, *De Profundis*

2

A SYSTEM OVERWHELMED

The correctional service has been described as "the system that cannot say no." It has no control over who its clients are, how many there are, when they arrive or how long they must stay. Prisons cannot tell the courts that they are full or that sentenced offenders must be put on a waiting list. They cannot refuse to admit anyone on the grounds that he or she is too crazy or too sick. Nor can they second-guess the courts by concluding that an offender's crime or criminal history is not serious enough for a federal prison term.

Nevertheless, the Correctional Service of Canada is committed to providing all offenders with programs to address their needs and reduce the risk they pose to society. It bravely maintains that it can do this and will continue to do so in spite of dwindling resources and an ever-increasing number of inmates.

The reality that I encountered, however, during the course of my visits to institutions in every region of Canada, was that people in the system are overwhelmed by the number of prisoners whom they are forced to accommodate and attempt to rehabilitate. The problem of overcrowding has been creeping up on the federal prison system for many years, as building and renovation programs have failed to keep pace with a rising number of prisoners. The auditor general of Canada noted in his 1994 report that the Correctional Service's inmate population grew from 10,500 to 13,200 between 1986 and 1993, but penitentiary cell capacity increased only from 11,656 to 12,061.

It is hard to say whether or not the rise in the prison population reflects an actual increase in serious crimes. Criminologists, statisticians, police chiefs and media commentators have been arguing for years about whether there is more crime or simply more fear of crime. There is much room for debate over whether the problem of violent crime is getting more serious or people are taking certain crimes more seriously. However, no matter how one interprets the cause, the effect is that courts are sending more people to penitentiaries and are imposing longer sentences. Public concerns about offenders committing crimes while on parole have also made the National Parole Board more cautious about releasing prisoners early in their sentences.

While there is public support for the idea of locking more criminals up for longer periods of time, few people are in favour of spending a lot of money on new prisons. Politicians realize that there are cheap votes to be won by talking tough on crime, but no political mileage to be gained by increasing the budgets of correctional services. When politicians have spent money on new prisons in recent years, their decisions have often been made in the interests of regional development or party politics rather than the rational deployment of resources for correctional purposes. The auditor general's 1994 report stated that decisions by Brian Mulroney's government to build two new prisons in remote locations, one of them in Mulroney's own riding, resulted in CSC spending an additional $20 million in capital costs and several million dollars a year in extra operating costs. The auditor also criticized CSC for costly renovation programs at Kingston and Dorchester penitentiaries, suggesting that the money would have been better spent replacing the existing facilities with new buildings.

Although CSC's current five-year building plan involves

spending $470 million to increase the number of beds by 2,000, no one anticipates that this will keep pace with the escalating inmate population. CSC's own population projections anticipate that prisons will have to rely more and more on the practice of double-bunking, putting two prisoners in a cell designed for one.

Double-bunking was introduced as a temporary measure in 1984, at which time CSC promised that the overcrowding problem would be solved within a year. The practice is in violation of United Nations standards for the minimum treatment of prisoners, which Canada has endorsed. As recently as 1990, the commissioner of the CSC told the government-appointed correctional investigator that double-bunking was "not correctionally acceptable."

When most federal correctional institutions were built, it was assumed that prisoners would be separated in small individual cells. Cells were not, therefore, designed to hold more than one person. The auditor general reported in 1994 that some of the double-bunked cells were only about 60 square feet, while others, including those at Kingston Penitentiary and the Saskatchewan Penitentiary were as small as 48 square feet. Jimmy O'Sullivan, warden at the 85-year-old Saskatchewan Penitentiary, told me that double-bunking in his institution was "atrocious." He said it was like making two people live on a billiard table.

In the older penitentiaries, conditions are sometimes little short of squalid. Many of the cells have no windows and the open bars at the front provide the only ventilation or natural light. The cells are often arranged in two levels, with the upper level accessible only via narrow metal walk-ways and stairs.

A typical cell contains a toilet, washbasin, a small desk, a chair, a bunk and some shelving that is usually crammed full of the prisoner's personal effects. When cells are double-bunked, the two occupants must share one desk and chair. At Kingston Penitentiary, I was told that some of the bulkier prisoners have great

difficulty turning around in a double-bunked cell and have to
edge in and out sideways.

While taking me on a tour of one institution, a senior administrator said, "Quite frankly, our cells are pissholes." He went on
to explain that prisoners are sometimes confined for days in
their cells for security purposes, while staff search for drugs
and weapons, investigate a violent incident or restore calm after
a riot. During these "lock-downs," food trays are given to the
inmates through the bars of their cells. "The only other place
where they do that is at the zoo," the administrator said.

At Matsqui Institution, a medium security penitentiary in
British Columbia, guards explained that overcrowding was placing a strain on plumbing and electrical systems. Opened in 1966
as a treatment centre for drug addicts and then converted to a
prison in 1975, the prison buildings were designed to be bare
and functional, but they have since become dilapidated and no
longer function very well. In some living areas, 35 prisoners
shared two or three showers, two toilet stalls and three sinks.
Unlike other prisons, Matsqui did not have toilets in all the
cells. Prisoners, locked in their cells, were supposed to signal
for guards whenever they needed to go to the washroom. Correctional officers did not always find that they could respond
promptly to these demands, and many prisoners consequently
kept jugs or tin cans in their cells as a precautionary measure.
One of the guards warned me not to walk too close to cell windows if I was making my way around the outside of a cell block
in the morning.

The experience of living in a double-bunked cell was described
to me by a group of prisoners I met in one of the cell blocks at
the maximum security Kent Institution in British Columbia.
One man explained, "You've got two guys living in a toilet. It
could be your best friend. After a while you want to kill him.
Everybody's entitled to some dignity, some privacy. You need a
time for quiet on your own. When you're double-bunked, there

is no such thing as time out. The pressure keeps building."

A rough-faced man with long straggly hair, who had been talking to some other inmates in French, momentarily interrupted his conversation to make a brief comment in English. "If they put anyone in a cell with me, I'll kill the fucking guy. What are they going to do? Send me to jail?" he proclaimed emphatically, before returning to his other conversation, apparently confident that his argument was irrefutable. It was later explained to me that the man was a contract murderer and might very well carry out his threat. I was told that there were no immediate plans to move him into a double-bunked cell.

By 1995, 25 per cent of CSC inmates were being held in double-bunked cells and the proportion was projected to rise to 30 per cent by the turn of the century. In a column in the correctional service staff publication *Let's Talk*, CSC Commissioner John Edwards wrote, "Like most staff, and most inmates, I do not much like double-bunking, but then, I don't much like paying taxes either. Indeed, double-bunking is today as unavoidable as taxes — and rising faster." Edwards predicted that proposed changes in criminal law will further increase the prison population. But, he wrote, "There is no money — or much desire — to launch a frenzy of prison building. With the Canadian incarceration rate being the second highest in the Western world (after the U.S.), it is doubtful if we need to increase significantly the overall prison capacity, even if funding was available."

The commissioner explained that the service is considering practical measures to "manage overcrowding as sensibly as possible." As examples of such measures, he suggested not double-bunking the tiny cells in older institutions, not putting smokers and non-smokers together, giving single cells to offenders serving long terms and minimizing the negative effects of double-bunking by increasing programming, employment opportunities and activities. Edwards stated that the service is also considering measures to speed up the release of prisoners without adverse impact on public safety by delivering programs more efficiently. He admitted, however, that ultimately a reduction in double-bunking is likely to come about only as a result of the long-term success of crime prevention measures or a decline in the current Canadian practice of sending non-violent offenders to prison.

Even prisoners and their advocates, who vehemently oppose double-bunking, agree that the answer lies in trying to reduce the flow of new inmates, rather than building new prisons. Graham Stewart, executive director of the John Howard Society of Ontario, a community organization that works with prisoners, compared the massive prison-building program in the United States to the absurdity of attempting to deal with a leaking bathroom faucet by filling one's house with a network of new bathtubs. Stewart, like many other people I interviewed, maintained that penitentiaries are full of people who do not need to be there.

People who end up in a federal prison are more likely than not to be functionally illiterate, to have a drug or alcohol problem and to have come from deprived, abusive or neglectful homes. Statistics also indicate that one in every ten federal offenders has a history of serious mental disorder. Such problems may not necessarily be recognized as causes of their criminal behaviour or accepted as excuses, but they certainly represent a substantial list of needs for treatment or educational programming.

With such a wide range of offenders continually arriving in the prison system, it is obviously important to determine quickly who are the most dangerous or disturbed and what kind of problems they might present. In order to do this, it is also necessary to probe beyond the actual crimes for which they have been convicted, since prisoners sentenced for non-violent offences may have mental health problems or personal histories of violent or sexually assaultive behaviour that could make them serious threats to public safety in future.

But the sheer number of prisoners entering the system sometimes makes it impossible for staff to do proper assessments or to follow up on their assessments by providing appropriate programs and facilities. The intake units located in maximum or medium security prisons are supposed to complete an assessment of all newly admitted prisoners before placing them in an appropriate penitentiary. Federal prison operations are divided into five regions: Atlantic, Quebec, Ontario, Prairies and Pacific. There is one intake unit for each region, except in the Prairie region where there is one for each of the three provinces. Staff at the intake units are expected to take between six and eight weeks to complete the standardized assessment process designed by the CSC national headquarters. This assessment involves a series of tests, evaluations and background checks to identify the factors that lead each offender to commit crimes. Case management officers, the staff members responsible for following up on prisoners' treatment needs, use the assessment data to develop a "correctional plan," a set of goals for each inmate. The final decision about where to place the offender in the penitentiary system is based on the needs identified in the assessment, the risks that the offender poses, the availability of specific programs in different institutions and logistical questions like where beds are available.

Most of the intake units I visited were overcrowded. Staff told me that it was often difficult to cope with the steady stream of new arrivals. Nowhere were the problems more acute than at the Edmonton maximum security penitentiary, a low-profile modern building that looks like a factory or warehouse, where the intake unit receives all offenders sentenced to federal prison terms in a province that is fabled for its tough responses to crime. I was told there that staff were not even coming close to following the standard assessment process. Alberta judges were meting out so many prison sentences of two years or more that the Edmonton reception unit was simply swamped with new admissions.

Even though new prisoners at the Edmonton unit were temporarily housed in segregation cells, health care cells and at a provincial jail, I was told that it was still sometimes necessary to cram three or four bunks into cells intended for one prisoner. Staff at the unit said that they did not have time to assess all the prisoners thoroughly before transferring them elsewhere in order to make room for more. With only 94 beds available, and 70 to 80 new prisoners arriving each month in 1994, staff could afford to spend only about four weeks on a process that normally takes from six to eight weeks.

Inadequate assessments of newly arrived prisoners can compromise public safety. If the risks are not properly identified at the reception unit, prisoners are far less likely to get the rehabilitative programs they need. There is also a far greater chance that mistakes will be made when prisoners are eventually considered for parole, since the risks that they pose will not be documented and no one will know about problems that have gone untreated. It is perhaps more than coincidence that many of the high-profile mistakes that have plagued the parole system in recent years have occurred in Alberta.

"We're trying to do good assessments and placements, when we've got no space and no ability to control inflow," said Jack Linklater, the warden of the Edmonton Institution, explaining that the rate of admissions in Alberta so far that year had been more than three times that of each of the other Prairie provinces. According to a manager in the reception unit, many new inmates are relatively minor criminals who would not have received a federal sentence in any other province.

In other provinces, offenders usually remain in provincial prisons for a few weeks after sentencing before being transferred to the federal system. This delay gives CSC staff time to gather background information about prisoners from their families, community agencies, police and other sources. In Alberta, however, the transfer process is often speeded up in order to cut provincial costs. This fast turnover further complicates the job of the CSC reception unit in Edmonton, since staff are sometimes forced to receive prisoners before they have even had time to request information from other agencies.

Overcrowding throughout the prison system makes it extremely difficult for intake and assessment staff to find appropriate placements for the new inmates. After the assessment process, the offenders are categorized as maximum, medium or minimum security prisoners, depending on the level of risk they pose and the seriousness of their crimes. In theory, offenders are then assigned to the institutions that can best provide the programming and level of security they require. In practice, it is often difficult to find a bed anywhere.

The majority of new admissions are not high-risk offenders who require maximum security. But minimum security facilities, which have no perimeter fences, are reluctant to take new admissions unless they have been assessed as presenting an exceptionally low level of risk. Consequently, the majority of offenders are sent from the intake units to medium security institutions, which have become extremely overcrowded.

John Junker, unit manager in the Edmonton reception centre, told me that it is often impossible to find beds for new inmates in either of the two medium security penitentiaries in Alberta. "Sometimes we have to take radical measures," he said, explaining that his staff occasionally put a group of twenty inmates on a bus and send them to Stony Mountain Penitentiary in Manitoba or the Saskatchewan Penitentiary in Prince Albert. Often prisoners are chosen for transfer at random, without any opportunity to consider their problems in maintaining contact with their families or their plans for reintegrating into the community after their release.

The theory behind CSC's security classification system is that prisoners who start at higher levels of security should be transferred to lower levels once they have completed rehabilitative programs and shown positive changes in their behaviour. The idea is that prisoners should "cascade" down through the system as they serve their sentence, gradually adapting to living in a less controlled and structured setting.

A practical reason for moving prisoners as quickly as possible to lower levels of security is that it saves money. It costs far more to keep prisoners in a maximum security environment where guards must monitor their every move than in a medium security institution where there is far less supervision. It is cheaper still to keep them in minimum security. In 1994, the cost of maximum security was $70,000 per inmate, compared to $42,000 in medium and $36,000 in minimum.

Until recently, senior managers put pressure on prison officials to transfer prisoners to minimum security as quickly as possible. But this trend was reversed by public outrage over violent crimes by prisoners who walked away from unfenced minimum security prisons. In 1995, a court awarded $394,000 in damages to a woman in Gravenhurst, Ontario, the victim of a vicious stabbing and sexual assault by Philippe Clement, a convicted sex killer who absconded from a minimum security prison in September 1992. A CSC administrator told me that staff in the Ontario region became very cautious about transferring offenders to minimum security as a result of this case. He noted that there were empty beds in minimum security institutions and triple bunking in some medium security prisons.

In every region, I encountered severe overcrowding in medium security prisons. This overcrowding was creating a bottleneck, which further prevented prisoners from cascading down through the three levels of security. In maximum security penitentiaries, inmates were often getting stuck where they were because there were no beds for them elsewhere. In some regions, newly admitted prisoners were sent to maximum security solely because there was no room for them in medium security.

At the maximum security Atlantic Institution in Renous, New

Brunswick, I was told that between 80 and 90 prisoners who were classified as medium security could not be placed in medium security prisons. Instead of being prepared for integration into the community, these prisoners were essentially being warehoused with more dangerous offenders in a remote prison, isolated from community agencies and services. They also had minimal access to the type of programming that the assessment process had recommended for them, since rehabilitative programs and occupational training available in maximum security are far more limited than those offered at lower security levels.

The programs that CSC offers to inmates attempt to address the problems and needs that lead offenders to commit crimes. They include cognitive living skills programs designed to provide offenders with insight into problems that they may have in dealing with everyday situations and relationships. Inmates learn methods for dealing with problems like family violence and substance abuse that directly contribute to crime, while general educational courses are intended to give them skills and knowledge that will help them find work when they leave prison. These "core programs," offered throughout the CSC system, are supplemented by a variety of therapeutic programs and activities offered in specific institutions to prisoners who need specialized programming.

In every institution that I visited, however, overcrowding was making it more difficult to deliver programs and other rehabilitative services in a timely and appropriate fashion. As Willie Gladu, of Kingston Penitentiary explained, "We don't have the capacity to meet the demand, and the mass of individuals are in a holding pattern, like planes waiting to land at an airport."

Kingston Penitentiary is a "multilevel" facility that holds maximum and medium security inmates. Its population includes sex offenders, prisoners with mental health problems and others who need to be held in protective custody. When I visited, the population was 510, but the official capacity of the prison at that time was 435. The prison's infrastructure, including workshop space and program areas, was not designed to accommodate that many inmates. Some prisoners were therefore unemployed, while many more were waiting to enroll in the programs that they were supposed to be taking.

"From an inmate's point of view, they went through a process to identify their needs and they say, 'Let's get on with it.' But the reality is that I can't plug them in as soon as they walk in the door," said Gladu, explaining that newly arrived prisoners are put on a waiting list for programs. He said the waiting list is prioritized according to factors like how great the needs of the prisoner are, how soon he is scheduled for release and how well motivated he appears to be.

The majority of newly admitted prisoners, about 56 per cent, face terms of two to three years and another 30 per cent will serve from three to six years. Most of these hope for a relatively short stay in penitentiaries, since prisoners may be released on parole after serving a third of their sentences and the law requires that most offenders be granted statutory release, by which they serve the last third of their sentence under supervision in the community, unless they have committed serious violent crimes in the past and are likely to do so again.

The average age of inmates has been increasing steadily in recent years. This change partly reflects demographics and partly results from a steady accumulation of long-term offenders in the system, ever since the 1976 legislation that abolished capital punishment also increased the period that murderers must serve in prison before being eligible for parole. Long-term offenders, prisoners with sentences of ten years or more, now represent more than 25 per cent of the federal prison population, even though they make up a much smaller proportion of the prisoners entering the system through the intake units.

Long-term offenders often mark time at the bottom of the waiting lists for programming, sometimes waiting years before their problems are addressed. There is a feeling among staff that there is not much point in doing a great deal for people who will be living for many more years in a prison environment. The problem is that by the time the long-term offenders' needs are addressed with programs, they may have lost any motivation they ever had and their anti-social attitudes may have become too deeply ingrained to change.

Prisoners with shorter sentences tend to get into programming sooner. There is a greater sense of urgency about changing the behaviour of people who may soon return to the community. Sometimes it already appears that their needs and problems are so great that it will be impossible to have much impact in the time available. It is not uncommon to encounter a prisoner who is at the same time functionally illiterate, addicted to drugs or alcohol, struggling with memories of sexual abuse in early childhood and suffering from a personality disorder that results in violent and impulsive behaviour. Barrie Friel, a senior administrator at the Prison for Women, told me, "With certain cases, the complexity and abundance of needs can be overwhelming."

With limited space available in programs, it is often impossible to get prisoners with relatively short sentences into all the programs that their correctional plan requires before their parole eligibility date. The parole board, which has become extremely conservative in its decision-making process, is reluctant to release prisoners who have not gone through all the programs designed to decrease their risk of reoffending. Thus, the board often denies parole to prisoners who would have been returned to the community at minimal risk, if they could have been scheduled into programs sooner. The result is that the overcrowding situation is further exacerbated because prisoners are being kept in jail for longer periods.

Prisoners and prison staff alike are caught up in a spiral of ever-increasing overcrowding, tension and frustration. As it becomes more and more difficult to place prisoners in the rehabilitative program that they need, offenders see their release prospects fading. This leads to more tension, violence and drug abuse. As a result, additional security measures often have to be employed in prisons that previously prided themselves on creating an environment that helped inmates turn their lives around. An administrator at the medium security Mission Institution in British Columbia told me, "This was a very therapeutic community, but we're becoming a jail."

Staff in medium security prisons, where the emphasis should be on programs and work opportunities, talk about prisoners "doing maximum security time in a medium security setting." In a medium security prison inmates are not locked in their cells or restricted to their ranges for as long as they are in maximum security. There is more double-bunking in medium than in maximum security, and it is justified on the grounds that prisoners do not have to spend as much time in their cells. But prisoners in medium security complain that they have nowhere else to go but to their cells when there is not enough work to go round and not enough programming.

Every aspect of prison administration is affected by overcrowding. "Even getting everyone fed is an adventure," commented one warden. Another administrator complained about shortages in supplies and told me that by early November he still did not have enough winter coats for all the newly arrived prisoners. In several institutions, I was told that prisoners were being allowed fewer visits from family and friends because of overcrowding and staff shortages in the visiting areas.

In many prisons, recreational space, including inmates' lounges and television rooms, has been cut back to make room for additional programs and programming staff. Prisoners in double-bunked cells therefore have fewer and fewer places where they can go to get away from their cell mates or spend time alone.

At Archambault penitentiary in Quebec, I talked about double-bunking with a man doing a life sentence. He told me that he had changed his attitude and gained control over his violent impulses through solitary reflection and meditation. He had also earned a university degree while in prison. He said he found it hard to imagine how one could study or meditate with another prisoner in the same cell. "If you're going to rehabilitate, you've got to work on yourself. You've got to have some solitude. How can you meditate or study when the other guy's watching TV? Where are you going to get some tranquillity?"

The lifer had been at Archambault during the period in the early 1980s when it was the scene of some of Canada's worst prison riots. It was a maximum security penitentiary then and is a medium now, but, according to this lifer, the tensions within it are mounting again: "With double-bunking, this is a powder keg. You're going to see the place blow up again."

I heard similar predictions from prisoners and guards in several institutions. Staff members told me that they were particularly worried about the risk of violent confrontation in medium security institutions where the overcrowding was worst and tensions highest, yet where inmates had more freedom to congregate than in the tightly controlled maximum security settings.

At the Matsqui Institution, the converted drug rehabilitation centre, a group of prisoners enumerated a long list of grievances concerning overcrowding, lack of programs and a shortage of recreational space. They compared the inadequate facilities at the jail with those at the old British Columbia Penitentiary, which remained in use for 30 years after it was first scheduled for closure, and finally closed only after a riot occurred in 1980. Gesturing with a clenched fist, one of the prisoners exclaimed, "Maybe we're going to have to do what we did in the late seventies and eighties when we tore those fucking places down."

One could almost feel the violent energy that the prisoner's comment inspired among the half dozen other inmates present in the room. Alarmed by the force of their anger I felt relieved that they were not angry with me. I was reminded — not for the

last time during the course of my tour of Canada's prisons —
that these are almost the only places in contemporary Canadian
society where violent insurrection is an everyday threat.

A few days after my visit to Matsqui, a guard was beaten with
a metal pipe by a prisoner angry about being denied a family
visit. The prison was locked down for four days, while the incident was investigated and cells searched for weapons. Ten days
after the lock-down ended, a prisoner was stabbed in the chest
by another inmate and suffered a punctured lung. Prisoners and
guards attributed both these disturbances to the tensions created by overcrowding. Their concerns drew a comment from
Randy White, Reform party MP for Fraser Valley West. White,
a strong advocate of tougher sentences and tighter parole
restrictions, expressed sympathy for prison officials who must
work in such a tense atmosphere, but reminded them that "the
public is in no mood to build prisoners more prisons."

This assessment of the public mood was undoubtedly correct. There is little prospect that more money will be spent on
improving prison conditions in the foreseeable future. It is also
likely that courts and parole boards will continue to follow the
popular sentiment in favour of sentencing offenders to longer
prison terms and denying them early parole. The people who
advocate such policies fail to appreciate, however, that overcrowding is undermining almost every aspect of prison operation
and that it constitutes a threat to public safety.

Processes designed to move offenders through the system
and gradually reintegrate them into society are getting clogged,
stalled and backed up. Prisoners' problems are festering while
they wait months or even years for programs that are supposed
to reduce the risk they will ultimately pose to society. Inmates
who should be learning productive trades or getting education
to help them cope in the work force are sitting unemployed
in their cell blocks exchanging practical tips on crime and
networking with other offenders. Problems that should be

identified are being missed, with potentially tragic consequences. Staff members are overstressed and overworked while violence and drug abuse increase, as prisoners grow more angry and more volatile.

3

THE LAW OF
THE JUNGLE

It is common knowledge that prisons are violent and brutal places. But it was not until I talked to guards and inmates about their experiences that I began to comprehend the stark horror and casual cruelty of penitentiary life. I also came to appreciate the horrendous impact this environment can have on prisoners and staff members alike.

"I don't think people realize the depression and anger that exists in places like this. Life is cheap. You can get somebody killed for $20. You know you can get killed," said Nick, a veteran guard at the maximum security Millhaven Institution, one of Canada's toughest prisons. He told me about a prisoner whose face was cut up by another inmate because he took too long in the shower. Speaking with the intensity that one encounters in survivors of severe trauma, Nick said that he had nightmares after seeing the prisoner with the skin torn from his face: "You want to talk about such things when you go home from work, but you feel that you can't. You bottle it up and this affects your personality." The impact on his personal life became clear to him when his own daughter was badly cut, falling through a plate glass window: "I calmly dealt with situation. Then, later on, I realized that it didn't bother me as it should have. I had become cold and distant."

Unlike the guards, prisoners do not take their frustration

and indifference home with them every night. When they eventually do return to the community, however, they are likely to be cold and distant, like Nick. Unlike the guard, they may also be angry and anti-social. Criminals may often be lacking in compassion and sensitivity to begin with, but many are evidently hardened by their exposure to violence in the penitentiary.

Maurice, an aging bank robber who had been in and out of prison all his life, told me that prison life reminded him of the nature shows he liked to watch on television where the strong were always preying on the weak. When a fight broke out, he said, other cons would swarm to the scene like sharks smelling blood. "Then the winner is placed on a pedestal and loser is treated like a piece of shit. When you drop, you're finished. You have nothing."

Anyone living in such an environment is bound to become emotionally callous, said Maurice. "How can you develop empathy?" he asked. "You're too busy surviving. Then parole board members will ask, 'Don't you feel sorry for scaring those people in a bank robbery?' But I can tell them stories that will make their hair turn white."

In rehabilitative programs, prison staff may talk about empathy, but it is a concept that seems totally alien in the cell blocks, where, as Maurice put it, "Kindness is an extinct animal."

During the course of my visits to several maximum security prisons, I never quite got used to seeing human beings caged, shackled and watched like wild animals. I realized that not all prisoners were treated like that and certainly not all the time. I was aware that those who were probably deserved it, and staff had good reason to be wary of them. Nevertheless, the situation seemed to compromise the humanity of everyone present.

I always left such prisons feeling somewhat sullied, as if by my presence I had silently condoned something that was essentially degrading. This was not a moral response. It was not based on a firm belief that prisons are wrong or that there is any obvious practical alternative. It was an emotional reaction, similar to the headaches that I experienced from the noise and poor air circulation in the buildings or the stiffness in my muscles that the tense atmosphere inevitably provoked. I suppose prisoners and staff get used to such feelings and come to accept them as an aspect of their everyday lives.

It is an environment where cruelty leads to indifference and indifference permits further cruelty. Nick told me that his attitudes toward prisoners were coloured by numerous disturbing and often disgusting past encounters. He said, "We hear criticism from the public that we don't care, that we're not sensitive. But they don't realize how many times I've gone into a cell, with people hollering at me, throwing bodily fluids. I've seen so much blood, so many slashings and hangings. You become cold."

The guards' attitudes evoke a negative response from prisoners. Maurice explained: "Deep in the bowels of the penitentiary, there is a 'Fuck you' mentality. You don't want someone near you and you tell them, 'Get out of my face.' The guards believe that guys like us will tear the place apart. That attitude is presented to you every day and you respond to it."

Serious attacks on staff, riots and hostage-takings are relatively rare events. But staff members who have lost a colleague or seen one badly hurt are likely to carry that memory to work with them every day for the rest of their careers. Prisoners at Stony Mountain Penitentiary in Manitoba complained to me that they were still suffering from lost privileges as a result of the murder of a staff member more than ten years earlier. I asked a guard about this and he told me, "Damn right, they are. But they've lost nothing compared to what we lost."

Prisoners' complaints about brutality and cruelty on the part of guards are seldom documented or substantiated. Alleged abuses are usually investigated by internal boards of inquiry, which are predisposed to accept staff members' version of events.

Prison staff depend upon one another for their personal safety, and it is almost unheard of for a guard to provide evidence against a fellow officer. There are normally no independent witnesses, and prisoners' accounts of events are not usually believed when guards contradict them.

Most prison staff members today are professional and deal fairly with inmates. Prisoners whom I interviewed attested to this. But even some prison staff members admitted that there are exceptions. Guards who abuse their power can do untold psychological damage and very quickly poison the atmosphere in units where they work. One notorious case of sadistic manipulation was recorded in a report of a parliamentary subcommittee in 1977: "At least nine inmates in one range slashed themselves on Christmas Eve 1976 after a guard left two razor blades in a cell and told them to 'have a Merry Christmas and a slashing New Year.'"

Guards can very easily abuse prisoners without resorting to physical assault. They can provoke confrontations and then lay charges for breach of prison regulations. Depending on the seriousness of the alleged offence, a prisoner may lose privileges or be sent to a dissociation and segregation unit, "the hole," where they are kept locked up for 23 hours a day. Inmates have the right to a hearing in a disciplinary court before being sent to the hole, but these courts, like internal investigations of alleged abuses, are inclined to give far more weight to the testimony of staff members than that of prisoners.

I visited the segregation areas in several prisons and they were invariably bleak, forbidding places. At Kingston Penitentiary, the hole was located at the end of a damp, musty corridor along which paint was peeling from the walls. The windowless cells had no bars, only metal doors with slots for sliding in trays of food. The moans and shouts of an evidently deranged prisoner echoed through the unit.

The exercise yards in segregation units are usually no bigger than a tennis court and may consist merely of a patch of bare earth or concrete between four high brick walls with a wire mesh over the top. At a modern maximum security prison in Edmonton, I watched an inmate pacing furiously around such a yard, as if looking in vain for someone whom he could punch or an object that he could smash in order to vent his frustrations.

Helen, a former long-term offender at the Kingston Prison for Women, explained how a short period in segregation could easily be expanded. She said that guards were supposed to go round every hour to give a cigarette to each of the prisoners in segregation, since they were not allowed to keep any tobacco products in their cells. In this tense and acutely boring environment, prisoners looked forward to their hourly cigarettes and could get rowdy if they did not receive them on time. But, when the prisoners raised a rumpus, the guard sometimes decided to go round delivering written charges instead of cigarettes. A prisoner might be prompted to tear up her charge in a rage, only to have the guard return a little while later with two new charge sheets. At this point, the angry prisoner could completely lose control and begin slashing herself or tearing her cell apart. This action would result in a further 30 days in segregation.

Prisoners have their own informal rules that make it dangerous for any inmate to be too friendly or cooperative with guards. Generally known as "the con code," these unwritten laws of the underworld exhort prisoners to maintain solidarity with one another, mind their own business, never to inform, or "rat," and have nothing to do with guards. These rules also provide some positive social values since they require prisoners to keep their word, respect one another's personal space and property. The code can help prisoners live with one another in a situation where the law of the land or official prison regulations carry little respect. In the past, the con code was a rigid law that prisoners breached only at extreme peril. One veteran guard told me about a prisoner being killed by other inmates for offering a staff member a doughnut.

At the intake unit in Millhaven, I interviewed a guard who was supervising a dishevelled and disoriented group of newly arrived prisoners, standing in a large wire mesh cage, waiting to be searched, fingerprinted, photographed and issued with clothes, bedding and toiletries. The guard told me, "The new-comers call you 'Sir,' and show respect. But after six months they are calling you 'Pig' and 'Asshole.' That's the training they get from the other inmates."

In recent years, CSC has been working hard at breaking down the con code, as it has been encouraging prisoners to par-ticipate in rehabilitative programs. Guards, now officially called "correctional officers," are supposed to be part of a team that provides counselling to prisoners and makes recommendations concerning access to programs, transfers and parole. Individual inmates must establish some kind of positive relationship with prison staff, if they ever hope to be transferred to lower levels of security or want a favourable report to the parole board.

The loyalty among thieves that the con code represents has also been eroded by destabilizing influences like heavy drug use and CSC's use of a network of informers within the prison population. Nevertheless, it is still a powerful influence, espe-cially in maximum security prisons, where there is less interaction between guards and prisoners. Inmates who are believed to have "ratted" on others are still likely to be killed and those who talk too much to guards risk falling under a cloud of suspicion.

"In prison you have to take sides," said Helen, who explained to me that it can be risky to decline to participate in an illegal act, like drinking "brew," prison-brewed alcohol, or smoking pot. If guards subsequently conduct a search and find the contraband items, the non-participant might well be suspected of informing.

At a parole hearing, I heard one prisoner claim that he had no choice but to participate in a token fashion in a brutal assault on another inmate. Everyone else on the range at the time was involved in the beating, he said, so he had to give the victim at least one kick. Sometimes prisoners will ask guards to lock them in their cells, because they believe that something is going to happen in which they do not want to be involved.

Prisoners can also draw suspicion upon themselves if they witness illegal acts by other inmates. For example, in the visiting area, prisoners never look at other inmates or their visitors for fear of witnessing an exchange of drugs.

If a dispute arises on a range and prisoners collectively resist the authority of guards by refusing to go into their cells or by staging a sit-down strike, any prisoner who does not get involved is likely to have a very hard time in future. Seasoned cons told me that they live in dread of such incidents when their parole eligibility date is approaching, because they know they have no choice about participating, but could never explain that satisfactorily to a parole board.

It was during the course of a collective protest by prisoners at Kingston Penitentiary on October 24, 1993, that Robert Gentles was killed. A black, 23-year-old, former high-school football star, 6 foot 2 inches tall and weighing 220 pounds, Gentles was serving a 31-month sentence for sexual assault, uttering death threats and possessing a stolen credit card. He died by asphyxiation, as five guards armed with Mace tried to get him out of his cell. Guards had been searching all the cells in his range for weapons and drugs, while the prisoners had been complaining that they had not been fed, banging on the bars of their cells and playing radios loudly in protest. When Gentles refused to turn his radio down, the guards decided to remove him forcibly from his cell.

Gentles' death was investigated internally by CSC and found to be accidental. But family and friends accused the prison system of racism and an administrative cover-up. They launched a private prosecution of the guards involved. After a hearing before a justice of the peace, manslaughter charges were laid, the first ever entered against Canadian prison staff in a criminal court. These charges were eventually withdrawn by the Crown on the ground that forensic evidence was inconclusive, though the family and its supporters vowed to continue to fight for their cause.

When I visited Kingston Penitentiary in the fall of 1994, the Gentles case was a burning issue and the air was heavy with tension. An administrator and another prison staff member accompanied me into a section of the prison that was clearly inmate territory. Prisoners were lining up to purchase goods from the inmate-run canteen, which sold items like pop, candy and toiletries. On the wall beside them someone had scrawled "Don't forget Gentles." The administrator appeared not to notice the graffiti and made a friendly comment to one of the prisoners. The inmate grunted a begrudging reply, while others beside him responded with a hateful stare.

I was slightly stunned by the impact of this scene and did not realize that my guide had quickened his pace somewhat and that I was lagging behind. The other staff member noticed this and came back to hurry me on through a set of metal bars that were threatening to close in my path. I realized that for a moment I was alone in a passageway with some of Canada's more dangerous criminals and that they were obviously in a very bad mood. I did not feel that I was seriously at risk but this experience made it clear to me that everyone is vulnerable in jail — prisoners and staff alike — in spite of all the locks, bars and security cameras.

Prisoners are well aware that the guards cannot protect them from other inmates and that it is in the company of their peers that they are most at risk. Prisons are intensely social environments populated by extremely anti-social individuals, many of whom have personality disorders, problems with drugs and alcohol, undiagnosed psychiatric problems and an inability to control their anger or their propensity for extreme violence.

As one ex-offender explained to me, "Every other prisoner is a significant other."

According to Helen, a veteran of the 1960s counterculture, being in jail was like "living in a commune with some really evil people." She told me, "On the first day, you learn never to make any moves until you know what's happening. It's super important to be hyperconscious. You very rarely walk around relaxed. You never forget for a second where you are."

Surveys and statistics have shown that prisoners are seven times more likely to be violently attacked or threatened with violence than people living in the community. Murders are by no means everyday occurrences in prisons, but there are usually at least three or four a year among the more than 14,000 federal prisoners. In September 1995, a CSC spokesperson estimated that the 56 inmate homicides that occurred during the previous decade translated into a murder rate almost twenty times the national average.

Many outsiders may well ask why we should care about convicts killing or maiming one another behind prison walls. Indeed, people sometimes hope that a notorious child killer or sex offender will "get what he deserves" at the hands of other prisoners. We should be worried, however, because most of the prisoners who live in this dangerous environment do return to society. Surely it is not in the public interest for penitentiaries to be training people to be ruthless killers?

A man serving a life sentence for murder told me that he believed himself to be far more dangerous after a few years in maximum security than he had been when he was admitted. He said he was convicted for an isolated crime of passion, but in the prison environment he became a vicious and desperate man. "I would have a knife in my belt every night, so that when the cell opened in the morning I would be prepared. If anyone came at me, I would take them out. I would not want to have to look over my shoulder forevermore," he said.

I asked how he could gain access to weapons in prison and he replied, "Snap off a broom handle and you've got a spear." He went on to explain how he could fashion a lethal knife from wood or plastic. He pointed to various items in the lounge where we were sitting, saying, "For me, that lamp is a steel bar. This may be only a chair to you, but I can see it as something holding four wooden clubs together."

Many prisoners learn for their own protection how to make a homemade knife, known as a "shiv," from almost any available material. I heard of one shiv that was made out of plastic garbage bags that had been melted down and then moulded into a blade. Sometimes the available material will be more easily fashioned into thin pointed weapons which are called "picks." Pieces of metal pipe or other metal objects, removed from prison plumbing fixtures or similar sources, are often used as clubs, which are known as "pipes."

Violent conflicts can arise over personal property, debts or drug deals gone sour. Violence may result from vendettas which have their origins outside the prison. Prisoners sometimes attack others as a result of gang rivalries or racial conflicts.

Intimidation, known in prison slang as "muscling," is a common problem, especially at maximum security prisons like Millhaven and at Kingston Penitentiary (which houses many very dangerous and unstable offenders, though it is actually categorized as "multilevel," because it contains sections with lower levels of security). An administrator at Kingston told me that inmate representatives lobbied against a plan to have prisoners eat together in a dining hall, rather than take their food trays back to their cells, because they were afraid that "heavies" in the population would charge weaker inmates a fee for sitting at the tables. Nick, the guard at Millhaven, told me, "Inmates pay other inmates to use the yard and to lift weights. Sometimes there are groups fighting for control of drugs, jobs, recreation, food lines. It's almost a caveman society where the strong prevail. I feel sorry for those who are just trying to do their time."

Helen, the former Prison for Women inmate, said, "You need to use your intelligence continually to avoid conflict. Those who are not so smart fail to do that and are continually getting themselves into trouble." She explained that a prisoner who wants to avoid conflict must also make sure that she is not perceived as being weak. If a prisoner loses face by failing to stand up for herself, her life could be made miserable for years. Helen gave the example of a situation in a food line-up when another prisoner stepped in front of her. Since she could not afford to be seen overlooking even such a trivial insult, she used to turn around immediately to talk to the person behind her, pretending that she had not noticed.

Violence often arises over issues relating to personal respect. For prisoners, who often lack self-esteem and are accorded little respect in the outside world, it is very important to preserve their honour and their reputations behind bars. Prisoners who lose the respect of their peers can find life almost intolerable. Someone who is not respected and does not respect other people is referred to as "a goof." In a society where many obscene insults are used with impunity, calling someone "a goof" is as sure a way of provoking a fight as a slap on the face with a glove was in the eighteenth century. One older offender bluntly described the etiquette of prison life by saying: "If you don't have respect and consideration here, you don't live too long."

Many prisoners told me that there is no such thing as a fair fight in jail and that it is normal for a prisoner to enlist several others to help in an act of revenge. At Millhaven, I was told, a prisoner who feels aggrieved or insulted may respond at first only with a cold stare, but retaliate days or even weeks later with a knife to the throat or a metal pipe to the back of the head.

Every prisoner has to be prepared to respond to a violent attack at any time, since it could easily be provoked by a misconceived word or glance, as well as by unfounded suspicions. I was told of one murder that occurred because a prisoner took a drag on a smoldering cigarette butt which he thought had been abandoned.

One older offender told me that there is more violence today because the positive values of the con code are no longer followed. He said, "People used to respect your space, your cell, your belongings. Now there are young punks, full of drugs, who respect nothing. They steal among themselves and from other inmates' cells. The only way to obtain respect now is to act with extreme violence. When you live in a place like this, you're always on standby to protect yourself. Every day I have to prove I'm going to survive here at any costs. Jail is a jungle where the weak do not survive or get taken advantage of."

Young and vulnerable prisoners are always at risk of being exploited by sexual predators. This does not usually take the form of overt coercion. The popular image of new prisoners being routinely gang-raped is derived from movies and perhaps some U.S. prison experiences. The Canadian prison culture does not generally condone rape, and predators try to preserve the illusion that their victims are consenting.

Prison psychiatrist Neil Conacher and colleagues at Kingston Penitentiary estimated in a study for a professional journal that, among the 400 inmates in the institution at the time of the study, there were at least five predatory homosexual prisoners, or "wolves." One of these used force to secure his victims and made no attempt to form a relationship with them, while the others denied using violence and claimed that they sought long-term relationships with younger prisoners. One of the predators described in this study was a 55-year-old man, eleven years into a life sentence for second-degree murder. He did not regard himself as a homosexual but as a "normal" man with strong sexual appetites that needed to be satisfied. The paper stated: "He describes a seductive approach involving the offer of drugs in his cell, but such is his reputation that youths approached in this way might often panic, and sign themselves into segregation or demand transfer. In his view, the kids that he approaches are already feminine, 'sluts' who lead him on."

This man's activities were tolerated by guards, the paper stated. "While he is frequently in trouble with authorities over other matters, they are curiously cooperative with this aspect of his behaviour, often agreeing to the 'double-bunking' of a young man into his cell and arranging a quiet transfer if the relationship breaks down."

According to Dorchester Penitentiary inmate Gerald Benoit, an advocate for prisoners with AIDS, predators often misapply skills that they have learned in prison therapy programs to manipulate their victims. He said they listen to the fears of the younger prisoner and then exploit them by offering protection. They may give them drugs and later claim that this was a loan from another inmate who was demanding repayment. In many cases, they isolate their victims from other prisoners by spreading false rumours about them. In the sick dynamics of these relationships, the predator usually passes himself off to others as a normal heterosexual man, while exploiting the shame that his victim feels and threatening to expose him as a "faggot."

Benoit maintains that such relationships are usually initiated without violence, but "once things are behind closed doors, intimidation can be used both to perpetuate and deepen the intimacy and to keep outsiders away."

Sex offenders and child killers, commonly referred to as "skin hounds" or "skinners," are universally hated by other prisoners and are always vulnerable to attack. Besides being fearful and extremely vulnerable, the sex offender population in prison tends to be different because it includes teachers, doctors, dentists, priests and a wide range of other professional men who have nothing in common with the average criminal. These cultural differences, of course, increase the mutual fear and suspicion between protective custody inmates and the general population. Sex offenders are more likely to establish relationships with prison staff than with regular inmates, not only because of their fears, but also because they often feel that they have more in common with the staff intellectually and socially.

In some institutions and for some offenders, the only safe option is to ask to be kept separate from the general inmate population by being placed in protective custody, or "PC" as it is commonly known. Often this means living in the segregation area, the "hole," where other prisoners are placed for punishment. Usually prison segregation units have separate sections reserved for protective custody inmates, but they often have to live under the same conditions as those being punished, remaining locked in their cells for 23 hours a day.

A decision to go into protective custody is a momentous one for any inmate, since it means being clearly identified as a target and therefore living in fear for the remainder of the sentence. It is not only sex offenders who may need protective custody. Intellectually handicapped offenders, often referred to as "inadequates," or those with mental health problems, known to other inmates as "bugs," frequently find their way into segregation because they are being persecuted or exploited by other prisoners. Some prisoners need to be segregated because they are victims of extortion, threats or personal attacks. Protective custody is also a necessity for anyone whom other prisoners believe to be an informant. Some institutions have a policy of requiring that prisoners who want to be placed in protective custody must name their aggressors. Consequently it is often assumed by other prisoners that anyone in PC is "a rat."

Many of the self-proclaimed "solid cons" whom I met boasted about attacking or threatening any sex offender with whom they came in contact. Most others professed sullen hatred for the men whom they described as "skinners." Sex offenders told me about being attacked with knives and beaten with baseball bats in prison yards. They talked about finding broken glass in their food and feces in their beds. One man told me, "They call you a piece of shit. They throw shit and piss at you. How long are you going to have faith that anyone's going to help you?" As a result of all this, many sex offenders try to hide their crime from other inmates and are afraid to identify themselves by attending therapeutic programs.

At the maximum security Kent Institution in British Columbia, I met with a group of lifers who described themselves as the "crème de la crème of bad guys in BC." They appeared anxious to get across the message that they would kill "rats" and "skinners" if ever they are given half a chance. Andy, a bearded middle-aged man who had been in jail for more than twenty years but was still in maximum security, explained his position: "I don't want no pedophile near me. The public is so naive. They think Clifford Olson lives with us. They expect us to accept people like Clifford Olson. But there are still some of us in Canada who will not live with them. I'm not living with them. Even if they're in the hole, I'll do my damnest to attack them."

The prison's security arrangements were geared to prevent this happening. Constructed in what CSC rather optimistically described as a "campus style," Kent Institution has two rows of living units facing one another across a central courtyard, with shared facilities accessible to both. With an influx of sex offenders in recent years, the number of prisoners needing protection mushroomed, particularly at Kent, the only maximum security penitentiary in the Pacific region. In 1990, the institution abandoned its practice of keeping protective custody inmates locked up for 23 hours a day in segregation. Instead, the prison was divided down the middle with each side getting equal access to visiting areas, programs, gym, yard and other amenities. When prisoners from one side were moved around the institution or using any of the facilities, inmates on the other side would be locked behind metal barriers.

The change did not sit well with the members of the general population who saw their use of recreational facilities cut in half. Andy and his friends complained about this, but they preferred to speak in more grandiose terms about their battle with PC inmates. They referred to the PC side of the prison as "the dark side" and wanted to give the impression that they were a sturdy band of solid cons fighting one of the most despicable evils of the world on behalf of the Canadian public.

"That is the code of ethics that we follow," said Andy, "the public should be aware that we try to stop skinners and stool pigeons from getting out and living in their community. The public thinks that we attack pedophiles and rapists because we're animals. Wrong. We all have families. As men in jail, we can't really take care of our loved ones. The only thing we can do to protect our families is preventing these predators getting out and trying to hunt down women and children."

This was probably more of a rationale than an explanation, especially in view of the fact that many of the group of solid cons with whom Andy identified were in prison for murdering their wives. Andy told me that he and his friends had only killed people they knew — "either business or domestic" — unlike sexual predators who may attack strangers.

Our interview was terminated when a guard arrived to inform the inmates that it was time for them to be locked up in their section of the prison so that the PC prisoners could get their lunch. The guard asked if I would like to meet a representative of the PC inmates and the lifers gave me withering looks as they departed, obviously disappointed that I would choose to interview a man whom they evidently regarded as the chairman of the inmate committee from hell.

I listened to the clanging of metal barriers and waited, while the general population was locked up and the protective custody inmates released from their quarters. Earlier in the day I had been given a tour of the institution and got a fleeting, but most memorable, glimpse of the shocking contrast between living conditions on the two sides. Each range of cells had common lounge areas where prisoners were allowed to spend their free time. The lounges were furnished and equipped by inmates using money that they had raised. On the general population side prisoners had made these places as comfortable and as aesthetically pleasing as possible. In one room that I visited, there were sofas, a stereo, a large tank of tropical fish and several striking pieces of art on the walls. On the protective custody side, I visited a lounge with bare walls and no furniture except for a small black and white television on a stand and one institutional, hard-backed chair. The chair had been knocked over and nobody had bothered to pick it up.

The chairman of the Protective Custody Inmates Committee was a lean, ragged-looking man. He had a jagged scar, running across his cheek and jaw. It looked as if it must have been made by a broken bottle or some similarly uneven weapon.

His name was Joel and he spoke with the intensity of a messenger from a dark and dangerous place. The prisoners whom I had interviewed before seemed cosy and complacent in comparison. Joel wanted to talk about the issues and problems that inmates on his side faced. He spoke of the tensions of double-bunking and the system's inability to find places in lower security levels for those who are no longer classified as maximum security inmates.

"We have incidents two or three times a week. In the kitchen somebody throws something at someone else. They are separated. Things happen because of tensions from double-bunking and from people being forced to sit here," Joel said.

Each side of the prison has its own segregation unit. Joel told me that there were 46 prisoners being held in 24 cells on the segregation unit on the PC side. One reason for this was that, even in protective custody, there were many inmates who could not get on with their peers. Some of those in segregation were there at their own request because they had conflicts with other inmates in PC or were afraid of their own shadows. He said there were cases of such inmates staying for three or four years in segregation. Others were there on institutional charges or because of ongoing investigations by the prison's security officers.

According to Joel, one inmate had been held in segregation for three months without even being told why he was being investigated. He said the Institutional Preventive Security Officers "have an answer for everything. When you try to push them on an issue, it's confidential information. They can deny transfer applications, deny paroles, deny jobs, harass visitors. There's basically nothing you can do. It's impossible to defend yourself against them because all they do is say it's confidential information. Accusations can be thrown at you by the dozen. They go on your file as fact without you being able to defend yourself."

Protective custody inmates are more vulnerable to being mistreated by guards, Joel maintained, because they have no solidarity. If prisoners in the general population have a grievance, they may stage a strike or a boycott, refuse to leave their cells or refuse to go in from the yard. But prisoners in protective custody are usually too frightened to assert their rights, and too divided among themselves to take any collective action. This affects the way that they are treated, Joel said.

Although Joel was courteous and spoke in an eminently reasonable way, he also impressed me as being one of the toughest and meanest looking individuals I have ever met. My curiosity got the better of my timidity and I asked him why he was in protective custody. He told me that he had spent many years in prison for various violent crimes and had done most of his time in the general population. In 1985, Joel got into an altercation with a fellow inmate at Matsqui and got the better of it. A friend subsequently warned him that the other man was planning to take revenge.

Joel went on to give me a colourless description of a vicious fight that ended in the death of the other inmate. He said, "I armed myself and waited for him to come. He had a pipe. I had a knife. After he went down on the floor, I went to the bubble and asked the guards to come. They threw me in seg."

While he was in segregation, Joel said, the institutional preventive security officer planted an informant in his cell to extract an alleged confession which was then used as the basis for a first-degree murder charge. But a lawyer was able to persuade the victim's friends to testify in court and Joel was acquitted on grounds that the killing was in self-defence.

Subsequently transferred to Kent, however, Joel found that he now had to deal with several of his victim's friends. There had already been six stabbings during a two-month period on the general population side and Joel realized that he would likely be killed if he did not go into protective custody.

Joel said he well understood the animosity that general population prisoners felt toward those in protective custody. He said, "I've been victimized by informants on a number of occasions. I don't like being grouped with sex offenders and informants. But for me it was a simple choice. Either risk my life or come to this side. I have to put my personal feelings aside. I have to deal with these people on a daily basis."

As Joel spoke, a picture emerged of a protective custody environment rife with paranoia and tension. He said most inmates were suspicious of one another and of the administration. Joel described sex offenders as living in fear of other prisoners, even while in protective custody, keeping to themselves and associating mainly with the guards. Prisoners in protective custody tend to stick to their cells, even when they are free to use common facilities. Joel said no one uses the sparsely furnished lounges unless they have to because "they're basically pretty depressing."

A guard told me that inmates seem to appreciate the security offered by cameras which have been installed in the penitentiary gym. He said that general population inmates wanted to rip them out when they were first installed, but many of those in protective custody usually make a point of staying within view. In prisons where there are no cameras, some inmates spend much of their recreational time sitting with their backs to the walls.

Prisoners who cannot cope with the violence, intimidation and other pressures of penitentiary life are sometimes driven to self-inflicted violence. Self-mutilation, slashing arms and other parts of the body with a blade or broken glass is relatively common in some prisons, particularly Kingston's Prison for Women. Women prisoners are far more likely to slash than men, but I have seen male as well as female prisoners with arms criss-crossed with scars from self-inflicted wounds. A prison psychiatrist told me of one inmate who literally bit a hole in his arm and then explained to staff, "I did it to get back at you guys."

Prisoners may slash themselves in order to vent their frustrations or to get taken temporarily away from the range, while they are given medical attention. Some prison staff members regard slashing as a purely manipulative technique for getting attention and causing trouble. When wounds are superficial, prisoners may be treated on the spot and returned immediately to their cells.

The suicide rate fluctuates from year to year, but it is sometimes more than five times higher than in the Canadian population as a whole. In 1993–94 there were twenty suicides in federal institutions, an alarmingly high figure that worried administrators and prisoners alike. Prison for Women has a dismal record for suicides among Native prisoners, five of whom took their own lives in recent years, but studies have indicated that male prisoners are actually more likely to take their own lives than females. At one medium security men's prison that I visited, an inmate representative told me there had been six suicides there during the previous two and a half years. He said some of them were young men who had been released on parole and returned to prison on minor parole violations.

Most of the prisoners who commit suicide do so by hanging themselves in their own cells, though some choose to die of drug overdoses. CSC research studies have noted that prisoners in overcrowded institutions are more likely to take their own lives. It is often impossible to know why prisoners have killed themselves. The possible reasons cited in various studies include: intimidation, drug debts, illness, mental disturbance, guilt and outside family pressures, such as divorces or denial of access to children.

As one might expect, prisoners who kill themselves are more likely to be serving long sentences. A large proportion of the suicides occur soon after the offender has been admitted to prison. But a more startling conclusion of CSC research studies is that another sizable proportion of the inmate suicides occur when the prisoner is soon to be released. While some long-term offenders take their own lives because they cannot cope with prison life, others commit suicide because they do not feel they can handle being out on the street.

The violence and horror of penitentiary life takes its toll on everyone who is exposed to it. A few are killed and maimed by it and some take their own lives. But most survive and learn to live within the warped prison culture. The attitudes and survival skills required in prison, however, can make people dangerous on the street and render them almost incapable of leading normal lives.

4

AT HOME IN HELL

Almost as disturbing as the violence and cruelty of penitentiary life is the way in which so many prisoners fit into this environment and feel perfectly at home there. It is frustrating for people who believe in harsh punishments to learn that prisoners often make themselves quite comfortable in jail. For those who hope prisoners will one day be rehabilitated, it is alarming to see how deeply they bury themselves in a world that is so disconnected from everyday life and decent human values.

Superficially, conditions appear much easier than many outsiders believe they should be. It is a basic principle of the correctional system that offenders go to prison as a punishment, but not for punishment. Prisoners are deprived of their freedom and forced to submit to whatever rules the system deems necessary in order to preserve security and protect the public. But inmates are otherwise considered entitled to basic civil rights and some of the amenities and comforts of everyday life.

Most institutions have well-equipped gyms, with weights or aerobic equipment. There are exercise yards with baseball diamonds and running tracks. The prisoners are allowed to have televisions, VCRs, computers and stereos in their cells, if they can afford to pay for them and providing the total cost of these items does not exceed limits that are stipulated in institutional regulations.

The prison food is adequate, if not always appetizing, and it can be supplemented with treats from canteens, which are usually run by inmate welfare committees, comprised of prisoners elected by their peers. These committees organize social events and arrange other services for inmates, including cable television. They also represent prisoners' interests in attempting to solve individual problems and collective grievances.

Prisoners may have access to barbecues in the summer and there are usually lounges or common areas with televisions, pool tables and, sometimes, microwave ovens or popcorn poppers. Long-term offenders often purchase furniture, artwork, aquariums, stereos and televisions for their lounges, which can be surprisingly comfortable and aesthetically pleasing.

One prison official explained that all these things contribute to reducing tensions and making an otherwise intolerable environment "liveable." But another staff member complained, "A lot of inmates are institutionalized. They don't pay taxes, don't have to deal with children, don't have to decide what movie to watch. They are placed in work, fed and don't have to deal with marital problems. They're so insulated from the real world. We're not doing them any favours. I think prison should be staying at home with your wife and kids for five years."

These concerns were epitomized by a prisoner at Matsqui, who told me, "It's easy to get meals. I have my bed. I don't have the burden of any responsibility. I don't even have to drive to get my dope. I can just walk down the tier and buy some."

Shortly before I interviewed Helen, a former inmate of Prison for Women, a tabloid newspaper had run a feature story about Karla Homolka, enjoying "all the comforts of home," in the prison where she was serving twelve years for manslaughter in the death of teenagers Kristen French and Leslie Mahaffy. I asked Helen what she would say to people who felt that prisoners were made to feel too comfortable and she replied: "We have the TV and the weight rooms, but they fade into insignificance compared to the suicides, the slashings, the helplessness to do anything to stop other inmates mercilessly persecuting weaker prisoners, the sound of crazy or mentally defective inmates ranting, screaming and throwing bodily fluids around." Helen said she found herself getting so shellshocked that she would withdraw as far as she could into the privacy of her own cell. She used to get mad when people were fighting on the range because she couldn't hear her television.

Prisoners and guards alike pointed out to me that television is one of the few things that keeps prisoners connected with the real world. Watching television also keeps prisoners out of trouble, since it keeps them in their cells and reduces their social interaction with other inmates. It is one of the strange paradoxes of prison life that a prisoner who is anti-social in relation to the people with whom he or she lives may have a better chance of leading a pro-social life on the outside. Those who get too involved with their peers are likely to adopt many of the warped values of the prison subculture. They also learn to deal with people in aggressive and manipulative ways that are not acceptable in the community.

Some prisoners serving long sentences deliberately cut themselves off from anything that might remind them of the outside world, never keeping track of the days and trying to lose themselves in the prison routine. Prisoners refer to this as "doing zombie-time." As contacts with the outside world diminish, inmates become more and more wrapped up in prison life. One ex-convict told me that Millhaven would sometimes buzz with rumours about a plan to "dump," that is kill, a prisoner who was unpopular or had made powerful enemies. "There was a sense of anticipation when somebody was getting dumped," said the ex-convict, who confessed, "I kind of looked forward to it. We got locked up for a few days. The police would come in. It was entertaining."

At Kent Institution, a modern maximum security penitentiary

set in the spectacular scenery of British Columbia's Fraser Valley, a man who had been in jail since 1973 said, "This is our retirement centre. Of all the pens in Canada, this is the treat. There's nothing here. We don't have any work. We just lay around and do nothing."

The only problem, he said, was that there were too many young people serving short sentences. "Older guys doing their time just don't want a screaming kid next door to them all the time. The youngsters realize they don't have to stay here long. In their minds, it's perfectly all right to raise hell. Those goofy fucking little kids should be sent home to Mommy," he said, explaining that the older cons do what they can to teach respect by knifing one of the rowdy young inmates every so often. "It's a sort of school here. You don't learn good things here. You learn how to do bad things the right way," he said.

When I asked Maurice, the former bank robber, about the impact of prison life on younger offenders, he replied, "Whatever propensity for evil he has, we will cultivate it, water it, feed it. We can sustain and nurture the dark side of a human being."

Hard core, long-term offenders, who also tend to be the prisoners with the most violent records, are a dominant influence on the prison environment. For major portions of their adult lives, prison is the only home and the only society or culture that they know, whereas for the steady stream of short-term offenders who pass through the system, it need only be a temporary interruption in their normal lives. But many of the younger offenders easily get caught up in the prison subculture. These are often people whose early lives have offered little that made them feel good about themselves or the community. As one case management officer put it, "It is only for very few individuals that prison is a culture shock. For those from disadvantaged backgrounds, it's no big deal."

Some want nothing more than to make their mark in the prison world. One offender told me that he had spent most of his early life associating with other delinquent youths and arriving at the penitentiary was the fulfilment of an ambition. He said, "I had heard stories about the pen before I got here. I already had an attitude. I was trying to carry the image that's supposed to be projected. I came here in 1983, a nobody. I came in and waited. I learned. I listened, until I made my move. Then I was looked up to. But I ended up turning a three-year bit into a twelve-year sentence." A big man with bulging muscles on his heavily tattooed arms told me that he enjoyed being in prison. He explained, "Introduce a kid to this environment and either he adapts, hits the weight pit and adopts an attitude or he doesn't survive. As soon as I adapted, I found that I liked it. I had acceptance by my peers — an identity."

The ways in which people attain status in prison are often deviant. Professional criminals, members of bikers' clubs and organized gangs are invariably well respected in prison, as are offenders who have committed crimes like armed robbery or escaping custody. Others may win respect in various ways and these include: defying authority; committing acts of violence against informants, sex offenders or other unpopular prisoners; and getting involved in drug dealing and other criminal activity inside the penitentiary.

Those who commit murders or other serious crimes behind bars, together with those who participate in riots, hostage-takings or escape attempts, may be sent to one of CSC's two "super maximum security" Special Handling Units, known as SHUs. Prisoners in the SHU are kept under constant control, cut off from the community and guarded more closely than most caged animals. It is the "end of the line" in the federal prison system, home to the most anti-social and most dangerous prisoners. Within the inmate subculture, however, it is a badge of honour to go to the SHU. When prisoners return to regular maximum security prisons after a period in the SHU, they are treated with respect.

SHU inmates are buried so deeply in the prison system, so cut off from everyday life, that they have little left to lose. Many of them have little self-control and the SHU provides them with an environment where they do not have to take any responsibility for their actions. They are controlled by external force and many prisoners actually thrive in such an environment.

The CSC has two SHUs, one at Ste. Anne-des-Plaines, Quebec, and the other at Prince Albert, Saskatchewan. They are both self-contained units, located within the perimeter of another prison. Each holds between 60 and 70 prisoners in small ranges of single-bunked cells. Each range has a small yard for outdoor exercise. Guards, armed with rifles, patrol catwalks above the ranges and common areas.

Segregation between protective custody and general population inmates is enforced, perhaps even more vigilantly than anywhere else in the prison system. The con code is strong at the SHU and there are many general population prisoners who would consider it a loss of face if they ever encountered a "rat" or a "skinner" and failed to attack him. Some prisoners, like the notorious Clifford Olson, who is held at the Saskatchewan SHU, are never allowed to associate with any other inmates. Others are allowed to share small day rooms where they eat their meals.

The furniture in the day rooms is bolted to the floor to prevent it being broken up to make weapons. Nuts and bolts are welded together. When pieces of equipment, such as the weights in the gym, cannot be welded together, they are secured by chains. In one room, I noticed a television that had been chained to a shelf, placed high out of reach. Beds in the cells are built into the walls and prisoners are not allowed metal objects like paper clips.

Yet the prisoners still manage to arm themselves with pipes, shivs or picks. The Quebec SHU was locked down when I visited, as a result of an assault in which one inmate stabbed another with a weapon made out of the metal housing for neon strip lighting. It had not occurred to anyone before that this could be used to make a weapon and guards were checking to see if any other light fixtures had been tampered with. While they were doing this, they were searching for any further weapons that might be hidden in cells. Staff members told me that they were not as concerned about the most recently discovered weapon as they had been a few months earlier, when they found picks made out of plastic windows. These were particularly alarming as they could pass unnoticed through metal detectors. About thirteen of these weapons were found among the 50 to 60 inmates in the unit at that time.

Some of the SHU inmates are dangerous men who will never see the streets again and cannot even live at peace with other prisoners. Jason, a former SHU inmate, described it as a very tense environment in which "everyone is there for a reason and everyone wants to prove that he is tougher than anybody else." He said it was a place where one can make enemies in an instant and violence can flare up without warning. But everyone is so carefully controlled and monitored by guards that there are relatively few fights and an uneasy peace is usually restored very quickly.

One unit manager described the SHU inmates as "a collection of very volatile men, who are potentially explosive at any moment and could not be held anywhere else." He said his staff were constantly called upon to deal with inmates screaming, spitting, kicking doors, verbally abusing them and threatening their lives. When guards slide food trays through the slots in cell doors, they will sometimes have the food fired back at them. Inmates will also sometimes resist being moved from their cells, slash themselves, throw bodily fluids, smash up their cells and destroy televisions or any other breakable object in the common areas. In other words, the unit manager said, "They tend to demonstrate that they do not have an appropriate attitude to authority."

Nevertheless, several SHU inmates and staff members told me that what they found most scary was not the occasional outbreaks of savage violence, but the unnatural calm that prevailed

most of the time. It was a calm that had been achieved by force
and suppression. The security measures that prevented dangerous offenders from behaving violently had also quashed their
initiative and spontaneity. The prisoners' personalities had been
shut down.

Particularly disturbing was the fact that some prisoners actually liked being in the SHU. Prisoners are transferred involuntarily to the SHU, but staff cannot force them to transfer out of
the SHU to a lower security level. Some prisoners refuse to leave
because they feel safer in the SHU than anywhere else in the
prison system. The cells have solid metal doors, which prevent
other prisoners throwing things at inmates who are considered
pariahs. The cells are also larger than average, usually fairly bright
and always single-bunked. Prisoners can make themselves comfortable there and be quite content, providing they do not mind
the fact that they will never see a visitor except through a metal
or Plexiglas screen. Although the average length of stay at the
SHU is from eighteen months to two years, I was told that one
prisoner had been in the SHU for more than fourteen years and
was terrified at the prospect of ever trying to live in another
environment.

"Guys get so damaged," said Jason, "you can see them dete-
riorating month by month. They get to feel comfortable there.
They are so caught up within the system. You get angry every
time they pull you out of the SHU and you end up fucking up."

Many of the people who spend most of their lives in jail are
not rapists or murderers, but comparatively minor criminals,
unable or unwilling to adapt to life in the outside community. In
prison slang, these people are described as "Doing life in broken bits," or "Doing life on the instalment plan." When I talked
to such inmates about their lives and their prison careers, it
became clear to me that, for many of them, the only places in
the world where they found any semblance of stability, status,
companionship or even happiness, were behind bars.

Particularly haunting and unsettling was the exotic story of a shy, slightly built man who had spent just over half his life in prison. A 54-year-old man, who had been on the street for only seven years since the age of nineteen, Joe was a prison drag queen. He told me that he had found friendship and love in prison, while on the street he was lonely and scared.

I realized how inside out his life was when I asked him about the guards at Millhaven, where he served much of his time. Millhaven is a maximum security penitentiary in which contact between guards and prisoners is limited. When prisoners are moved around the institution they are usually separated from staff by means of metal barriers. Prisoners spend a lot of time locked in their units and guards tend to watch them mainly from security posts. Joe described this situation by saying: "The guards were segregated from us. They hardly ever came out of the cage they were in."

As soon as I realized that from Joe's perspective the guards were the ones behind bars, I began to make more sense of the looking-glass world of convict life that he described to me. Joe gave me a view of a world that was completely beyond the range of my experience and even stranger than I would have imagined. But at the same time he reminded me that the everyday world that we take for granted seems almost as alien to offenders like Joe when they return to society. What the prison system has made of Joe and thousands of other offenders — what it has done for them or failed to do — is an aspect of reality that anyone might encounter walking the streets of any Canadian community today.

Joe had already spent many years in federal prisons and provincial institutions for a series of robbery and burglary convictions before he found his special niche in the inmate culture. He had been present at the infamous riot at Kingston Penitentiary in 1971, which resulted in sex offenders and suspected informants being tortured and killed in a horrifying orgy of violence. He told

me that this was "a good riot," until it turned ugly, since prisoners had been protesting intolerable conditions in "a dirty old
penitentiary."

During the next few years, Joe escaped from prison twice —
not from any burning desire to get away, he explained, but in
order to put something over on the guards. One of these escapades
was a spectacular mass break-out of fourteen convicts from the
supposedly escape-proof Millhaven Penitentiary, soon after it
was opened in the early 1970s. Prisoners were able to cut through
the bottom of the perimeter fence, Joe said, because the view
from the security towers was obscured by the coils of razor wire,
designed to stop anyone climbing over the top. Joe said he and
other inmates gave themselves up to police soon after they got
away, because they did not know where to go or what to do. He
explained that they had escaped in order to prove something,
but not to gain freedom, because "we had no freedom. We were
lost in the world, after doing too much time inside."

After spending time in segregation, Joe was transferred to
Dorchester Penitentiary in New Brunswick, a dark, foreboding
building that looks like a Victorian workhouse. At that time, it
had the reputation of being one of the toughest jails in the country, but for Joe it was a haven. "They pampered us," he said.
"They were afraid of another Kingston riot."

When he arrived, Joe said the deputy warden told him, "If
anybody tries to escape from my prison, I'll be outside the wall
to blow your head off." But, inside the prison, staff turned a blind
eye to how some prisoners dressed and behaved during their
leisure hours.

Soon after he arrived, Joe saw a beautiful young man, with
long auburn hair, wearing make-up and women's clothing. He
was enchanted with this person, but intimidated by "the big brute"
who was with "her." Joe told me that he wanted to get close to
this "queen" but the only way he could find to do that safely was
to become a drag queen himself.

Officially, the prison service did not then, and does not now, permit homosexual activity in penitentiaries. But in practice it would be almost impossible to prevent and, unless there is obvious coercion involved, there is no reason to interfere with activities that may make prisoners calmer and easier to manage. Prisoners themselves tend to have ambivalent attitudes in this area. Many prisoners who would not consider themselves homosexual can get involved in a close relationship, casual sex or a marriage of convenience, when no other sexual outlet is available. According to Joe, some drag queens were attacked by other prisoners during the Kingston riot, but generally they are tolerated as part of the prison subculture.

During the time that Joe was at Dorchester, he said, there were fifteen drag queens, each with a formidable partner. They were treated with respect "because if you bothered any of our group, you'd be lucky if you made it out of the prison alive."

The queens all worked in the prison tailors' shop and made their clothes there. One prisoner who claimed to have been some kind of minister on the outside performed marriage ceremonies. When Joe got married, he said, the other queens helped to dress him and put on make-up. After their wedding ceremonies, they used to have dances in the gym to which other prisoners were invited. It was the only time that the husbands let the girls dance with the other guys.

"I was protected and pampered, even by the other queens. All of us were close. We'd each got a man. People looked after me. I found somebody to love me," said Joe.

The life that Joe led in jail made him passive. Prison tends to do that to most inmates, since it takes care of basic needs like food and shelter, removes them from family responsibilities and denies them most of the choices that people make in everyday life. But Joe was also shielded from the kind of personal decisions that most prisoners have to make every day to function in the environment and stay alive. He did not have to worry about conflicts with other prisoners as long as his husband and friends protected him. Describing what seemed to me like a parody of an old-fashioned marriage, Joe said, "If you're more on the feminine side, all these people do your thinking for you." As time went by, Joe said, "I became meeker and milder. I needed more and more of these people's help in prison."

It was not a safe environment, although Joe was usually protected from the dangers that surrounded him. He mentioned in passing that one of his best friends, another queen, got killed. Joe said that he himself at one time became too close with another queen and their husbands threatened their lives.

After Joe broke up with his husband because of his relationship with other queens, he began hanging out with a young guy called Billy. On Saturday and Sunday mornings the cells would be left open and Joe would join Billy in his cell. Prison staff would allow this as long as there was no trouble. Billy and Joe used to sleep together all morning, but never once had sex during the three years that they were friends. Joe told me, "It became such an affectionate love affair and the prison was permitting it."

"They had a hard time getting me out of that prison," he said, "I was happy. I had more in there than I had ever had in my life." When he was released from prison, Joe felt that he had been expelled from the only world where he belonged. He felt as if he had landed on Mars. All the important things in his life were completely outside the frame of reference of anyone whom he might encounter on the street. "How can they believe this on the street?," he said. "It's hard to go out on the street and say, 'I'm married. My husband's in jail. Here's my ring.'"

During his brief periods on the street, Joe was terrified. He used to carry knives around to protect himself. He felt he could not do anything for himself. He had no idea how to relate to people after years in an environment where he was always being pursued and admired by men who found him attractive. Then there was usually a friend or loved one in jail to whom he longed to return. He used to work hard at getting sent back to prison, committing brazen, careless burglaries, and feeling frustrated when he did not get caught.

Although Joe's prison experiences were quite different from those of other offenders whom I met, his problems were similar to those of many other prisoners who have become so wrapped up in the prison culture that they no longer see a role for themselves in the outside world. At a parole hearing, I heard a female offender explain that she had committed two senseless crimes in order to be able to rejoin her lover in prison. She twice assaulted older people, using just enough violence to make it likely that courts would sentence her to federal time. She explained that she had to commit two such crimes because she did not get caught on the first occasion.

Helen, the former inmate of Prison for Women, told me the tragic story of a young Native offender who had lost contact with her home community and her adoptive family. In jail, the young woman had a series of passionate and stormy relationships with other prisoners. A waif-like woman, with tattoos on her face as well as her arms, her appearance seemed normal in the prison environment, but would have appeared freakish to people whom she encountered on the street during brief periods of release. In a state of deep depression, the young woman asked Helen, "Is there anyone out there who cares about me?" Helen was unable to name anyone, because there really appeared to be nobody outside the prison who cared. Soon after this conversation, the young woman hanged herself in her cell.

It is very important that prisoners be able to maintain some contact with family and friends in the community, as those who do are far less likely to give up hope of ever making a life outside the jail subculture. To this end, friends and family members are allowed to visit prisoners regularly.

But family visits take place within a prison environment which tends to distort all relationships. In most prisons, the visiting areas are large lounges, where inmates and their families can sit together at cafeteria-style tables. The lounges are monitored by guards from a security post with the aid of video cameras and sound-recording devices. Families and friends are also sometimes allowed into prisons to participate in dances or socials. For security reasons, some prisoners are not allowed "contact visits," where they may be in physical contact with outsiders. They can receive "non-contact visits," in booths where they are physically separated from their visitor by a Plexiglas screen.

The guards who monitor visits are also responsible for going through prisoners' mail. They are not supposed to read the letters, merely check the packages for contraband. From casual conversations with guards in Visits and Correspondence units, I got the impression that many of them knew far more about prisoners' private lives than could be gleaned from looking at the insides of the envelopes.

Most federal prisons also have family visiting trailers, which are small furnished apartments, where prisoners are allowed to spend up to 72 hours with their spouses and children. Usually there are no more than two such units in each prison. Since most penitentiaries house several hundred inmates, there is always a long waiting list for the use of the trailers. Prisoners are normally allowed conjugal visits, providing there is no security risk involved, if they can prove that they are legally married or were living common-law for at least six months before they were incarcerated.

Many victims of crime, other members of the public and some prison staff members are offended by the notion that prisoners, including murderers and other vicious criminals, should be allowed conjugal visits in comfortable, furnished apartments. But the visits can save marriages, provide comfort and hope for spouses, as well as prisoners, and allow children to maintain bonds with parents. For female offenders, separated from their children, the need is often even more intense. The trailer visits also serve as an antidote to the poisonous influence of prison culture by providing a semblance of ordinary community life and a brief return to civilized values. Evaluations of the family visiting program have indicated that it improves the morale and behaviour of inmates, reducing the number of offences that they commit in institutions and cutting down dramatically the risk of prisoners escaping.

The possibility of conjugal visits is an incentive for unmarried prisoners to seek relationships with members of the opposite sex in the community with a view to marriage. It is not unusual for wedding ceremonies to be held in prison chapels or visiting areas. Some "prison brides" are members of community groups doing volunteer work in the prison, while others may be friends or relatives of other inmates. It is also quite common for prisoners to come in contact with their future spouses through advertisements in personal columns for pen pals or companions.

Many such relationships are apparently healthy and mutually beneficial, but several prison guards told me that they viewed some of these marriages as little more than commercial transactions in which sex was bought and sold. There is also a danger that the spouse may be a very needy individual whom the prisoner has deceived and manipulated. Prison staff members are not supposed to divulge personal information about prisoners, but individuals may take it upon themselves to warn fiancées if their husband-to-be has murdered his previous wife. Usually prisoners are persuaded to disclose such information, if they have not done so already. In many such cases, fiancées are satisfied with the prisoner's explanation and convinced that he has rehabilitated. Many prison wives firmly believe that their husbands were wrongly convicted of their crimes.

Trailer visits provide prisoners with a tenuous link to their families and spouses, but they also tend to foster unrealistic expectations and preserve relationships that could not survive in the outside world. The visits allow prisoners and their spouses

to enjoy intimacy without necessarily sharing any of the responsibilities of everyday life. As one prison guard put it, "When
they have trailer visits, it's always a honeymoon."

There is also a grave danger of spouses and their children
being exposed to abuse. Background checks are conducted on
the families before visits are approved, but what goes on in the
trailer is not monitored. The risks were most clearly and tragi-
cally demonstrated by the death of a prisoner's wife in a trailer
unit at Kent Institution in 1993.

Patricia Williams, a 46-year-old former antiques dealer with
two adult children from a previous marriage, had left her home
in England in order to live near the man with whom she fell in
love after answering a classified advertisement. Initially, she was
perhaps unaware that her husband-to-be, 31-year-old Greg
Williams, was serving a life sentence for beating a woman to
death with a steel pipe. But she presumably knew that when
the couple married inside the prison in July 1992. After the
ceremony, the prisoner told a newspaper reporter, "no man, no
prison, no guards, no wars" would ever separate them.

Fifteen months later Patricia was found dead in the family
trailer unit at the end of a 72-hour visit, her husband unconscious beside her. Greg Williams subsequently confessed to
injecting her with a fatal overdose of heroin. He pleaded guilty
to manslaughter, claiming that the couple had made a suicide
pact after learning that they would be separated because she
had been denied immigrant status in Canada.

After Patricia Williams' death, a CSC report on the family
trailer program noted that there had been 10,000 family trailer
visits in 1992–93, but only 36 security incidents were reported,
a tiny fraction of the 1,278 incidents reported in prisons that
year. Only five of the incidents in trailers were major assaults
and 21 involved contraband.

There is clearly grounds for concern, however, when prison
programs put members of the public at risk. Particularly trou-

blesome is the potential threat to children. An administrator at one prison that I visited said that there have been occasions when child protection agencies have become involved in situations where children were allegedly abused. The trailers in this prison had small backyards with picnic tables that were surrounded by steel fences topped with razor wire. It was hard to imagine what the emotional impact would be on a small child forced to spend three days in such an environment with an abusive father, perhaps serving a long sentence for a violent crime.

The risks and problems associated with the family visiting program present the correctional service with dilemmas that are not easily solved. The program is widely regarded within the prison system as too valuable to scrap. Past experience has shown that problems do not often occur — though it is hard to know for sure, especially with regard to child abuse. Security checks and stricter regulations for approving visits can minimize the risks. But is any risk acceptable? Patricia Williams' family would say not, though she herself, like other prisoners' spouses, fought hard for the right to visit her husband. Restricting family visits could make some children safer, but it would also impoverish the emotional lives of others by depriving them of a few days of family life. There are no easy answers and prison officials are forced to choose what they see as the lesser of two evils, persevering with the program and doing what they can to prevent another tragedy.

In the isolated and artificial world of a penitentiary, there are few solutions to any problems that do not involve, at best, a compromise. Often, the solutions create more problems. Violence and the distorted values of the prison subculture force prisoners to adapt in unhealthy ways. Security measures designed to control the violence result in prisoners becoming passive. The more isolated prisoners become, the less chance there is that they can ever lead a normal, law-abiding life. Yet programs to preserve prisoners' links with the community may expose outsiders to risk.

5

PRISONERS OF THE DRUG WAR

"Where there are drugs, there is violence," commented Joe, an aging ex-offender, as he recalled one of several brutal murders he had witnessed during his prison career. He described with graphic detail how a young man was savagely stabbed to death and sexually assaulted by a cell mate, high on drugs. The killing resulted from a dispute over a small piece of hashish that the assailant believed the younger man had taken. The two men were locked in their cell, Joe explained. The murderer, he said, "didn't care about nothing, didn't even try to hide the fact he killed the guy. And the cell was half-filled with blood."

For Joe, this murder was a symptom of a drug problem in penitentiaries that has destroyed much of the old inmate culture, distorted relationships and made prisons increasingly dangerous and unpredictable. Many other prisoners, particularly older ones, described drugs the same way. As one man put it, "Drugs have weakened the convict."

Prison staff members also told me that drug trafficking and the intimidation associated with it were an overwhelming problem that invaded and corrupted every aspect of prison life. Guards told me that drug-related violence was out of control and creating an unsafe environment for everyone. Therapists said that the purpose of rehabilitative programs was being defeated by drug abuse.

But they were all describing extremely complex issues that

are inextricably linked with other problems that are endemic to prisons. While drugs may have precipitated the murder that Joe described, sexual assault may also have been a motive. The pressures of double-bunking were obviously a factor, since the two men were locked in a cell together. However drug-crazed the murderer may have been, it is hard to imagine such a sense-less crime and such indifference to the consequences, except in a prison environment.

The correctional service has declared drugs to be one of the crucial problems facing penitentiaries. In 1995, the CSC com-missioner announced a series of new strategies designed to combat this menace. Many people inside the prison system are convinced, however, that the problems are so widespread and so deeply ingrained that only drastic measures will work. Some prisoners and staff members fear that any attempt to deal with the drug problem will actually result in more harm than good.

Drug abuse and trafficking in prison, like most other prison problems, begins in the community. Whatever happens in prison, either to reduce the problems or to escalate them, will have con-sequences in the community. Drug smuggling does not respect prison walls any more than it does international borders. Pris-oners' families and other community members are directly affect-ed by the prison drug trade and the violence associated with it. When drug abusers leave prison untreated or with more serious problems, society is faced with untold costs and inestimable risks.

It would be naïve to expect that there would not be a major problem with drugs in federal penitentiaries, given that the pop-ulation includes about 1,300 drug offenders, all of whom were convicted of serious offences, such as trafficking and smuggling, that merited a sentence of two years or more. Not included in this figure are the many drug users sentenced to penitentiary for other crimes. According to data gathered in penitentiary intake units, approximately 70 per cent of offenders say they committed their crime under the influence of drugs or that drugs were a major factor in the offence.

Canada is second only to the United States in the number of drug arrests per capita. We may have more serious drug problems than other countries, but it also suggests that we favour law enforcement over other ways of dealing with the problem. This tendency is illustrated clearly by the fact that there are more drug users in Canadian prisons than in treatment centres. It is also likely that prisons are increasing the number of drug users on the street. Many prisoners told me that they acquired drug habits in jail or moved from soft to hard drugs during the course of their sentences.

People addicted to drugs like heroin or crack cocaine will do almost anything to feed their habit. Many of the addicts who find themselves in prison have got there because of desperate crimes committed to obtain drugs or money to buy them. It is only to be expected that they will resort to any means to get drugs in prison. Other drug users, who have relied on drugs in the past to relieve stress or avoid problems in their lives, are likely to want them all the more to cope with the tensions of prison life. Occasional users and even people who have never taken drugs before are likely to be tempted to indulge in an intensely boring and stressful environment. Peer pressure in the overcrowded jails may force some prisoners to take drugs in order keep the trust of cell mates or others on their range.

Prisons are therefore a very lucrative market for the drug trade. For some dealers, especially those who are well connected with organized crime, a prison sentence is a promising business opportunity. According to the 1994 report of the Expert Committee on AIDS in Prisons, drugs may increase in value by as much as 500 per cent when they are sold behind prison walls. In spite of the high prices, many prisoners find ways of paying for drugs or obtaining them by other means. Evidence of this was provided by the results of a CSC random drug-testing program which showed that at any one time, approximately 20 per cent of inmates' urine samples contained a drug. Most of the positive samples contained more than one drug, thus indicating that prisoners were using a number of drugs at the same time.

The AIDS task force report, which was commissioned by CSC, also estimated that only 5 per cent of the drugs entering penitentiaries are intercepted by authorities. Since pills and small quantities of hard drugs are easier to smuggle, heroin and Valium are common commodities traded on the underground economies of the penitentiaries, though hashish remains the drug of choice for many prisoners and is also available.

Friends and relatives visiting individual prisoners or attending socials are the most common sources for the drugs that find their way into prison. Many members of CSC staff maintain that the only effective way to limit drug trafficking would be to cut off all visits in which outsiders may have physical contact with inmates. On the other hand, the goal of eventually reintegrating prisoners in society is best served by preserving their contacts with family and other community members. In fact, the Corrections and Conditional Release Act requires that prisoners be allowed visits, except for reasons of safety or security. CSC staff do not normally refuse visits unless the visitor has a serious criminal record or the Institutional Preventive Security Officer, the IPSO, has reason to believe that the visitor is likely to bring in contraband or otherwise jeopardize security.

The correctional service is therefore faced with the extremely difficult task of limiting drug smuggling in areas where two or three guards monitor up to 100 visitors a day who may remain in close contact with prisoners for several hours. Staff can watch and listen in on the conversations of individuals whom they suspect, but the situation is complicated by the fact that the major drug dealers pressure other prisoners, who are not likely to arouse suspicion, into persuading their visitors to bring in drugs.

Visitors often wrap drugs in balloons or condoms and conceal them in body cavities. Even baby's diapers may sometimes provide a hiding place. The drugs may be exchanged while kissing or embracing. Prisoners may then swallow the condom containing the drugs or go to the washroom where they can conceal it on their own bodies.

Basic human decency as well as civil rights limit the options of prison staff in responding to such situations. By law, prisoners, as well as visitors, can refuse to submit to full body searches. Prisoners can be placed under 24-hour observation in what is known as a "dry cell," where there is no flush toilet and any concealed drugs can eventually be retrieved. But monitoring a dry cell is not a duty that guards relish and staff cutbacks have made it difficult for institutions to provide the level of supervision required to do it on a routine basis.

Visits to prisoners are not the only potential source for smuggled drugs. No matter how secure a prison is supposed to be, there is a steady stream of outsiders passing in and out of the doors. Food and other supplies must be delivered. Tradespeople are required for repairs and routine maintenance. Numerous professionals and volunteers visit prisons for many different purposes. CSC employees routinely pass in and out of prison gates without being subjected to even a cursory search.

An administrator at one prison told me that it was counterproductive to be too efficient at stopping visitors from bringing in drugs. "Drug dealers are very ruthless," he said. "They will go to any length to try to get drugs in. If you cut down on the personal avenues, the pressure is going to increase on staff."

Prison reform activist Clare Culhane pointed out to me that drugs used to get in to the old British Columbia Penitentiary in the days when all visitors were required to remain behind glass screens. She said she once asked the warden how he thought the prisoners were getting their drugs and he merely looked out of the window to see if it was snowing. A prisoner at Matsqui said to me, "If visitors are not bringing drugs in, staff will. If not staff, the walls are not that high."

At the Prison for Women in Kingston, prisoners frequently received packages of drugs "by air mail," thrown over the wall by accomplices on the outside. A report on a security incident at the prison noted, "This problem is not easy to solve. The area is large and any initiative will be expensive." One prison administrator told me, "For every system we create, they will come up with a way to beat the system."

Prisoners with the means to do so can buy drugs with funds transferred directly to drug dealers using third parties on the street. Sometimes inmates will beg or borrow money from friends or relatives for this purpose.

Inside the prison, there is little cash available and the economy operates on a barter system. Prisoners are given a wage for the work they do in prison or for participating in programs and classes. But this allowance does not usually exceed $6.90 a day and is placed in an account from which prisoners can make direct payments for items like soft drinks, cigarettes, candy and toiletries, which they obtain at prison canteens. Cigarettes are hoarded and used as a currency for drug purchases. Major debts or purchases could be paid off with stereos, clothes or objects filched from workshops. Services like tattooing may also be traded and some prisoners perform sexual favours for money or drugs.

Prisoners who allow others to "front" them drugs or other goods when they first arrive may find their debts growing rapidly beyond all proportion. They may soon find themselves pressured to hide items of contraband in their cells or to persuade their visitors to smuggle in drugs. They can very quickly find themselves far more deeply involved in the prison drug culture than they ever intended.

Those who build up heavy debts risk being badly beaten or even killed, if they cannot pay. Some resort to stealing from other prisoners, a recurring problem, which is becoming more difficult to prevent as a result of double-bunking. In several prisons that I visited, the inmate-run canteens had suffered heavy losses through break-ins and petty theft. At Matsqui, the inmate committee was struggling to pay off an $18,000 debt as a result of a canteen break-in.

The correctional service has long been concerned about the prison drug trade and its connection with violence and death. According to the report of a 1991 Task Force on Substance Abuse, 49 people were killed in Canadian penitentiaries, between 1981 and 1986, and many of these crimes were a direct result of alcohol or drug use and trafficking in drugs. During 1985–86 alone, 181 major violent incidents occurred, of which 106 (58 per cent) were believed to be related to drug use.

People working in the prison system believe that the problems of drug abuse, drug trafficking and related violence have got even worse since then. Overdoses and suicides prompted by drug debts were among nine inmates' deaths in 1993–94 that CSC attributed directly to drugs.

In some cases, murders and assaults are committed by prisoners stoned on drugs. In others, the violence arises from a dispute over drugs or as a reprisal for an unpaid drug debt. One former inmate of Millhaven recounted the story of a wealthy businessman serving a life sentence for murder who tended to throw his money around and spent a lot of it on drugs. My informant told me that the prisoner eventually got wise to the fact that prison drug dealers were "ripping him off mercilessly" and stopped giving them money. The drug dealers responded with a vicious attack in which they injected battery acid into him. The victim survived the attack and was transferred to another prison.

A series of inquests in Ontario in 1994 focussed public attention on a prison drug problem that seemed to have run far out of control. One of the most sensational of these cases involved the murder of 22-year-old Trung Ky Duong in an exercise yard at Millhaven on December 16, 1993. Duong was with a group of other Asian prisoners in the yard of "J" unit, home to some of Canada's most violent criminals, when they were charged by about 40 white inmates. Steven Poutsoungas, a dangerous offender who had previously stabbed one other prisoner to death and beaten another unconscious with a baseball bat, was seen by a guard chasing Duong through the crowd and stabbing him five times with a homemade knife. As is often the case in such incidents, there was nothing that prison staff members could do to protect the victim without endangering themselves or the other prisoners in the yard.

Soon after the killing, Poutsoungas was seen giving drugs to other inmates in the prison gym. Guards also saw him and other inmates burning his blood-soaked clothes. When Poutsoungas was subsequently searched and interrogated, a metal detector indicated that he had something hidden in his anus. Guards suspected that it was either a weapon or drugs wrapped in tin foil, but the prisoner laughed as he reminded them of his rights under the law which does not allow X-rays or internal searches without an inmate's consent.

Prison security officers believed that Poutsoungas was a major drug dealer at Millhaven, while Duong, whose body contained traces of Valium and marijuana, was known as a "muscle" for other drug traffickers. Duong had been serving sentences for the murder of a Toronto teenager and the beating death of a Winnipeg shopkeeper. At Millhaven, he was implicated in the stabbing of two other Asian inmates who had refused to pay a drug debt. Other prisoners told police that Duong was killed because he had "not shown proper respect." Poutsoungas was transferred to a prison in Quebec and hanged himself in his cell in February 1994, before he could be brought to trial on a charge of manslaughter.

According to testimony at another inquest, three film canisters were discovered during an autopsy, hidden in the anus of a man who died of a heroin overdose at the minimum security Frontenac Institution near Kingston in October 1993. One contained hashish and there were 118 Valium pills in another. The third canister was filled with $40,000 worth of 62 per cent pure "Mexican Brown" heroin, small amounts of which could constitute a fatal dose.

The drug trade is often controlled by powerful, well-organized groups with strong underworld connections on both sides of the bars. Not only can they have prisoners killed inside the penitentiary, but they are also sometimes capable of threatening the lives of relatives on the outside. Depending on the prison, its location and the demographics of its population, there may be one dominant group, several groups catering to different clientele and respecting one another's turf, or different elements vying for control in often vicious turf wars. A spectacular example of this was in Montreal, where members of two rival biker gangs deliberately committed crimes in order to get into the provincial Bordeaux jail in the fall of 1994 and then engaged in a violent war over control of the prison drug trade.

At the federal Edmonton Institution, the warden, Jack Linklater, described a vicious turf war that ensued when the prison was converted from a medium to a maximum security penitentiary institution. Ten inmates were seriously stabbed during a ten-month period, he said, "and it was nothing like the movies. Without exception, each of the stabbings was in the back. These were cowardly attacks of vicious men trying to get control."

The large-scale drug dealers, however, generally want to have a peaceful prison environment in order to pursue their business. When there are serious conflicts, institutions are usually "locked down," with prisoners confined to their cells. Lockdowns frustrate the drug dealers because they disrupt trafficking within the institution and cut supply sources, since visitors are not allowed in. It is in the interests of the drug dealers to avoid such situations, and they therefore try to reach an accommodation with their rivals.

In almost every prison, there is a powerful group of insiders who act like underworld crime bosses, controlling many aspects of inmate affairs. One of my sources referred to these people as "the intelligentsia" of the prison population, others called them "wheels" or "players." These people keep track of who comes and goes to the prison, what their backgrounds and skills are — in much the same way as the intake and assessment staff, though for very different reasons. They will broker deals and form alliances with various groups involved in drugs and other criminal activities.

Mark, an ex-offender, told me that his life was once threatened at Millhaven because he tried to organize a social evening for prisoners and visitors from the community. A prison drug dealer assumed that the social was an attempt to hone in on the drug trade, since such occasions can provide good opportunities for smuggling in contraband. The drug dealer told Mark that he would have him killed, a threat that could never be taken lightly at Millhaven. Mark went to the prison power brokers for help. Having heard his case, they told Mark that they would intervene to stop the drug dealer from carrying out his threat. They explained that a killing would be counter-productive as it would inevitably result in a lock-down, which would temporarily dry up the drug supply and bring a lot of heat on their operations.

The inmate power brokers sometimes control the inmate welfare committees, which run the prison canteens, represent the interests of prisoners and organize social events. Like prohibition era city bosses, members of these groups often use the committee and other channels of influence to help favoured individuals get the most desirable inmate jobs within the prison. Some of these jobs can then be used to gain further advantages, such as access to areas where drugs can be hidden, opportunities to make weapons or a freedom of movement that makes it easier to distribute drugs.

In several prisons that I visited, however, inmate committees appeared to be working conscientiously for the benefit of other prisoners. In some they seemed to have a close relationship with administrators and were, perhaps, less well trusted by fellow prisoners. The majority of CSC staff members with whom I discussed this issue took the position that inmate committees serve a valuable purpose in providing prisoners with some form of representation and mechanism for helping one another, organizing social events and charitable activities, improving morale and self-esteem.

Prison administrators and guards sometimes see even the prison underworld power structures as stabilizing influences on the inmate population. Their activities are tolerated and even tacitly encouraged because they make it easier to manage a very volatile situation. In describing the activities of an inmate committee, one union representative told me, "These are no heroes standing up for the rights of the little inmate. But the management is using them to keep a lid on the institution."

Jack Linklater, the warden at Edmonton Institution, described inmate committees as "a power house group up to no good." He said prisoners were muscled into voting for the strongest and most powerful inmates, who would use the committee to further their ends in controlling the drug trade and laundering money through the canteen. Linklater abolished the inmate committee in his institution, replacing it with a system of representation that prisoners boycotted on the grounds that it was undemocratic. In an attempt to disrupt the underground economy in the institution, the warden also took over the administration of the inmate-run canteen, a move that prisoners compared to the heavy hand of a tin-pot dictator.

These steps were part of a series of measures at Edmonton Institution designed to curtail the heavy drug trade and deal head on with the problems of the prison underworld. Many of these measures would subsequently be incorporated into the tough new anti-drug strategies announced by CSC in 1995. The problem that I encountered when I visited Edmonton in November 1994 was that the new policies had contributed to an environment that was more tense than almost any other prison that I visited and was described by one prisoner as "merciless, degrading and miserable as hell." Edmonton Max, as the prison is commonly called, was haunted by memories of past violence and bristling with tensions that promised more to come. My tour of the building took me through recreation rooms that had been closed and converted to staff offices. My guide pointed out the spot where a prisoner had been murdered under a pool table, before the poolroom was closed. They had not closed the gym, where a guard was stabbed by an inmate who asked him to fetch a basketball. But I noticed that it was untidy and dirty, unlike almost any other room in any prison that I visited. The assault on the guard was a recent event which left staff tense, fearful and angry with prisoners.

Linklater explained that he used to be a social worker with liberal views on prison administration. The violence that he had encountered in the prison changed his attitudes. It became obvious, he said, that one cannot help inmates without first taking firm control of the prison environment and acting decisively to combat the negative influences of the inmate subculture and the drug-driven underground economy.

"The business of control is so important to doing significant work. The collective mentality works against people trying to help. You have to create an environment where inmates can be individuals. They need to be controlled and safe," Linklater said. The administration began to take control by strictly limiting prisoners' freedom of movement, separating them into small groups before they were allowed to pass from one section of the prison to another for programs, work, meals or recreation. Prisoners were frisked frequently as they moved within the institution and additional armed guard posts were set up. In an aggressive attempt to dry up the drug trade, the institution purchased a dog that had been trained by Canada Customs to detect drugs. Staff members explained to me that the chocolate-coloured

Labrador, which they called Max, was used for cell searches and also placed in a cage in a corridor outside the prison visiting area. Visitors would sometimes have to walk between a fan and the dog's cage. Whenever the dog appeared to detect drugs, the visitors would be asked if they would consent to be searched. Those who did not consent would be asked to leave and not allowed further visits.

When there is a major social event at Edmonton Max, officers stationed at the entrance are accompanied by police. They have a list of the people authorized to attend. When they are suspicious, they direct vehicles to a separate parking lot and ask permission to search the vehicle using the drug dog. Many vehicles drive away as soon as they see the police and the dogs.

Prisoners whom I met were angry about these Draconian measures. "I don't think it's positive to oppress people and put them down," Craig, an unofficial prisoners' representative told me. He said inmates were becoming depressed, angry and more anti-social than ever before as a result of cutbacks in self-help groups, recreational facilities, hobby craft opportunities and social events.

Craig said drugs were still readily available, but more expensive. He said this was perhaps a result of the stricter controls, although it was hard to be sure because drug prices on the street had also gone up. In any event, he said, the practical result was that there was more extortion and intimidation, since prisoners were having to go deeper into debt to buy their drugs.

Prisoners with long sentences ahead of them have very little to lose once they had already been stripped of their privileges, Craig told me. He said, "A result is that we're going to have more acts of violence. When you oppress people for lengthy periods of time, you're going to have revolt and instability." A former Edmonton inmate, whom I met in another institution, agreed: "The problems in there are going to get worse. The attack on the guard was just a beginning. Now the guys are going to stand together and say, 'Fuck you.'"

In other prisons, some staff members told me that cracking down too hard on drugs can cause more problems than it solves. Many violent and volatile prisoners are calmer when they have drugs. An official at a woman's prison said that she can always tell when there is a shortage of drugs because tensions rise and the inmates become more cranky.

In the absence of drugs, prisoners are likely to resort to making "brew," a highly potent, often sickening, alcoholic beverage concocted in makeshift stills from kitchen scraps or whatever the prisoners can find. Several veteran guards informed me that brew can make prisoners more crazy and reckless than almost any hard drug. It is especially dangerous because it tends to be shared by all the prisoners on any range where it is brewed, unlike drugs which are usually sold on an individual basis. An administrator, who has traumatic memories of riots in which colleagues were killed, said, "Brew in prison is poison. We snuff it out like wildfire." At Edmonton Max, a young administrator boasted about the success of the anti-drug policies by saying, "We can tell that drug use is way down, because now we're having to deal with a brew problem."

The new CSC drug strategy had the ambitious goal of creating a drug-free and safe prison environment. CSC Commissioner John Edwards told a parliamentary committee in April 1995 that prisons were already seeing the benefit of new policies, such as strengthened search procedures, better screening of visitors, more extensive drug testing and tougher sanctions. But, in what was perhaps a huge understatement, he admitted that the drug problem had not disappeared entirely and was unlikely ever to do so. He said, "When you confine some of the country's biggest drug dealers and many serious drug users within the same four walls, it shouldn't be too surprising that they will continue trying to ply their trade."

In British Columbia, where heroin addicts are relatively

common in the prison population, many CSC staff members acknowledged that drug-control programs were doomed to fail. A middle-management staff member at the maximum security Kent Institution told me that the institution takes every precaution it can to stem the flow of drugs, but "as long as we have a front gate and people come in, drugs are going to be moved."

The supply could be slowed down by tightening procedures and strictly following rules with respect to visits and searches, the staff member said. But he wondered what end it would serve, if visiting time were cut and the drug supply dwindled "to the point where tension becomes unbearable."

The CSC drug strategies do not include any measures that would routinely restrict visits or reduce contact between prisoners and their families. But visits may be denied and suspended indefinitely if the institution believes that drugs may be exchanged. Prisoners who have been found to be involved with drugs may be denied any future contact visits.

Prisoners and their families have complained to CSC that this is unfair and counter-productive. Graham Stewart, executive director of the John Howard Society of Ontario, called this policy "perverse" in a letter to CSC Commissioner Edwards. He wrote, "Many inmates will tell you that the people who are often most important to them in helping them deal with their drug problem are their families and visitors. Depriving people of these contacts will only lead to greater despondency and frustration and, in that state of mind, they have little motivation to refrain from drug use."

In principle, visitors are supposed to be monitored more carefully with the use of sniffer dogs and more rigorous searching. In practice, however, with an ever-increasing number of prisoners and decreasing levels of staffing, it is likely that the situation will remain one in which policies cannot possibly be implemented because there is no one available to do the job.

CSC relies a great deal on informants in its effort to combat drugs. Prisoners at Matsqui told me that they call the place "Ratsqui." They claimed that it has become almost routine for prisoners with drug debts to "rat out" their creditors and then get authorities to transfer them to another institution. The prisoners told me that it is also common for drug dealers to inform on their rivals in order to eliminate competition.

A staff member who disapproved of the use of informants told me, "Snitching destabilizes. A lot of programs run on trust, but the security people are creating an environment where there is no trust." He said that using informants can actually increase risk to the public, citing the notorious example of Daniel Gingras, a convicted killer and prison drug dealer, who was rewarded for his activities as an informant at Edmonton Institution by being allowed to go to the Edmonton Mall under guard on his birthday. He escaped from his escort and went on to murder two people.

Informants are often unreliable and self-serving, though this does not seem to prevent security officers from putting their information in other prisoners' files. Prisoners are frequently penalized on the basis of anonymous reports that they can never challenge. Information gleaned from such sources will often remain on their records and eventually be reviewed by the parole board, even if it remains unproven.

Prisoners and prison rights advocates have made strong protests against another tactic that CSC has employed in its assault on drugs. Recognizing that the underground economy is largely based on barter rather than hard currency, CSC has begun aggressively seeking out and confiscating any goods that prisoners have in their cells without official permission.

Prison regulations specify what inmates are allowed to possess and require that all personal effects be recorded on a list and approved by the administration. For example, prisoners are usually allowed to possess computer equipment, not exceeding a value of $2,000. In the past, prisoners have cheated on these rules with the tacit consent of administrators or guards, who recognize the value of keeping the inmates as comfortable and content as possible.

During "lock-downs," when prisons are searched for drugs or weapons, guards also look for other "contraband" items, which may be as innocent as a television that has been traded for a stereo or clothes that have not been authorized. Prisoners in double-bunked cells may be charged with possession of contraband, because of something that their cell mates have brought in. The drug strategy also gave institutions the right to change their regulations so that prisoners would be allowed fewer personal effects in their cells.

According to prisoners at Collins Bay Institution, a medium security penitentiary in Kingston, Ontario, articles removed during a lock-down and search included books, clothes, hobby craft tools and supplies, personal documents, Tupperware containers, cups, photo albums, canned food and toiletries. Wooden shelving was also removed from cells, although metal shelves and cabinets that were supposed to replace it were not yet ready. The warden justified these actions on the grounds that prisoners had accumulated excessive amounts of articles that could be used for barter or trade.

Roy Glaremin, a prisoner at Collins Bay responded to this in an article in a prisoners' journal: "Imagine someone coming to your home and commenting on how much you could sell your clothes and furniture for, as though you had no other use for those things. By describing our belongings this way, the warden misrepresents us and misleads you, all in an attempt to defend his heavy-handed and, I think, reckless management of Collins Bay." New regulations, similar to those applied in Edmonton, resulted, according to Glaremin, in the prison becoming unstable, with prisoners openly discussing civil disobedience. His article made this comment: "Regardless of where in this situation one's sympathies lie, one would, I hope, acknowledge that CBI [Collins Bay Institution] has become a meaner place. Making prison conditions meaner hardens the people living in those conditions, making them less friendly and less peaceful. In turn, this leads to a more difficult reintegration into the community at large. What does that mean? More drug use, more crime, and more prison sentences."

In his letter to the CSC Commissioner, Graham Stewart of the John Howard Society wrote, "While recognizing the problems of drugs within institutions, one cannot help but feel that the concern about drugs has become a 'licence' to introduce tyrannical policies and arbitrary punishment."

The CSC drug strategies include provisions for drug-treatment programs in prison. But resources are limited and up to 20 per cent of the prison population report substantial problems with drug or alcohol addiction. The prison system has tried to provide some programs and will no doubt attempt to make more available. The reality is, however, that the pressures and temptations to take drugs in prison probably far outweigh the limited impact that can be achieved through programs that do not have the resources or expertise to focus on intensive treatment, but tend rather to be drug awareness courses that merely inform prisoners about the consequences of drug abuse.

A crucial component of CSC's anti-drug strategy is an increased use of urinalysis drug tests. The law requires that tests be administered either on a random basis or when there is reasonable cause to believe that a prisoner is intoxicated. Information from informants, obvious intoxication or sniffer dogs can provide grounds for a non-random test, but frequent tests on the same individual can be judged to be a form of harassment. The random tests are administered by following computer-generated lists. When prisoners are found to have drugs in their system, they may lose privileges or spend time in segregation. They may also be transferred to another institution and may be denied family visits until they can prove that they are drug free by testing negative in three successive tests.

But the testing program only makes the drug problem more serious in one important respect. Heroin is metabolized far more quickly than marijuana and other soft drugs, traces of which can stay in the system for several weeks. In order to reduce the chances of being caught out on a random drug test, many soft drug users in prison are switching to the harder, potentially deadly and far more addictive drug.

Drugs remain plentiful in prison, in spite of all attempts to keep them out. Peer pressure and the tensions of prison life encourage prisoners to use drugs or to use them more often and in greater quantity. Many people who enter prison as occasional smokers of marijuana or hashish will have become heavy heroin addicts by the time they return to the community.

Many of the problems of drugs and violence in prison begin in communities that choose not to treat drug abusers, but to send them to jail. Ill-equipped to solve these problems, prisons often make them worse, returning offenders to a society that still has no help to offer them and will now be exposed to even greater risks.

6

PLAGUES BEHIND BARS

For more than two weeks, early in 1995, prisoners at Kingston Penitentiary were afraid to come out of their cells. They were alarmed by an outbreak of tuberculosis, a contagious lung disease spread by coughing and sneezing which, in the past, claimed hundreds of lives in the damp, ill-ventilated prison. Tests on 468 prisoners, in February 1995, revealed that more than 100 had been infected. These tests detected an early stage of TB infection, where the disease is not active or contagious. But somewhere in the prison there were presumably active carriers of the disease who had already come in close contact with about 20 per cent of the penitentiary population.

Many of the newly infected prisoners worked in the kitchen and inmates feared that someone there might be the source of the contagion. Staff took over kitchen duties. Some inmates were placed in isolation in the prison's health centre, while further TB tests were conducted. Meanwhile, the inmate committee asked the administration to impose a lock-down, whereby programs were cancelled and prisoners remained locked in their cells.

Tensions mounted, as prisoners waited and staff investigated. Many of Kingston Penitentiary's tiny cells are double-bunked and most of them have open bars through which stale air recirculates around the overcrowded ranges. When an inmate coughed, a dozen others held their breath.

Nowadays, in normal circumstances, tuberculosis infection can be easily detected through tests and, once detected, drugs can prevent the infection from becoming active. If the infection is allowed to take its course unchecked, only one case in ten will normally develop into active TB and those cases can be treated with medication. But strains of TB have recently emerged that have proved resistant to the medication. A 1993 article in a U.S. medical journal reported that an epidemic of multidrug-resistant TB took more than 100 lives as it spread through east coast hospitals and prisons.

Tuberculosis is more difficult to identify among people with HIV, intravenous drug users and others with weak immune systems. People with histories of poor nutrition, inadequate health care and low standards of personal hygiene are also more likely to catch the disease and are less easily cured. In other words, the lifestyle and background of many prisoners puts them at a high risk of contracting TB and makes it more likely that their infection may not be detected until it reaches a contagious stage. Penitentiary inmates could take little comfort from the fact that drug-resistant strains of TB had so far not been detected in Canada, since those infected with TB included drug traffickers from overseas, arrested at international airports.

A 1994 CSC task force on AIDS received a stark warning from a Kingston prison outreach worker who observed that a number of TB cases had recently been detected in Canadian prisons and it was only a matter of time before the disease became a plague. Noting that TB is far more easily communicable than AIDS, particularly in confined spaces, the outreach worker warned that TB might spread through the overcrowded prison system like "wildfire death."

In fact, it was soon discovered that the Kingston TB outbreak had spread through several prisons in the area. This spread was to be expected since prisoners are frequently transferred from one prison to another. Tests determined that about 18 per cent of the inmate population in Kingston area prisons had been exposed to TB. At least twelve cases were suspected of being active and contagious.

Staff members also tested positive for TB, as did at least one community volunteer, who had visited prisons regularly. It is likely that other members of the public were also exposed to infection, since prison gates are regularly opened to receive numerous visitors, including volunteers from community groups, prisoners' relatives and friends, contractors and other trades people, lawyers, dentists and other professionals. One Kingston Penitentiary employee refused to go to work because of the risk and a union representative observed that staff "worry about taking TB back to their homes."

To everyone's relief, the TB outbreak in Kingston proved not to be of a drug-resistant strain. No active cases were confirmed and those infected were urged to take a six-month course of medication that should prevent active TB from developing. There is no way of forcing them to complete this treatment. Some prisoners, especially those with drug or mental health problems, are notoriously careless about complying with health care programs. Many of those infected will have completed their sentence or returned to the community on parole before their course of treatment is over. Some of these will forget to take their pills. A few of them may well develop active TB and pass the disease on to others in the community. When people contract TB after being partially treated with antibiotics, the bacteria that they pass on to others may have begun the process of genetic change that leads to a tougher, drug-resistant strain.

The Kingston TB scare was soon over and the issue quickly disappeared from the media, but it served as a timely reminder that our prisons are potential breeding grounds for deadly plagues. It demonstrated clearly how quickly such a plague might spread and how futile it would be to hope to contain it behind the prison walls.

Medical services in prison are designed to provide the equiv-
alent of normal community health care for inmates. Penitentiary
health centres are like well-equipped doctors' offices, with the
addition of a few beds that are available for short-term care.
Nurses are on duty full-time, while general practitioners and
other physicians are on call or available for consultation. The
clinics deliver first aid, and staff are usually adept at dealing with
slashings and suicide attempts. In cases involving serious illness
or major injuries, prisoners are taken under escort to community hospitals. Prisoners frequently complain about the quality
of the health care that they receive, but staff maintain that the
inmates have unreasonable expectations and do not realize that
people living in the community have to wait just as long as prisoners do to see family doctors and specialists.

Many prisoners actually get better health care in prison than
on the street. The lifestyle and social skills of some chronic
offenders is such that they do not take good care of themselves
in the community and tend to use medical services only in an
emergency. Prison staff provide routine preventative care. Visiting dentists are available and many prisoners, who could not afford
adequate dental care in the community, get long-neglected problems fixed before their sentences end.

Prison food tends to be heavy on carbohydrates, but probably provides a better balanced diet than most of the prisoners
would have if left to their own devices. Many prisoners work out
in order to increase their body strength for self-protection or to
preserve their morale. Prison health surveys have shown that prisoners generally carry far less excess body weight than most people
in the general population.

But prisons are not caring environments and the healing role
of medical staff is often compromised by security needs. Guards
as well as nurses are on duty in the health units and prisoners'
requests for medical attention are often treated with suspicion.
Prisoners who feel sick are sometimes sent away by staff who

believe that they are malingering or seeking medication for non-medical purposes.

Some prisoners seek medication to deal with the stress of prison life, and these requests sometimes create dilemmas for staff. Giving prisoners tranquillizers may keep them happy and is often encouraged by guards who would like an easy shift. But there are risks. Valium, or diazepam, for example, which is frequently used as an anti-depressant, is a popular recreational drug among prisoners. It is supposed to calm patients down, but people on Valium can act erratically. Some prisoners are particularly wary of their fellow inmates when there is a lot of Valium around. It is also a valuable commodity. As one psychiatrist pointed out in a paper on prison medical services, "Five 'v's or 5 mg tablets of diazepam have paid for a man to be 'piped' or beaten about the head with a baseball bat."

With limited resources, prison health services are continually facing new challenges, as prisons become more overcrowded and the populations become more diverse. Like other institutions in society, prisons are required to become increasingly attuned to the needs of disabled people and others with special health or social needs. The proportion of older inmates in the prison population is growing more rapidly than that of the society as a whole, partly because of the large number of inmates serving terms of life imprisonment with no parole before 25 years. Before the death penalty was abolished in the 1970s, life sentences required only fifteen years without parole. Another reason for the sharp rise in the population of aging inmates is the presence in prison of numerous sex offenders, convicted recently of offences that took place many years ago. A 1994 report by the CSC's research staff noted that the increased medical needs of older inmates is likely to put "a serious strain on correctional medical budgets."

A serious outbreak of a contagious disease could very quickly overwhelm the resources of penitentiary health units. Prisons bring together the people most likely to be victims and carriers of certain diseases, and provides the ideal environment for the disease to flourish and spread. The conditions are particularly ripe for spreading HIV, the AIDS virus. Unlike TB, the human immunodeficiency virus (HIV), which leads to the fatal deterioration of the body's immune system known as AIDS, is not easily spread. People can contract the virus only through contact with infected blood or the exchange of bodily fluids. Sexual activity is the most commonly recognized way of becoming infected with HIV, but even more risky than unprotected sex is the practice of sharing needles while injecting drugs intravenously.

If an evil despot wanted to spread HIV in order to wreak havoc in the world, it is hard to imagine a more efficient method than rounding up drug addicts, locking them up for a few years in a place where needles are routinely shared and clandestine homosexual activity is common, then returning them to the community. As the U.S. National Commission on AIDS observed in a 1991 report, "By choosing mass imprisonment as the federal and state governments' response to the use of drugs, we have created a *de facto* policy of incarcerating more and more individuals with HIV infection."

In December 1994, out of a total population of about 14,000, there were 120 federal prisoners in Canada infected with HIV. But AIDS activists believe that, for every prisoner who has tested positive for HIV and disclosed that information, there are many more who do not know they have the virus or choose not to acknowledge it. Unofficial estimates put the number of HIV-positive prisoners at one in twenty. It is believed that the rate is even higher in women's prisons, where more than 20 per cent of the inmates are serving sentences for drug offences and many have been involved in the sex trade on the street.

On the street, public education and needle exchange programs have been at least partially successful in convincing drug addicts not to share needles. But, in prison, many drug addicts find that their options are limited. Drugs are usually available, but needles, which are far more difficult to smuggle into prison, are in short supply. Faced with a choice between sharing needles and "going cold turkey," many drug addicts will be desperate enough to throw safety to the wind. One needle is often shared by fifteen or more prisoners without being cleaned between uses. The needles are frequently hidden in common areas and regarded as communal property. Sometimes, drug users resort to homemade "sharps," made out of hardened plastic and ballpoint pens. These can cause blood poisoning, scarring and damage to veins, in addition to the risk of HIV, if they are shared.

Needle exchange programs, like those in place on the street, are considered out of the question by prison authorities, concerned about the security threat and the legal implications of providing prisoners with equipment for illegal and self-destructive activity. Since cleaning needles with bleach reduces the danger of spreading HIV, though it does not eliminate it, CSC has agreed to make bleach available to inmates of institutions, providing staff members agree to the move. Staff have in the past objected to providing bleach on the grounds that it could be used as a weapon, but a pilot project in which bleach was distributed at one B.C. prison was completed without incident.

HIV can also be spread by sharing of tattooing and body piercing equipment. CSC has endorsed recommendations from the Expert Committee on AIDS and Prisons that prisoners be allowed to hire professional tattoo and body piercing services. But prison tattooing is a traditional communal activity that is likely to continue in spite of the fact that it is contrary to regulations.

Nor will regulations stop sexual activity between prisoners. Staff tacitly acknowledge that this takes place and prisoners are supplied with condoms, water-based lubricants and dental dams in order to encourage them to practise safer sex. Because sex is officially prohibited, however, prisoners often engage in furtive activity in shower stalls and other situations where they are less likely to bother with condoms. For this reason, CSC has been urged to officially condone consensual sex, but the problem with that is that it is hard to know in a prison environment that both partners are really consenting. There is obviously little that can be done to protect prisoners who are the victims of sexual assault by other inmates, besides attempting to prevent further incidents by identifying perpetrators and segregating them from other prisoners.

The risk from AIDS and hepatitis, both of which are passed on through exposure to blood, has added a new element of fear to the stressful work of prison staff. Nurses working in prison health care units are usually aware of the problems that individual patients pose, but rules of medical confidentiality prevent them passing on information to security staff who deal with the same prisoners on a day-to-day basis. Correctional officers insist that they should have the right to know if a prisoner is afflicted with a communicable disease. Guards must respond to emergency situations when prisoners slash themselves or stab other inmates. Prisoners sometimes collect blood and other bodily fluids to use as weapons to throw at guards. Violent prisoners sometimes threaten to infect guards with AIDS by splattering them with blood.

Prison authorities maintain that there is no need for correctional staff to know the medical status of individual inmates, since they can best protect themselves by taking precautionary measures whenever they are exposed to risk. Protective gloves and suits with helmets are available for use in emergencies when staff risk being exposed to blood, but it is not always possible to anticipate such situations.

Prison staff everywhere were terrified by the potential implications when a staff member at Prison for Women was allegedly stabbed with a syringe during a confrontation with prisoners. Staff are also exposed to danger when they conduct routine searches of cells, since they may be cut by a razor or pricked by a needle as they put their hands in a crevice or run their fingers along a ledge. They can protect themselves against this risk by wearing very thick rubber gloves, but these tend to reduce sensitivity to the point where it is difficult to find whatever has been hidden.

Guards and nurses in health units often have bodily fluids thrown at them. A prisoner may suddenly produce a razor and threaten to slash himself or herself. In some emergencies, guards may be inclined to respond instinctively to provide aid or attempt to prevent injury, rather than walk away in order to get help and put on protective clothing. Many of them feel that they could make better decisions if they were informed about the risks that each prisoner might pose.

A prison guard, who was president of his union local, told me that AIDS was not as great a concern as some new potentially deadly strains of hepatitis. He cited a study of 110 Prison for Women inmates who volunteered to be tested. He said only one proved to be HIV positive, whereas 48 tested positive for hepatitis. He told me, "When you're dealing with inmates, you don't know who has what. Their right to confidentiality overrides your right to protection. But we usually know which inmates have AIDS because they're on double rations. From things done at the hospital we figure out who has TB. Hepatitis, we don't know. There are a lot of situations where you're dealing with body fluids. In the old days, I went home with my shirt soaked in blood. Now, I put on rubber gloves. You miss a lot of the human contact because of that."

While security staff are officially told nothing about the medical status of inmates, they can often gather information through unofficial channels. Donna Dixon, Chief of Health Care at the medium security Joyceville Institution, was quoted in the CSC journal *Let's Talk*, as saying, "I'm continually amazed at the amount of information that inmates and staff have. It doesn't seem to matter how much confidentiality is respected by medical staff,

there is always a leak from somewhere." A prisoner at the maximum security Atlantic Institution in Renous told me, "The grape-
vine doesn't take long to get something through the jail. They
call you for testing over the intercom. You can't talk to the doctor without a guard in listening distance. They can call people
down for blood work. People start to wonder. Then they leave
you on the range with nineteen other guys."

Prison AIDS activist Gerald Benoit, who was serving a life
sentence for murder, told me that other prisoners staged demon-
strations at Dorchester Penitentiary when they discovered in
1987 that he had HIV. They wanted the prison authorities to
place him in segregation. But Benoit and an enlightened prison
administration stood their ground, with the result that he
became the first HIV infected prisoner in Canada to be placed
with the general inmate population. Since then, his own efforts
at educating his peers, together with an increasing level of general knowledge about the virus, have resulted in prisoners
with AIDS being accepted by other inmates at Dorchester, as in
other institutions. "Now the people ostracized are the ones who
harass people with AIDS," said Benoit, who told me that there
were five prisoners with AIDS at Dorchester, three of whom
were double-bunked with HIV-negative inmates. He said, "We
encourage everyone to disclose his status. The guy who has tested positive needs to hear that they are going to treat you as
they've always treated you."

Benoit was a 40-year-old Newfoundlander, who had a habit
of speaking very fast, perhaps conscious of the fact that he had
much to say but little time left. He told me that he spent several years during the early 1980s working as a transsexual prostitute in various U.S. cities. After testing positive for HIV in 1985,
he returned to his home province, where he participated in a
brutal murder. Once he had been sentenced, Benoit came to
terms with the fact that he had HIV and was certain to die
before his prison term expired. But, he told me, he went into

denial about the fact that he was a murderer and was not able to acknowledge his guilt until more than five years later. Now, he said, he wanted to devote what was left of his life to helping other prisoners with HIV and trying to prevent its spread. He said he would feel that what he has done is worthwhile, "if I have saved one boy from leaning over and taking contaminated body fluid." He added, "Each guy I reach is for Greg, the guy who died."

Benoit said his own experience in testing positive for HIV enabled him to indentify closely with those of other HIV-positive inmates. He said he felt particularly close to a 23-year-old prisoner serving a sentence for armed robbery. The young man was a victim of childhood sexual and physical abuse. His prison files recorded 43 attempted suicides. Benoit explained that he and members of the Prisoners With AIDS peer group that he founded "aren't just dealing with the HIV issue. We're dealing with things like being sexually abused as children and having made some pretty rotten choices in our lives."

Prisoners with AIDS face even greater health problems and discomforts than people living with the syndrome on the outside. Benoit, who is also infected with TB and hepatitis, told me that he takes eleven pills every day in order to survive. He said, "When someone in the next cell gets a cold, I get a flu shot. It's like having 30 people in your living room all the time — and they don't realize that their germs are more dangerous to me than I am to them."

In the terminal stages of AIDS, patients often develop numerous ailments and complications that require extensive medical attention. Prison medical facilities have great difficulty meeting their needs and giving them the quality of care that they could get elsewhere. Prisoners with full-blown AIDS and those in the terminal stages of other fatal diseases are transferred to hospitals or hospices whenever it is possible to do so without compromising security. CSC also has a policy of regularly recommending to the parole board that inmates with progressive life-threatening diseases be released earlier, before they are at the point of death, if they do not constitute a threat to society. The reason for this is that it serves no purpose to keep such prisoners in custody and they can get better care in the community with families and friends.

It is not always possible to find a place in the community for terminally ill offenders, as I discovered when I attended a parole hearing for a prisoner with AIDS, whom I will identify as Gordon. At the age of 35, Gordon was facing a three-year sentence for numerous property offences, but had been told that he could not expect to live for more than two years. He had spent most of his adult life in jail, usually for break-ins and petty theft, and he freely admitted to the parole board, "My record is disgusting, I know. I very much regret that record."

A case management officer conceded that there would be very little chance of Gordon staying away from crime after his release, were it not for the fact that he no longer had the strength and mobility to commit a burglary. In these circumstances, the parole board was told, his risk of reoffending was zero. Gordon said he was ashamed of his past crimes, but did not think that he should be punished by having to die in a humid, sometimes cold prison cell.

The parole board agreed to release him, providing a suitable community placement could be found for him. He had believed that family members would look after him, but they did not show up for the parole hearing and did not return the case management officer's phone calls. Gordon explained that no hospice would take him in because he once attempted to commit suicide, while he was in prison, by rolling himself up in a sheet and setting fire to it. He thought he could survive on his own in the community, living in a room, if he had some support from friends. This plan seemed to unravel, however, when he explained, "I don't have many friends in the community. I have a few, but they're drug addicts."

A few months after the hearing, prison staff were still trying to find a suitable arrangement for Gordon's release, but it was beginning to appear that there was nowhere else for him to go. Like many other prisoners, Gordon had been unable to find a viable way of living on the street. Now, he could not even find a place to die.

There are many other chronic offenders who can find no place in the community after their release. Many of them went to prison in the first place largely because of a lack of resources in society. Prisons can scarcely even begin to address the mental health problems that they represent.

While prison populations have been exploding in recent years, psychiatric hospitals have been emptying their beds and closing their doors. The "deinstitutionalization" of mental health services has been carried out in the interests of cost savings and to protect the rights of patients who might be unnecessarily institutionalized. With few services available in the community, however, many ex-psychiatric patients have been "left to rot with their rights on," as criminologist Barbara Hudson put it in her 1993 book *Penal Policy and Social Justice*. Noting that many of these people have found their way into the prison system, Hudson went on to comment, "As the welfare net has contracted, the penal net has expanded to become the new catch-all."

A 1990 study of penitentiary inmates in Quebec reached startling conclusions about the prevalence of mental illness. Inmates who participated in the study were asked a series of questions about their mental health and their responses were analysed in relation to a standard manual which lists the symptoms of all recognized mental illnesses, which are more commonly described by psychiatrists as "disorders." The study found that one-quarter of those surveyed had at some time in their lives suffered from symptoms that fit the diagnostic criteria for a major mental disorder. Another half of those surveyed presented a problem of substance abuse, while a further 13 per cent met the criteria for other, less serious, mental disorders. Only 5 per cent of prisoners in the study group did not present symptoms for any mental disorders. The study found that even the seriously "disordered" (mentally ill) prisoners were not getting the treatment they needed. "Whereas 40 of the 112 inmates suffering from a major mental disorder reported that they had discussed their symptoms with a professional, only 24 were transferred to psychiatric care while in the penitentiary," a report on the study noted.

CSC has recognized that the number of mentally disordered prisoners has been increasing at an alarming rate in recent years. The service has responded by opening psychiatric or treatment centres in each region. These are fully equipped psychiatric hospitals which treat disordered prisoners in a secure setting. These facilities are also expected to provide treatment to sex offenders, whose numbers have also increased dramatically. Bram Deurloo of CSC's research department observed in a 1993 presentation to the Ontario Psychological Association, "We must do the seemingly impossible — create a safe but therapeutic environment for disordered offenders within the correctional milieu."

In fact, many disordered patients end up in segregation cells because they tend to be victimized by other inmates, who refer to them as "bugs." CSC has responded to this problem by establishing mental health units in some penitentiaries to provide programs and care for mentally disordered inmates, though at a far less specialized level than those offered at CSC's five regional psychiatric centres. The focus of these smaller units is mainly on helping disordered prisoners survive in the prison environment.

A mental health unit was established at the Saskatchewan Penitentiary in Prince Albert after a 1980 survey revealed that more than 14 per cent of the prison population had chronic mental illnesses, and that all these prisoners were being held in segregation cells. During nine years of operation, the 26-bed unit has admitted 581 inmates, about 60 per cent of whom were previously in segregation cells. When I visited the unit, I was told that staff were also providing services to 86 prisoners living in the general population. About half of these were former inmates of the segregation unit who were able to survive in regular cells after a period in the mental health unit.

For the individual prisoners and for the system as a whole, it obviously makes sense to enable inmates to survive better in prison than they do now. The ultimate aim of prison psychiatric and treatment services must be to reintegrate prisoners into society, but places in psychiatric centres are limited. Few psychiatrists and psychologists are prepared to undertake the thankless task of working in a prison environment for the limited pay that the correctional service can offer.

Prison mental health services are not equipped to deal with a population in which almost everyone has mental disorders, any more than health units and other prison services can handle the complex medical, social and ethical problems associated with AIDS. The prison system was never designed to provide a caring or therapeutic environment. On the contrary, prison overcrowding, together with the prevalence of drug abuse, violence and sexual assaults, create conditions in which infectious diseases and particularly HIV and AIDS are likely to spread. Far from being cured in prison, mental health problems are likely to become aggravated, with the result that prisoners may be more unstable when they are released and pose far greater risks.

Prisons inherit the problems that society cannot handle or choses to ignore. But prisons cannot control them either and sometimes make them worse. Most of these problems will ultimately return to a community where people still believe that all they have to fear is crime.

7

RACIAL TURMOIL IN JAIL

Racial conflict and the disadvantages of visible minorities are other problems that inevitably find their way into prison. When these issues become inflamed and intensified by the conditions of penitentiary life, the resulting anger and lingering bitterness can produce an explosive mix.

Penitentiary inmates include people from more than 50 different ethnic or racial groups. In a violent environment where racism is rife, some visible minority prisoners feel that they need to organize for mutual protection against other inmates. They feel safer in numbers and ask to be housed together in neighbouring cells. Prison staff often comply with such requests. Guards recognize that they cannot protect prisoners from one another. Housing members of ethnic minorities together on the same range can result in less friction and reduce the risk of someone being isolated and victimized. It also makes sense to let people live close to those who perhaps share the same culture, language, customs or religion.

But ghettos are being created and gangs are taking root. Many visible minority prisoners who used to be members of small street-level gangs feel they need to join, or to form, closely knit criminal organizations. As one CSC staff member put it, "The federal prison system actually encourages them to organize."

In the Prairie region, where there is a shockingly disproportionate number of aboriginal people in the prison system, gangs have long been established. Groups that originated as street gangs for disenchanted urban youth have solidified their power in prisons and used the penitentiaries as a base from which to further their interests in the streets. In Winnipeg, which has a larger population of Native people than any reserve in the country, there is a large gang that calls itself "The Indian Posse." A prisoner at Stony Mountain explained at a National Parole Board hearing that it was hard for him to avoid being involved in the Posse because "these are the people I grew up with. When I talk about going straight, they laugh at me. They are friends I've known for a long time. Relatives are in it. They are everywhere I go."

At another parole hearing in Toronto, I heard a young man of Italian-Canadian origin explain how he came to be associated with a group of known drug dealers during his four-year penitentiary term. He told the parole board that he had been involved in a confrontation in which a Jamaican drug dealer was killed and therefore needed to stay close to powerful inmates from his own ethnic background. He said, "They were the people who ran the institution. My life was on the line every day. They watched over me. For me not to get killed, I had to associate with them."

In making his case for day parole to a halfway house, the young man said, "In a halfway house I won't have to hear in my ear, 'He's selling dope. He's smoking this. They're fighting tonight.' You hear you're going to get punched out tonight. That's why I go and talk to them. I'm being protected. I'm being watched. When I get out, I'm going to try to forget about prison life, all that I have heard and seen that's scared me."

Although gangs and little ghettos within prisons can provide protection to individual inmates and reduce friction on a one-to-one basis, they can also result in territorial disputes involving widespread violence. In the long run, they can make the prison more unstable and render everyone less safe.

The medium security Collins Bay Institution in Kingston has a facade of pointed towers that makes it look like a fairy tale castle in a Disney movie, but inside, it is notorious for its over-crowding, violence and racial tension. In March 1995, about 200 prisoners in the weight room of the prison gymnasium watched Donzel Young being stabbed to death, apparently trying to break up a fight between a black and a white prisoner.

A 33-year-old black man who had been campaigning to prove that he had been wrongly convicted of murder, Young was known as a peacemaker in the prison and frequently attempted to ease tensions between warring factions in the prison. Guards tried to clear the gymnasium immediately after the incident, but about 30 prisoners, both blacks and whites, refused to leave and a prisoner was injured by a ricochet from a warning shot fired by a guard. Order was restored and the institution remained locked down for several days, but there was a lingering fear that the tensions and frequent interracial skirmishes could easily escalate into a prison war between blacks and whites.

Since crime is often a symptom of deeper social ills, prisons usually contain a large number of people from disadvantaged groups. In prisons all over the world, one can find an overrepresentation of aboriginal people and racial or ethnic minorities. Canada is no exception to this: members of visible minorities make up just under 19 per cent of the federal prison population.

It would be hard to argue with those who maintain that the number of aboriginal people in Canadian prisons is a national disgrace. In the Prairie region, people whose ancestry is North American Indian, Métis and Inuit represent about 5 per cent of the general population, but 32 per cent of the federal inmate population. Aboriginal groups make up approximately 3 per cent of Canada's general population, but they comprise 12 per cent of the population of men's penitentiaries across Canada and 17 per cent of the inmates in federal prisons for women.

In Ontario, it would appear that black people are also being imprisoned in disproportionate numbers, though it is hard to find accurate figures. Statistics relating to crime and race are not always kept because they are politically sensitive and subject to bias or error. CSC's own data showed that black inmates comprised about 9 per cent of the federal prison population in the Ontario region in 1992–93. Black men were recorded as making up 4.7 per cent of the national male inmate population, while black women comprised 6.5 per cent of the female inmate population. According to the same statistics, whites comprised about 80 per cent of the male population and 70 per cent of the female population. The only other category recorded in the published figures was "Asiatics" who comprised 1 per cent of the male and 1.5 per cent of the female populations.

Since these figures were published, the visible minority population in prisons has apparently continued to increase in the size and diversity. The broad categories of CSC's somewhat crude statistics contain dozens of different groups, many of which have huge linguistic and cultural barriers between them. "It's astounding how cosmopolitan prisons are compared to ten years ago," said Graham Stewart of the Ontario John Howard Society, who added, "Now a John Howard meeting in a prison is like a meeting of the United Nations." To some extent, this transformation of the prison population reflects changes in Canadian society at large. But it also results from patterns in the international drug trade and enforcement of laws against drug smuggling.

Many of the visible minority prisoners are foreign nationals, arrested at international airports for attempting to bring drugs into the country. These are usually poor people who had been paid to act as "mules" for international drug dealers. Some of those arrested at the airports speak no English or French and know nothing about Canadian society or its laws. They are often shocked to find that importing narcotics carries a minimum sentence of seven years. I was told of one case in which a convicted smuggler believed that he would be able to bribe his way out of prison and tried to kill himself when he realized that Canadian justice does not operate that way. Most of the foreign drug mules never know any more about the country than what they learn in prison, since they will be deported after serving their sentences.

The diversity of the minority population creates serious administrative problems for CSC staff. Interpreters have to be found for as many as 50 different languages or dialects, but the interpreters obviously cannot be available all the time. In spite of recent efforts to hire new staff from visible minorities, most CSC employees are white Anglophones or Francophones. Language barriers make it difficult for prisoners from some minority groups to participate in everyday activities or programs. Members of these groups consequently have more time on their hands and are forced to rely more upon their own resources. These factors inevitably intensify the ghettoization effect.

Food has to be provided that is appropriate to the diets of people from a variety of cultures. Arrangements must be made to accommodate many different spiritual needs, including access to spiritual advisers, special services, ceremonies and periods of fasting. All these considerations tend to reinforce the tendency to put people from similar backgrounds into the same living area, especially where there may be some members of the group who speak English or French and can translate for others.

Some CSC staff have racist attitudes, as may be expected in any large work force. I encountered only a few examples of overt racism, however, during the course of my interviews and casual meetings with hundreds of CSC staff members. The most noteworthy of these was a former penitentiary warden, still in the employ of CSC. He told me that he would always prefer to be carrying a gun, if he encountered a group of black males on a city street at night.

Prisoners sometimes complain of racist taunts by guards, and allegations of racism were made in connection with the death of Robert Gentles, the black man who died while white guards attempted to remove him from his cell. There is no way of proving or disproving such allegations. In the Gentles case, no evidence has been offered to support the allegation and a CSC investigation found that there was no racism involved.

Penitentiary inmates have many reasons to fear one another, and race sometimes plays a part in these concerns. Prison violence is seldom precipitated by racism alone, but racial tensions and gangs are often a factor in disputes over drugs and a variety of other issues. For example, the murder of Trung Ky Duong by Steven Poutsoungas at Millhaven was essentially the result of a dispute between two drug dealers and perhaps part of a war between rival groups, but it would be foolish to ignore its racial overtones, given that the stabbing took place during the course of a melee in which a group of white prisoners stormed a group of Asian prisoners. In this case, however, as in many other similar incidents, CSC's concerns appeared to revolve around the issue of drugs.

Drugs, rather than race, have been the focus of CSC's efforts to combat prison violence. This may be a big mistake, according to Graham Stewart of the John Howard Society. He argues that racial conflict in prisons is "a sleeping giant," a dangerous problem to which "CSC is turning a blind eye." While acknowledging that there are no easy solutions to these complex problems, Stewart says he is concerned that CSC does not seem to be preparing any strategies to deal with the threat posed by different ethnic minorities organizing to defend themselves and building territorial control. In searching for solutions to this issue, Stewart maintains, CSC would have to confront the problem of overcrowding, since the lack of available space in prisons makes it hard for staff to defuse tensions and break up gangs by moving prisoners around.

In some prisons, staff prevent ghettos from developing by creating a racial mix within each range. But, in overcrowded prisons, this policy can also result in problems. According to a CSC official, a murder at one Prairie institution resulted from an incident in which a white prisoner complained about his cell mate burning ceremonial sweet grass in their cell. The two men got into a physical fight, which escalated into a political dispute involving members of an organization representing Native prisoners in the jail. The white man ended up being stabbed to death.

A conservative prison system has been taken by surprise by the new realities of a multicultural society and international crime, but the problems of aboriginal prisoners are long-standing and deeply embedded. CSC has been well aware of these problems for a long time and has recently begun to address them. In attempting to do so, however, the prison system must confront the impact of crimes that white society has perpetrated against Native people throughout Canadian history.

There were sad reminders of this history at Stony Mountain Penitentiary, which now houses 280 aboriginal offenders in a total population of just over 600. Built in 1877 on one of the few hills to be found in the Prairie landscape northwest of Winnipeg, Stony Mountain is a grimly imposing fortress-like institution. In the hallway outside the warden's office, I was shown pictures of the penitentiary's most famous inmates, the Cree chiefs Big Bear and Poundmaker, imprisoned in 1885 for their participation in the Louis Riel Rebellion. When he was sentenced to imprisonment, Big Bear exclaimed, "I would rather be hanged." He died soon after his release from prison two years later. The prison's first warden Samuel Bedson noted that Native prisoners "languished in confinement, sorely missing the freedom of their outdoor life."

One of the pictures of the two chiefs shows them on the prison steps with the warden and three priests, a reminder of the fact that the penitentiary used to run a school in which Native prisoners were taught to abandon their "superstitions." Just over a hundred years later, the consequences of these policies is evident in our prisons, as in our society.

An overwhelming majority of the Native people who find their way into the prison system today have no knowledge of their language and understand little about their traditional culture. Many grew up in cities, where they learned to see their culture through white people's prejudices and stereotypes about "Indians." Many Native prisoners were separated from their families and culture early in life to be brought up in foster care, group homes, residential schools or other institutions. Even many of those brought up on reserves were not exposed to their traditional culture either because of family circumstances or because the culture had been eradicated from their community.

"The system created me and made me dysfunctional," said one Native prisoner, a man who was apparently dealing with his identity problem in his own way, since his voice and mannerisms, together with his decorative silver earrings and carefully manicured fingernails, made it difficult to accept that one was not talking to a woman. During his last release, he told me, he had gone back to his Native community, but found "there was no place for me there."

The same social problems that have brought aboriginal people to jail in grossly disproportionate numbers have disrupted Native communities and families. Native prisoners are even more likely than their non-Native counterparts to suffer from problems like illiteracy, alcohol abuse and life-long exposure to family violence. But they are even less likely to benefit from the standardized programs that are offered in prison.

CSC research has determined that even the tests that are used in assessing new prisoners during the intake process are not relevant to the cultural backgrounds of Native people. One man provided me with a colourful explanation of this problem, saying, "They ask you, 'Do you have visions?' That's part of my culture, but when I answer, 'Yes,' they think I'm some kind of psychotic."

Problems of language, education and cultural background often make it difficult for some Native inmates to understand how the system works or what is expected of them. For example, a National Parole Board report cited one case where a man disclosed that he was embarrassed by his limited ability to speak English and just answered "Yes" or "No" to any question that he did not understand. A Native inmate liaison told a 1992 Royal Commission on Aboriginal Peoples, "I was recently involved with one man who did not realize that he had signed a paper waiving his request for parole. He thought he was signing an agreement for treatment for alcohol abuse."

A Native offender from Ontario told the same commission that he had experienced racial prejudice from some prisoners and guards in institutions where Natives were a small minority. He said, "A lot of people, particularly from isolated reserves, are very shy and distrusting of anybody who is non-Native. They get into the system and they find it hard to talk to people or anything else. Some of them might make progress on their own in changing their way of thinking and their way of doing things, but the system does not get to see it because of their shyness and their distrust."

Prisoners from isolated reserves often find themselves incarcerated hundreds or even thousands of miles from home, deprived of any contact with family or friends, particularly when they or their families are illiterate. An inmate representative at Stony Mountain told me that many of the prisoners who come from northern reserves find themselves "in a world that doesn't belong to them. It's not their world. They're lost."

It is sometimes very difficult for prison administrations to make provisions for people from remote communities, since there are many different aboriginal cultures and sixteen distinct languages still in use in different parts of Canada today. It is also difficult for institutions to provide programs specifically geared to the needs of Native people, when they have only a handful of aboriginal prisoners.

From this perspective, the Native prisoners in the Prairie region have an advantage over their counterparts elsewhere in the country. With their high concentrations of aboriginal offenders, penitentiaries in the Prairies have experienced many periods of interracial violence and ugly confrontations between inmates and staff. Over the past twenty years, Native prisoners have not only organized powerful gangs, but have also become politically aware of the historical injustices suffered by aboriginal people. They have formed a representative body called the Native Brotherhood Organization, which is present in most prisons in Western Canada.

The Brotherhood is a powerful group that frequently takes strong stands on issues of concern to Native inmates. Administrators or white inmates ignore the Brotherhood at their peril, although prison staff members sometimes cynically observe that people active in the Brotherhood are also involved in drugs and gangs. It sometimes appears that the genuine grievances of aboriginal peoples are used by Native offenders as an excuse for ongoing criminal behaviour.

When I visited prisons in the Prairies, there was a great deal of optimism among aboriginal offenders as a result of a cultural renaissance that Native societies have recently experienced. Aboriginal people are rediscovering their traditional spiritual values and practices, many of which young Natives are learning for the first time. Recognizing the value of Native culture as a means of rehabilitation, CSC has encouraged participation in traditional ceremonies, incorporated Native culture into programs and hired Native elders to provide prisoners with spiritual guidance.

When I first made arrangements to visit Stony Mountain, administrators were bubbling with enthusiasm about their new programs for Native prisoners. They suggested that I participate in a traditional sweat lodge ceremony at which I could experience for myself the exuberance and profound sense of spiritual awakening with which aboriginal inmates were rediscovering their culture.

By the time I arrived, however, a crisis had arisen that was threatening to undermine the new programs, erasing the good will that they had created and replacing it with the renewal of long-standing tension and bitterness. Instead of attending a joyous ceremony, I was permitted to sit in on a potentially explosive meeting over the future of sweat lodges in the institution.

A Native sweat lodge is a sacred ceremony of purification that revolves around a form of sauna, in which stones are heated on an open fire, before being brought into an enclosed space where water is poured on them to create steam. The problem that had arisen at Stony Mountain was that the sweat lodges were located in a prison courtyard, close to the institution's health centre, where staff were bothered by smoke from the open fires. Some of the staff members complained to federal health and labour authorities, while a few were refusing to work and seeking compensation. The prison administration wanted to move the sweat lodges to another location, but many of the Native prisoners believed that this would be sacrilegious because the courtyard had now been consecrated as sacred ground.

The meeting, called by the Native Brotherhood Organization, was held in an assembly hall that now forms the hub of the penitentiary's Native cultural centre. Except for the bars on the windows, the room resembled a church or school hall. When I arrived with assistant warden Al Maclean, there were 50 or 60 prisoners present and some were preparing for the meeting by clearing away beads, twine and half-completed "dream catchers," left over from a handicraft class. Coffee was being served in styrofoam cups from urns at the back of the room.

It was not until later, when the meeting was under way and passions were inflamed, that it occurred to me that there were no guards present in the hall, although inmates outnumbered prison staff and visitors by about ten to one. It was then that I started thinking about stories that Maclean had just been telling me of a period ten years earlier when the prison was racked with riots and hostage-takings, culminating in the murders of two guards.

According to Maclean, prison violence had decreased enormously during the past few years, largely because of the introduction of Native programming. The programs, led by an elder and two Native liaison officers, were introducing or reintroducing prisoners to traditional values and culture. A family violence program, designed by staff at Stony Mountain, helped prisoners understand how the cycle of abuse that afflicts many Native communities is linked to a history of oppression, in which Native people learned to lose respect for their culture and themselves. Prisoners with apparently deep-rooted anti-social attitudes were suddenly latching on to traditional Native concepts like tolerance and respect for others. The sweat lodge ceremonies that are supposed to cleanse the body and spirit of impurities were a focal point of these programs. Prisoners particularly liked the sweats because they felt emotionally and physically high after them. Maclean told me that he was certain that prisoners did not take drugs while they were participating in sweats.

Many of the prisoners attending the meeting gave moving testimonials to the value of the Native programs. They spoke about reliving past abuse and recovering feelings and experiences from their childhoods. Although the prison environment usually makes people wary of displaying emotion, several prisoners said that they cried when they came to understand these things. They spoke about a sense of brotherhood that they experienced with peers who had seen them cry but had not laughed at them.

"The sweat lodges help us find who we are. The elders and people that know about our culture give us an identity," said a prisoner who had been institutionalized for more than twelve years. He went on to explain, "All through my years in the system people were telling me how bad I was. I heard that. I said, 'That's who I'll be.' Now, they're telling me I'm a caring person. I am learning about myself. It is painful. I still have hatred for the system, but I feel a big change."

Behind many of the prisoners' speeches, however, there was a veiled threat. They continually hinted that they would quickly go back to their old ways if the sweat lodges were taken away from them. One warned that they might "get out of hand." At one point, one of the Brotherhood representatives became frustrated with an argument that an administrator was making and exclaimed, "Fuck!" He immediately apologized for his language and wafted some sage and tobacco smoke on his face in a gesture of symbolic cleansing.

The chairman of the Brotherhood, a thick-set man who wore his long hair in a ponytail, explained that Native people easily get "edgy," and when that happens elders tell them that it is time to go to the sweat lodge. He went on to say, "I'm getting edgy. I'm concerned I'm about to do drugs. The program is not having an effect on me. If you take away the effect, the culture will crumble."

Maclean and another administrator explained that they were not trying to suspend Native programming and that the problem was simply a practical one caused by the legitimate concerns of some staff members. One of the Native liaison officers, however, greatly dismayed the assistant warden by expressing the belief that the health and safety complaints were merely a "smokescreen" and that the real issue was "non-acceptance based on racism."

Rhetoric became more inflamed as the meeting progressed. A representative of the Assembly of Manitoba Chiefs, invited by the Brotherhood, made a speech in which he promised to help the Native prisoners regain their rights. One prisoner expressed the somewhat paranoid fear that "staff are worried about losing their jobs because there will be no Native guys here when we've healed ourselves." Another prisoner suggested that the number of Native activists, not the amount of smoke, was what bothered staff. He said, "Sweat lodges only became a problem when 250 brothers began fuelling the fire."

A prisoner whose arms were decorated with tattoos prefaced his comments by saying that he had done time in the Special Handling Unit, the prison within the prison system for those who commit serious crimes while in jail. After proclaiming in this way that he was not afraid of prison authorities, he went on to say that the sacred ceremonial grounds should not be moved and "once that sacred fire is lit, I will not let anyone put it out. I will go up against anyone who tries and only one of us will walk away alive."

Another prisoner rose to say that he too had been to the SHU. In a speech that seemed like an open call for insurrection, he urged other prisoners to join with him in "going up against the wall and together tearing it down."

It was easy to imagine how an ill-judged move by administrators at this point or a few more fiery speeches from prisoners could have precipitated a riot. I could not help reflecting that there were several hostages readily available and that I was one of them. But the administrators retained a firm, though respectful position, explaining that the issue was a practical one and they had no intention of violating Native rights. The Brotherhood leadership was anxious to negotiate and more moderate prisoners told the militants that the ceremonial grounds could be located anywhere since all the earth is sacred.

The meeting moved on to a discussion of where the new sacred grounds would be and how soon the sweat lodges could be moved. There was also a wrangle over when the next meeting would be. The Brotherhood tried to insist that the administration meet with them every month, but Maclean, careful not to relinquish any authority, would only say that they would consult with the Brotherhood when it was appropriate to do so. The Native leaders saved face by saying that they were sure that the administrators would not insult the Brotherhood by refusing to parlay, if the prisoners made the traditional overture of offering a gift of tobacco.

After the meeting, Maclean told me that he had been involved with prison riots before and was well aware how easily they could start. He believed that the man who talked about killing to protect the sweat lodges would probably carry through with his threat if given any encouragement to do so. It is important in such situations, he said, to be sensitive to the dynamics of the group, attempt to solve problems publicly and "manage prisoners as a collective."

The original concept of the penitentiary was one of dividing and conquering. Prisoners were supposed to be separated into cells, locked together in small groups, kept under armed guard and supervised carefully whenever they were moved from one place to another. But this is no longer possible in the over-crowded modern prison. Nor is it desirable to control prisoners' movement too much within institutions, as this will make them more passive and restrict their participation in rehabilitative activities.

In most prisons today, inmates routinely congregate in groups, and there are many occasions when prisoners outnumber staff or visitors. There are risks involved, but these are part of the reality of prison life. When prisoners respond to racial tensions by organizing themselves into powerful groups, the risks increase substantially to prisoners and others. In an environment where drug abuse and individual acts of violence are common, it is easy to see how collective animosities could be inflamed by a perceived injustice or a racial slur. When disadvantaged people feel that they are being persecuted, they may decide that they have nothing left to lose. There is an ever-present possibility of race war or riot.

The racial turmoil in prisons is a result of problems in the outside community. The disproportionate number of Native people in prisons can only be explained in the light of generations of poverty, abuse, prejudice, exploitation and social injustice. The overrepresentation of other ethnic groups and the tension between different races also reflects divisions and inequalities in Canadian society, as well as law enforcement policies that jail many foreign nationals for drug smuggling. The tensions in prison will probably continue to escalate, unless society comes to grips with these problems and their underlying causes.

As the prison system struggles with these complex and often overwhelming problems, there is a lack of policies and guiding principles. The system is apt to respond in two different ways. On the one hand, staff may try to integrate minority prisoners, and to provide programs to address their needs. On the other hand, prison managers may resort to increased segregation and repressive measures in response to the ever-present threat of riot and racial violence. In a prison system that is often at odds with itself, one can expect that many administrators will vacillate between repressive and supportive measures. Prison staff may try to provide humane solutions to massive social problems that society dumps on the correctional system, but in the final analysis, prisons are expected to keep a lid on explosive issues that the broader community refuses to address. That is why prison administrators sometimes believe that they have no choice but to call in the riot squad.

8

WOMEN IN PRISON: VICTIMS OR MENACE?

On February 21, 1995, television viewers were confronted with shocking images of female prisoners being stripped naked, shackled, prodded with batons and forcibly removed from their cells by male guards in riot suits and helmets. These scenes, from a videotape shot at the Prison for Women in Kingston ten months earlier, conjured up images of political atrocities, pornography and extreme sexual abuse.

A Native woman who had been stripped while she was apparently half-asleep looked disoriented and totally humiliated, as she was forced to back up against a wall with a transparent plastic riot shield pressed against the front of her naked body. Another naked woman kneeled with hands behind the back of her head, motionless as if in a yoga position, asking in vain for a gown, while a chain was fastened around her waist and two guards stood in front of her with their batons raised like erect penises. But perhaps the most disturbing images were of a woman protesting and struggling as two men pinned her, face-down on the floor, and helped a female guard rip her clothes and tear them from her body.

"This is degrading. I can take anything, but this is degrading," one of the women told the guards. Another prisoner subsequently disclosed that she felt as if she was reliving her past experience of being raped by several men.

The men who were subjecting the female prisoners to these indignities remained as calm and courteous as customs officials searching through baggage. They were members of Kingston Penitentiary's Emergency Response Team, specialists in the task of "extracting" rebellious prisoners from their cells. They apparently performed the job with professional detachment and even paused at one point for a coffee break.

Almost as disturbing as the scenes depicted on the video, were the abysmal conditions at the women's prison and a series of ugly clashes between prisoners and guards that led to the riot squad being called in. The whole story as it emerged in subsequent investigations was one of stark horror. It confronted everyone with some extremely distressing realities concerning female offenders and the conditions under which they are imprisoned.

This shocking episode and the outrage that it provoked crystallized the issues in an ongoing debate about how society should deal with women who break the law. It is a debate in which the central question is whether women's prisons should be places of healing or repression.

It is an obvious and incontrovertible fact that it is mainly men who are responsible for violent crime. Comparatively few women are arrested and charged with any serious crimes. This fact is reflected in prison populations, where women are invariably a tiny minority. In Canada's federal prison system, female offenders represent about 2 per cent of the population.

One might expect that the tiny proportion of women who end up getting sent to federal penitentiaries would really deserve to be there. Nevertheless, the majority are serving time for nonviolent crimes. This situation also exists in men's prisons, though the numbers are, of course, far greater. Whereas most nonviolent offenders in men's prisons are there for property offences, drugs is a far more common crime among women than burglary. Another obvious difference between male and female offenders is that violent male offenders include a large number of sex offenders, whereas only a handful of women are ever convicted of such crimes. Compared to men's penitentiaries, women's prisons contain a higher percentage of murderers and offenders convicted of manslaughter, but one crucial difference is that many of the women who kill did so in domestic situations under the pressure of extreme abuse. They do not therefore necessarily represent a threat to the population at large.

As a tiny minority in a male-dominated prison system, female offenders have consistently been given short shrift. Throughout the history of the federal prison system, women have been, to quote the title of an influential study of the problem, "too few to count." This book of essays on women in conflict with the law, quoted Sheelagh Cooer, who characterized the past treatment of women as "a mixture of neglect, outright barbarism and well-meaning paternalism."

Until the 1930s, female offenders were housed in a series of different makeshift sections of men's prisons. The Prison for Women in Kingston, now universally known as P4W, was opened in 1934 to correct that situation. But it was plagued with problems from the very beginning. A dismal and depressing building, with two-tier ranges of cage-like cells, it was designed as a maximum security institution, in spite of the fact that the majority of female offenders do not pose a threat to society. Its architects also apparently assumed that women do not need as much exercise as men and therefore failed to include adequate outdoor recreational space. Since it was the only women's penitentiary in Canada, it housed offenders from all over the country, many of whom were thus imprisoned thousands of miles away from their homes and families.

The suicides of five Native women between 1989 and 1991 were a damning indictment of the isolation and the sordid conditions at P4W. It was an environment in which self-mutilation and suicide attempts were routine and drug use endemic. Acts of violence and intimidation were not as common, or usually as savage, as in male institutions, but were nevertheless an inescapable aspect of everyday life. With no other institution to which disruptive prisoners could be transferred, staff at Prison for Women frequently resorted to sending prisoners to the segregation unit, which, unlike most such units in male prisons, was simply another two-tiered range with open barred cells.

A former prisoner, a Native woman, wrote in a report to a government task force in 1990, "The segregation unit continued to hold us hostage without heat in the dead of winter, without toothpaste or a toothbrush. More seriously, medical treatment for crisis situations was so deplorable that we often believed that death was inevitable for Sisters who slashed."

"Essential to an understanding of the destructive nature of P4W is the history of violence that most of us share," the report continued, citing the results of a survey in which "27 of the 39 women interviewed described experiences of childhood violence; rape, regular sexual abuse, the witnessing of a murder, watching our mothers repeatedly beaten, beatings in juvenile detention centres at the hands of staff and other children. Twenty-one had been raped or sexually assaulted either as children or adults."

P4W had been scheduled to close for many years. It had been described in a 1977 a parliamentary subcommittee report as "unfit for bears, much less women." But it was not until the last few years that plans were finally made to replace it with a series of regional women's prisons. These smaller regional facilities, most of which were due to open in 1996, represent a new direction for the treatment of female offenders in Canada's federal prison system.

For generations, women's prisons have been punitive institutions geared to accommodate the small proportion of female offenders who are violent and dangerous. The new regional women's prisons were designed primarily to accommodate the vast majority of female offenders who do not constitute a threat to society. In order to house offenders close to their home province and give them access to the surrounding community, CSC has constructed a network of small, open prisons. These are located in Edmonton, Alberta; Kitchener, Ontario; Joliette, Quebec; and Truro, Nova Scotia. A Native healing lodge has been opened in Maple Creek, Saskatchewan, and federal female offenders in British Columbia are accommodated at the provincially run Burnaby Correctional Centre for Women.

The physical design of the new facilities and the programs that have been planned for them were conceived as a "woman-centred" approach to corrections. The underlying assumption is that most women prisoners are non-violent and many of those who committed violent crimes in the past did so in the context of an abusive relationship. A high proportion of female offenders are victims of childhood sexual abuse and domestic violence. The regional prisons were founded on the belief that segregation and punishment merely perpetuate the abuse and compound the damage that most female offenders have suffered in their lives.

The new prisons have a flexible approach to programming, based on each woman's needs and goals. The new programs begin with the understanding that female offenders need to be empowered rather than coerced. They encourage offenders to use community facilities and get involved in outside activities. Each facility has a small secure unit for maximum security offenders, but it is assumed that only a few prisoners will have to be locked up.

What happened at P4W in 1994 and the problems that these events exposed is likely to have a profound impact, however, on policies that will be followed in the new facilities. Some CSC staff want stricter security measures at the new prisons in the light of the violence and rebellion at P4W that the riot squad was called in to quash. Others fear that compassionate and humane policies may easily be undermined by belligerent staff and a few unruly inmates. As women prisoners move into more pleasant and comfortable surroundings, they carry with them a powerful reminder that the prison system's rhetoric about rehabilitation is always backed up by its power of brutal repression.

The fact that P4W was soon to close had a significant impact on what happened in April 1994. Many experienced staff members — those who had seniority in the correctional service — had anticipated the closure by transferring to new jobs in other institutions, taking advantage of a trend toward hiring more female guards in male institutions. Most of the correctional officers who remained were women with less than one year's experience. On the other hand, many non-violent offenders had been transferred to various interim regional facilities in anticipation of the move, leaving P4W with a population of 129 inmates, more than 80 of whom had committed violent crimes.

Although female offenders are generally far less violent than men, there are some women whom authorities consider to be extremely dangerous. P4W gathered the most dangerous women in Canada together in one place. In 1994, they were among the sixteen inmates of "B" range, a unit that housed prisoners identified as aggressors in the general population, the women referred to as "the heavies."

Some of the women subsequently seen on the video were very scary individuals. It is easy to forget that as one sees them being victimized by guards. The presence of dangerous women in the prison population can easily be overlooked in the valid generalization that most female offenders are not a threat to society. We oversimplify all the issues involved in crime and punishment if we fail to accept that a person can be both a victim and a menace.

For example, 31-year-old Brenda Morrison, who was seen on the video being held face-down by guards, had a criminal record which included manslaughter in the shooting death of her boyfriend. In 1994, she was serving time for an attack on a man, whose hands were tied behind his back with electrical cord while he was beaten with a baseball bat, stabbed with a pocket knife and cut on the throat and the penis. Morrison threatened to cut off the man's penis if he did not give her the PIN number to his bank card, and then abused him for six hours before stuffing him into the trunk of his car, from which he eventually escaped. During her prison term, Morrison allegedly attacked other prisoners and guards. A report by an internal CSC board of inquiry into the April 1994 events described Morrison as extremely dangerous with an "ongoing capacity for violence and a total disregard for the well-being of others."

Joey Twins, who was seen on the video being pushed with a riot shield, was serving a life sentence for the second degree murder of a 63-year-old man, whom she beat and stabbed eighteen times, while under the influence of alcohol. According to the CSC report, she played a major role in a 1991 disturbance at P4W, threatening to assault and kill staff and barricade the entrance to a range. On November 16, 1993, she threatened staff members with a broken broom handle, refused to come out of her cell and subsequently slashed herself. In a subsequent search, she was found to be in possession of razor blades and a homemade knife fashioned out of a toothbrush with a razor embedded in it.

The conflicts that led to the riot squad being called to the prison, on April 26, 1994, began four days earlier. Twins, Morrison and four other prisoners from "B" range, who had been waiting for medication in a corridor near the prison's hospital unit, entered into a violent confrontation with staff on April 22. Some of the prisoners were under the influence of a particularly potent batch of prison "brew," home-brewed alcohol that is made in makeshift stills, which can cause more violent and erratic behaviour than any other drug. According to guards, the prisoners were attempting to escape. The prisoners denied this, although they subsequently pleaded guilty to various criminal charges, including assaulting a peace officer, attempted prison break, forcible confinement, possession of a weapon and uttering threats. The prisoners would later claim that they confessed to these crimes only in order to get out of the segregation unit where some of them were held for nine months following the April 1994 disturbances.

During the course of the confrontation near the hospital unit, one guard believed that she was stabbed with a syringe and feared that she had been deliberately infected with HIV. The syringe was not recovered and she did not test HIV positive. Another guard was kicked in the knee, an injury which subsequently resulted in a blood clot travelling to her chest and causing a life-threatening condition. According to the guards' account of events, they were attacked with a pair of scissors and one prisoner ripped a telephone from the wall, threatening to take a guard hostage and "string the bitch up" with the cord.

After being subdued with Mace, the prisoners were placed in the segregation unit. A CSC investigative report noted that P4W staff failed to comply with standard procedures in that they did not search inmates prior to their being placed in segregation. If an effort had been made to ensure that the prisoners did not have any weapons with them when they went into the segregation cells, the subsequent events might have been averted.

This security lapse was typical of the inconsistency with which P4W was being run. Staff members apparently had conflicting or ambivalent attitudes to prisoners, showing great tolerance in certain circumstances and undue severity in others.

These inconsistencies were subsequently noted in the report of the CSC investigative team. The report stated that some staff members played favourites with certain inmates, while others gave in to prisoners' demands in order to buy short-term peace. "Inmates run the institution," according to some staff members quoted in the report. The investigators maintained that there was a pattern of inmates engaging in self-mutilation and suicide attempts as a manipulative way of gaining control over guards. It was noted that prisoners involved in an intimate relationship with one another were allowed to live on the same range. The partners of violent offenders, some of them vulnerable, non-aggressive prisoners, were therefore housed with the "heavies" on "B" range.

The report also criticized the prison administration for allowing prisoners perks such as regular parcels from home and numerous personal possessions in their cells, policies that the investigators saw as making drug smuggling and possession much easier. The investigators noted that prisoners were apparently able to make phone calls at CSC's expense and that the institution's phone bill included calls made by inmates to Hong Kong, Jamaica and Portugal.

Although most people would agree that prisons should not be allowing inmates to run up phone bills of more than $5,000 a month, many of the criticisms made by the investigators' report alarmed those who advocate better treatment of women prisoners. For example, it may be true that suicide attempts are sometimes manipulative, but they may also be responses to intolerable living conditions and life histories of extreme abuse. Women involved in the correctional system have long argued that it is inappropriate to punish a prisoner for mutilating herself and would be far better to provide therapy and support. Many of the practices at P4W that the investigators criticized as lax were attempts to create a more humane and supportive environment for female offenders.

What happened in the segregation unit in April 1994 illustrated clearly how prisoners can be, at the same time, vulnerable and manipulative; needy and aggressive. As the events unfolded, staff members were seen as considerate, as well as callous. Having allowed themselves to be outmanoeuvred by the prisoners that they supposedly had under their control, prison administrators responded with repressive force.

The CSC investigative report recorded an incident that clearly illustrated how staff members responded harshly after a prisoner had taken advantage of their initial compassion. The incident occurred on the day after the fight outside the medical centre, two days before the riot squad was called in. Florence Desjarlais, a prisoner in one of the segregation area's upper-tier cells, slashed herself. Other prisoners reacted by shouting, screaming and clanging the bars of their cells. While nurses bandaged her wounds, prisoners demanded that they be allowed to speak with Desjarlais. They threatened to slash themselves if they were not allowed to do so. When Desjarlais herself pleaded to be allowed to speak to fellow prisoner Sandra Paquachon, guards decided to let her sit on a chair outside Paquachon's cell.

Paquachon had just been sentenced to life imprisonment for the second-degree murder of another prisoner who was found hanging in her P4W cell. The victim's death had originally been ruled a suicide, but Paquachon confessed in September 1993 that she had killed her friend, a heroin addict who was unable to care for herself as a result of a drug-induced seizure a year before her death. When she was convicted of murder, Paquachon was already serving an eight-year sentence for armed robbery and a concurrent five-year sentence for taking another prisoner hostage in May 1993.

The guards who allowed Desjarlais to sit outside Paquachon's cell did not notice at the time that Paquachon had been able to get her hands out of the cuffs she was wearing. She then slipped a noose around Desjarlais' neck and produced a four-inch-long nail, which she held to the other woman's throat, yelling, "I've got a hostage. This is a hostage-taking. I'm going to stick her."

The guards called for reinforcements, who arrived with a Mace canister. When Paquachon was threatened with Mace, she began to tighten the noose, saying, "I'm going to stick her."

Mace was fired at her face and her hostage was rescued. As inmates continued to shout and scream at guards, two more threatened to hang themselves. One woman was throwing liquid at anyone who walked past her cell. A few minutes later, a prisoner was found hanging in her cell. She was cut down, attended to by nurses and then examined by a doctor, who determined that it was not necessary to send her to hospital, in spite of the fact that the woman was pleading for more attention and banging her head against the bars of her cell.

Prisoners maintained that the disturbances in the segregation unit two days later, on April 26, 1994, were precipitated by a racist taunt on the part of one of the guards. Many of the women considered by the administration to be the most dangerous and violent were of Native ancestry. Most of these harboured bitter memories of the five suicides by Native women at P4W. According to the inmates, one of the guards in segregation that night made a hateful reference to these tragedies by saying to Native prisoners, "Why don't you string yourselves up like the rest of them?"

Guards denied making any such comment. From their perspective the fresh round of disturbances began when correctional officer Tracy Ostrom, a 23-year-old former waitress, with three months' training and five months of experience as a guard, was trapped at the end of the upper-tier walk-way with prisoners threatening to take her hostage. Although all the prisoners were locked in their cells, they had armed themselves by taking their beds apart and putting metal brackets in pillowcases that they could swing between the bars. The CSC report noted that Paquachon, the prisoner involved in the earlier hostage-taking, was threatening the guard by stating, "We're going to fucking kill you" and "I have a knife and I'll cut your fucking throat out."

A supervisor arrived with Mace and rescued Ostrom. While he was doing so, a prisoner threw urine on him. Prisoners were unable to flush their toilets because the water supply to the cells had been cut off in order to prevent them from deliberately causing a flood. They were retaliating by throwing the contents of the toilet bowls at guards.

A prisoner on the upper tier began setting fires by lighting paper and throwing it down to the common area on the floor below. Those in the lower tier fed the fires by throwing garbage, toilet paper and blankets from their cells. When guards arrived with fire extinguishers, inmates threatened them with their improvised weapons and threw urine on them.

Staff decided that it was necessary to remove prisoners from their cells so that they and their cells could be thoroughly searched. But removing prisoners from cells in situations where they are uncooperative and might be armed is a job for a specially trained riot squad. Members of the team have to know how to handle prisoners in a way that will prevent injury to themselves or others. The team members must also be disciplined enough to keep their own tempers while being subjected to abuse. Since none of the guards at Prison for Women had been trained for this work, it was decided to bring in the male emergency response team from nearby Kingston Penitentiary. As one P4W guard explained, "How were we going to get near their cells? It would have taken eight or nine females wrestling with them just to get the search done."

Nevertheless, the Correctional Investigator, who serves the function of ombudsman for the federal prison system, reviewed reports of the incident and did not find that there was sufficient evidence to justify bringing in the male team. Describing the CSC investigative report as "at best incomplete, inconclusive and self-serving," he noted that the supervisor who first recommended the use of the riot squad seemed to be primarily concerned about the morale of staff, as much as for their safety. The supervisor referred in his report to "the fragile psyche of the officers in the institution at this time" and stated, "I do not feel that our officers should have to continue to suffer this type of abuse when we have the means to put a stop to it.

Otherwise, I fear that we will have more staff requesting stress leaves and a diminished credibility toward management."

The decision to call the riot squad was made at 8:45 p.m., but the squad did not begin their operation until three hours later, by which time the prisoners had calmed down. Morrison told a reporter that they were singing Native spiritual songs and trying to make themselves happy, prior to the arrival of what she referred to as the "goon squad."

After reviewing the videotapes of the cell extractions, the Correctional Investigator concluded, "The exercise was, in my opinion, an excessive use of force and it was without question degrading and dehumanizing for those women involved."

On the day after the cell extraction, Margaret Beare, a member of the Citizen Advisory Committee, which acts as a liaison between prisoners and administration, visited the segregation area. She noted in her diary, "Women naked or in torn paper gowns, in shackles, no mattresses, no hygiene items/utensils etc. Segregation was quite cold — at least it would seem so for a person with no clothes on."

That evening, Beare was asked to witness internal vaginal and rectal examinations of the women. She noted that the women agreed to the searches in exchange for showers and were each given a cigarette afterward. According to her notes, "Women were given security gowns and had one blanket to sleep on at this time. No toilet paper except as requested piece by piece — no hygiene products."

After noting that there had been no use of force in conducting the internal examinations, Beare added the following comment in her journal: "Issue of sanitary napkins very barbaric — great discussion over old dirty underwear — was there any clean? Image of women walking from showers with pads between their legs naked — quite unnecessary."

Four days later Beare returned and was told that the women had not been allowed to take another shower.

Prisoners complained to her about their treatment by the Emergency Response Team and said they were still without items of personal hygiene, including soap, toothbrushes and clean underwear. They also blamed the Citizen Advisory Committee for not going to the media about "these atrocities."

Beare mused in her journal, "I question myself in that I have been busy ensuring that the 'process' is carried out professionally and as 'gently' as possible — need to keep asking if the process is the right one — i.e. how long should they be treated like caged animals/was the ERT team necessary/what 'privileges' are in fact rights?/is the exchange of a shower and freedom from shackles vs. an internal examination a fair exchange???"

On May 6, two weeks after the original incident, Beare noted that the prisoners were still sleeping on the cement floor with only two security blankets. They were still denied books and toothbrushes. A senior CSC administrator explained to the citizen volunteer that these were not punitive measures but security precautions. He said toothbrushes were a potentially lethal weapon once a blade was welded into the plastic head, and books could be used to start fires in order to force guards to release the women from their cells.

Five of the prisoners were due to be moved to the Regional Treatment Centre at Kingston Penitentiary. They told Beare that they were nervous and angry about the prospect of being moved to a male institution where there were rapists and "diddlers" who might "jerk off" in their food. According to Beare's journal, two of the prisoners said that they regarded P4W as their home, as they had been there for seventeen years. She quoted Paquachon as saying "If the guards can't take the violence, they should go out on the street and take jobs as cleaners."

The women were moved to the male institution, but were subsequently returned to P4W as a result of a court order. Most of them remained in segregation for about eight months, during which period their possessions, privileges and amenities were gradually restored to them. In December 1994, a plea bargaining agreement resulted in six women being sentenced in criminal court to additional prison terms ranging from 60 days to twenty months.

As the sordid history of P4W ends with the opening of the new regional prisons, it would be comforting to believe that the events of April 1994 were merely an ailing institution's last bouts of feverish rage and the last stand of an old punitive regime. The new prisons with their compassionate philosophy and innovative programs are promising to initiate a new era in the treatment of women. But it is salutary to remember that P4W was once seen as a solution. It too was the result of years of campaigning and optimistic promises.

There is no doubt that the public outcry prompted by the video will ensure that never again will male guards be ordered to strip female prisoners. To avoid this eventuality, CSC has trained female guards to serve in emergency response teams, although the ideal of the new prisons is that such force will not have to be used.

When CSC investigators reported on the April 1994 disturbances, they raised the concern that a few extremely violent women could disrupt the new prisons and cause them very negative community reactions. Many of the new facilities have been forced to work hard at convincing their host communities that the women will not constitute a threat. Members of the public have been assured that they will be safe because the few high-risk offenders will be held in the secure units within the prisons. But these were designed to accommodate only 10 to 15 per cent of the inmates. With members of the surrounding communities nervous about their safety, it is likely that there will be pressure on prison administrations to put more prisoners in the secure units or to make the other sections of the new prisons more secure.

If women are not allowed out of the new prisons, they may

end up being worse off than they were at P4W. The new facilities have fewer amenities built in, as they were designed to make use of resources in the community. For this reason, some of the more hardened offenders at P4W were nervous about being transferred. There is also a concern that the new facilities will quickly become overcrowded, since judges will be more inclined to sentence women to federal prison terms, now that more appropriate facilities are available.

None of the new facilities were yet open when I did my tour of federal prisons. But while I was in Edmonton, I met with Karen Smith-Black, deputy warden of the new Edmonton women's facility and Evelyn Zawaski, a citizen who had become involved in the prison's planning process. They were both enthusiastic about the prospects. Edmonton citizens had created a furor about a site that was originally proposed for the facility, and their protests resulted in an intense consultation process and the selection of a new site that was more acceptable to neighbouring residents.

Zawaski told me that the new prison is in a light industrial area, bordering low-income neighbourhoods. She said single-parent families in the area had been persuaded that the prison could be a valuable community asset. They have discussed the possibility of people in the community gaining access to recreational space in the prison which has a gym, a baseball diamond and soccer field. At the same time, it is proposed that prisoners participate in volunteer activities in the community and be allowed to use the local swimming pool and skating rink. Some area residents were proposing business ventures, such as a print shop and a telephone answering service, which would employ prisoners. Although plans for the prison included facilities for some prisoners to keep their young children with them, local residents also saw opportunities in providing foster care for children who could not stay with their mothers in prison. "We are making the institution mirror society. We're not making women so dependent on us. They go to community clinics for health care. They cook their own meals and are responsible for the cleanliness of their homes. We haven't been helping them by waiting on them hand and foot," said Smith-Black.

While the benefits of this approach were obvious, I saw a completely different version of the future of women's prisons in Canada, when I visited BCCW, the Burnaby Correctional Centre for Women in British Columbia. This provincial prison also houses female federal prisoners from the Pacific region. CSC decided not to build a new women's prison on the west coast because the arrangements at Burnaby were considered adequate.

Unlike the new federal prisons which house offenders in small cottages, BCCW is a large modern building. It is a pleasant, airy institution that looks from the inside more like a university residence than a prison. There are solid wooden doors instead of bars and they have silent electronic locking devices that guards can operate with coded plastic cards. It is, nevertheless, as secure as any maximum or medium security penitentiary and many people feel that this is unnecessary for a largely non-violent population.

BCCW does have an open custody annex that provides accommodation to a small number of prisoners who are considered not to pose a security risk. But an administrator at BCCW told me that he believes CSC is overly optimistic in believing that it can house 85 per cent of its population in an open prison. He told me that only five of the 40 federal offenders at the Burnaby prison were being housed in the annex.

Feminist prison activists see the Burnaby prison as a prime example of the tendency to overestimate the security risks that female offenders pose. There certainly seems to be less justification at BCCW than at P4W for keeping prisoners under tight security. While violent incidents were regular occurrences at P4W, there has been just one act of violent aggression in the Burnaby institution's short history. That was a stabbing which left other inmates feeling nervous and insecure. In the words of one administrator, it caused "a loss of innocence" among inmates. A prisoner told me, "It jolted a lot of us. Never in the whole five years that I've been inside a prison have I ever seen or heard about things like that."

Although there is very little violence and aggression, an administrator told me that there were problems with slashings and attempted hangings, none of which had so far been successful. I was told that many of the inmates had drug problems and there was no doubt that drugs were getting into the prison, but there had been no overdoses during the three years that it had been open.

My own impression of the female offenders whom I met there was that they were a far cry from the fierce women who were causing the problems at P4W. One of the Burnaby prisoners told me, "All the women here are hard core criminals till the lights go out and you hear them crying with their teddy bears." A woman who had been at P4W viewed the Burnaby prison as a haven in comparison to where she had been before. She said, "If I was sent back to a P4W type environment, I would revert to my old anger."

Most of the women whom I met at Burnaby talked about abuse that they had experienced throughout their lives. One woman said, "This is actually a safe place for a lot of women. Boyfriends, pimps, whatever, can't get you. You get decent food. You're clothed. There are people around that care about you, even though it's only your fellow inmates. That says something very sad about our society that you have to go to jail to be safe."

Another woman said, "A hug is a new thing for me. To do it now is somewhat miraculous. But you have to be careful here because if you try to hug some women they think you're getting in their space. To many of them a touch means pain."

Prisoners complained about what they saw as a lack of programs that would help them change. One woman said, "They

call it a correctional institute, but what are they correcting?"
Another women said, "There's no preparation for the outside
world. You don't have to make any decisions for yourself. You
may feel like it's a holiday for two weeks, but it wears off. You get
hysteria. Then fear sets in."

Federal prisoners serving long sentences are housed with
short-term provincial offenders at BCCW and this causes conflicts. One of them explained, "It's difficult, when looking at
being here a long time, to hear some little cookie saying 'I've got
nine more days.'"

Some of the federal prisoners said they used to get new
clothes supplied to them more quickly at P4W and received better medical care. A staff member explained, however, that some
of the complaints about medical care may be due to the administration's attempts to avoid making prisoners too drug-dependent.
This was a major problem at P4W, where the medical profes-
sion's tendency to overprescribe psychotropic medication to
women was exaggerated by the nature of the population and the
conditions. One P4W prisoner told a CSC research study that
she took prescribed medication continually for four years and
felt like a zombie. A staff member told the same study, "When
one of my goals is to increase a sense of self-control and sense
of personal power, it's working at odds with medication."

Prisoners at Burnaby, however, also felt that they were being
denied control over their environment. One of them explained,
"You have no personal space in here. You have nothing personal in here. They try to annihilate your personality. It starts in
admitting when they spell your name wrong. You're given a
number. Then you are taken out of street clothes. If you've been
in city cells, you have to be deloused. You wouldn't treat your
children or your family members like that, so why are they doing
this to us?" This woman's grievances appeared trivial in comparison to the trauma depicted on the P4W video. But what
she was describing was a part of the same continuum. She was

complaining about the dehumanizing, routine cruelty that most people would accept as a part and parcel of prison life. Prison staff and others who have spent a lot of time around prisons accept as normal the fact that people are being locked up and sometimes shackled when they move. It is normal that guards can look into a cell and see a prisoner sitting on the toilet. It is a given that prisoners can expect to be punished if they get too angry or assertive with guards. Strange though it may seem, many prison insiders saw nothing wrong with the way the women at P4W were treated when they were strip searched by masked men in their cells.

The new network of women's prisons, built to replace P4W, was designed with the belief that a more open, humane and woman-centred environment will help heal past abuses and bring out the best in offenders embittered by previous experience. The events of April 1994 at P4W provided many people with irrefutable evidence that the old way of treating female offenders is unsuccessful and unacceptable.

For the CSC investigators and other correctional insiders, however, the same events provided a clear illustration of how dangerous and intractable some offenders can be, whether they be male or female. These people saw the violence and anger of the prisoners as a warning of what could be in store for the staff and administrators of the new "cottage-like" women's correctional centres.

Some of those who have fought hard to change the way that women are treated in the correctional system are afraid that the concerns of the CSC investigators could become a self-fulfilling prophecies. They are concerned that administrators of the new facilities will lock too many women away in their small secure sections, where inmates will be even more confined than they were at P4W and have less access to programs and services.

There is no doubt that long after P4W has been closed, it will remain a traumatic memory for many prisoners and employees alike. One ex-inmate, a woman who had lived for years with the anger, pain, profanity and violence of P4W, sobbed and struggled for breath, as she told me about seeing friends slash and hang themselves in their cells. She said, "I can't forget the things that happened in there. I'll never be free."

Part Two

PROTECTING THE PUBLIC

There are a thousand hacking at the branches of evil to one who is striking at the roots.

Henry Thoreau

Quoted by MP Bob Horner in *Crime Prevention in Canada: Towards a National Strategy,* the Twelfth Report of the Standing Committee on Justice and the Solicitor General.

9

CHANGING THE GUARDS

Prisons are expected to provide a quick fix to problems that have taken a whole lifetime, or perhaps several generations, to develop. A growing number of people are terrified and outraged by violent crime, but society seems unable to come to grips with its underlying causes. We look to prisons for the protection that these foreboding buildings, with their armed towers and razor wire, appear to promise but have so far failed to deliver.

When Kingston Penitentiary was built, crime was seen as an evil that might be driven away by hard work, harsh punishment and repentance. But there was little hope of repentance in a place without light or grace. More recently, crime was treated as a social ill that could be "cured" by education and rehabilitative programs. But prisons were like underequipped hospitals overwhelmed by a war or a plague, soon becoming places of disease and contamination, rather than healing.

In the post-modern prison, a management model is applied. Crime is regarded as a threat to public safety which may be minimized with the help of risk assessments and pragmatic decisions, made with an eye to the bottom line. But the bottom line is always changing, as the prison system struggles with pressures and problems beyond its control. Prisons are expected to maintain costs, accommodate more inmates and reduce risks. While prison administrators try to balance conflicting political demands, their employees easily become cynical and confused. The result is a system that often seems to be at odds with itself.

The Correctional Service of Canada, which used to be a militaristic organization, has become a huge bureaucracy, generating an endless flow of rules, regulations and directives. Many prison employees feel hemmed in by nit-picking procedural rules and weighed down by the sheer drudgery of complying with them, as surely as inmates are oppressed and confined by stone walls and coils of razor wire. Some staff members also believe that the bureaucracy's appetite for paperwork is self-serving. In a climate where any mistake or oversight may be minutely examined and publicly criticized, CSC administrators require that every piece of information is recorded and every decision documented.

In every office that I visited, shelves were filled with thick manuals, bulging files and piles of forms. This seemed to be a constant, even in offices where information was also being retrieved, filed and updated on networked computers.

I was so used to finding similar manuals everywhere that I was filled with eager anticipation when the warden of Stony Mountain penitentiary offered to show me a book that I had never seen before. Explaining that it was a treatise on prison management that he himself had authored, Art Majkut produced a thick, magnificently bound hardcover bearing the title, "How to be the Warden of Stony Mountain."

While I examined the cover and opened the book, the warden bounced up and down gleefully, waiting for me to see the punch line of his elaborate joke. The pages were all blank. "That's all you need to know," said Majkut, still chuckling to himself.

I often thought about Warden Majkut's blank book, as I left other offices with briefcase-splitting loads of reports, program descriptions and brochures. It came to symbolize for me the more flexible and pragmatic side to prison administration that does not appear in any of the official documents. The warden's book also suggested the unwritten rules and the underground culture of prisons, the unregulated realities of a hidden world. The contrast between the book's empty pages and the stacks of manuals and reports on the shelves beside it represented in my mind the continual conflict and frequent contradictions that I discovered between the way the prison system is supposed to work and what actually happens behind prison walls.

The basic goal of the federal prison system is spelled out in the CSC Mission Statement, a document drawn up in 1988 to give direction to the prison service. This requires that prison staff do far more than simply keep prisoners in custody, try to keep order and prevent them from escaping. It states that CSC "contributes to the protection of society by actively encouraging and assisting offenders to become law-abiding citizens, while exercising reasonable, safe, secure and humane control." The mission statement includes a set of values and objectives that define what is expected of staff and the system as a whole. These include a duty to respect the dignity and rights of offenders, to recognize and encourage their potential for change.

When the mission statement was introduced, it represented a radical new direction for an organization that had always been dominated by punitive attitudes and a preoccupation with security, in spite of all the lip-service that has been paid over the years to rehabilitation. The mission statement told staff very clearly that it was their duty to act humanely and that the best way to protect society was by helping prisoners to change their lives.

These principles were enshrined in new law in 1992, the Corrections and Conditional Release Act, which governs all aspects of the prison and parole systems. This legislation states that the fundamental purpose of the prison system is to protect the public, but recognizes that the long-term protection of society is best assured through the safe return of offenders to the community as law-abiding citizens. The act made it more difficult for violent offenders or drug offenders to get parole, while speeding up the parole process for non-violent offenders. It was drafted in the aftermath of a series of high-profile blunders involving the release of prisoners on parole who went on to commit murders. The National Parole Board and CSC shared the blame for some of these errors in judgement, since the parole board relies a great deal on information and assessments provided by prison staff. The legislation placed stringent requirements on CSC to gather information about prisoners and share it with other agencies, such as the parole board and police. It also gave victims the right to receive information and made it possible for victims and other interested parties to attend parole hearings, which had previously been closed to the public.

Widely recognized as being one of the most comprehensive pieces of correctional legislation in the world, the Corrections and Conditional Release Act also stipulated that the correctional service should respect the civil rights of inmates and provide programs to respond to the needs of all offenders, paying special attention to the previously neglected needs of women and Native people. The correctional service was ordered to use "the least restrictive measures necessary" to ensure the protection of the public, staff and offenders. Punitive measures, transfers to higher levels of security and other restrictions on inmates have to be justified and prisoners are entitled to hearings at which basic rules of fairness must be applied.

The mission statement and the new legislation have both placed a tremendous burden on a system that was already struggling just to keep a lid on problems like overcrowding, violence and drugs. Nevertheless, CSC administrators believe they can achieve this goal if they can get all their staff to contribute toward creating an environment in which prisoners might be cajoled or inspired into making changes in their lives. To do this involves attempting to transform the culture of an organization that has always been governed by punitive attitudes and rigid routines. It requires altering the institutional mind-set that dominates the prison system and often weighs it down with the inertia of people who have spent most of their lives marking time.

"We're trying to turn a big ship around," said one personnel manager, who acknowledged that some correctional staff are actually trying to steer the ship in the opposite direction, while others are standing aside and watching the manoeuvre, fully confident that the current set of reforms will end up like all previous attempts to change the system and that the ship will eventually turn around a full 360 degrees.

One of the most crucial changes that CSC managers are trying to implement involves the role of the front-line correctional officers, the people whom everyone still calls "guards," much to the chagrin of those who are trying to make them change their ways. The guards supervise inmates on a day-to-day basis and are therefore the staff members with whom prisoners have most contact. In the past, their function was essentially one of keeping order, maintaining security, making sure that prisoners' basic needs were provided for and ensuring that the day-to-day operations of the prison ran smoothly.

The new policies attempt to ensure that the correctional officers are actively engaged in helping prisoners change their lives. The guards are now expected to work as a team with case management officers. Case management officers represent what guards tend to see as the "soft" side of corrections. They are the staff members directly responsible for making sure that prisoners get whatever programs or treatment is appropriate. Case management officers draw up a "correctional plan" for each prisoner on the basis of assessments and information gathered during the intake process. They are responsible for making sure that the plan is followed, keeping track of further information gained from programs, security reports and other sources. On the basis of all this information, case management officers are supposed to prepare documents and recommendations for parole hearings and decisions about transfer to other levels of security.

Since case management officers spend far more time with prisoners' files than with the prisoners themselves, it makes sense that they should team up with correctional officers who have an opportunity to get to know the prisoners well. Guards are therefore expected to perform a counselling role with individual inmates and make reports on their progress. They are also supposed to participate in decision making about transfer requests. Many older guards hate this system because it requires them to do more paperwork and exercise "people skills" that they do not necessarily possess.

At Millhaven Penitentiary, home to Ontario's most violent and dangerous convicts, a correctional officer told me that he and most of his colleagues were proud to be called "guards." Nick was one of many prison employees who explained that he had seen three different philosophies in the correctional service during the course of his career and therefore saw no point in following the latest trend. He said it made more sense just to "wait until the pendulum swings back."

Staff who have been in the correctional service for about twenty years have seen two changes in the style of prison uniforms and they often cite these as examples of the system's failure to steer a steady course. In the early 1980s, prison staff were issued with new military-style uniforms on which veterans could wear their campaign medals. The idea was that this would contribute to a new sense of discipline among correctional officers. One veteran guard told me, "We looked like banana republic dictators." When the mission statement was introduced, it was felt that a more casual look would be appropriate, so new uniforms were designed and issued to all guards. The guards felt their new uniforms, with their blue-and-white striped shirts, made them look like staff in a fast food restaurant and they quickly got tired of prisoners teasing them by asking for "a Big Mac and fries."

Guards were also uncomfortable with the new casual prisoners' uniforms, which replaced institutional green shirts and trousers with jeans, running shoes and casual shirts bearing the prisoner's name on a tag stitched to the front. In minimum security prisons, guards are not required to wear uniforms and some of the older guards get irritated because younger staff members tend to dress like the prisoners in jeans, running shoes and casual shirts or sweaters. "You can't tell players without programs," complained Nick.

The violence and hostility that guards encounter in prison tends to give them a cynical and jaundiced view of inmates. The stress and secrecy of their jobs also serve to isolate them from the community. Tired of being harangued by neighbours about the failings of the prison system and unable to talk about the realities of their work, they are likely to prefer the company of their co-workers. Their view of the society can easily become limited and out of date. As one prison staff member put it, "We become almost as institutionalized as the inmates do."

Guards who are negative and cynical about inmates do not really believe that rehabilitative programs will work. They see them as window dressing and hypocrisy. When other staff members get fired with enthusiasm about a particular program or an inmates' progress, there are always some guards who will label their colleagues as "bleeding hearts" and conclude that they have been conned by the convicts.

The personnel officer whom I interviewed suggested that the negative attitudes of some guards is akin to industrial sabotage, given that the goal of the prison system is to create an environment in which inmates will be encouraged to change. "Imagine how long they would last on a production line saying 'This is garbage. I'm not putting this piece on,'" he said.

Nick, the guard at Millhaven, railed against policies that require all correctional officers to rotate through all the different jobs in the prison. The purpose of this rule was to get all staff members involved in working with prisoners in their living areas, and to ensure that no employees work exclusively at armed security posts where they have nothing to do with inmates. But Nick said that some guards prefer to sit at security posts and want nothing to do with case management teams and filing reports. At Millhaven, Nick told me, the system is just "a big lie," because many of the officers simply divide the tasks up unofficially among themselves.

What the people who designed the programs and the mission statement do not realize about the inmates, Nick told me, is that a lot of them "don't give a shit." He went on to explain that his job was not to punish inmates but to protect the public by maintaining security in the institution. To do this, he said, you have to understand that "there are three things that keep inmates happy: food, recreation and their own space." Like many other guards of the old school, he preferred to leave inmates to their own devices, as far as possible, maintaining a reasonably tolerant attitude, as long as there was no trouble. Most of his interaction with prisoners occurred when someone stepped out of line.

Many CSC administrators believe that the attitudes of guards are beginning to change as a result of recent increases in the number of female correctional officers hired to work in men's prisons. According to CSC research, as well as informal observations, female staff members tend to take a less confrontational approach to inmates and use verbal skills rather than force to resolve conflicts. They also rely more on proper disciplinary channels, rather than violence or intimidation. Women employees are also seen as being more open to the cooperative, team-building approach that is favoured in CSC's new policies.

But women in men's jails are subject to harassment, not so much from prisoners, as from male guards. The harassment reported in surveys of female prison staff ranges from unwanted touching to various forms of discrimination and prejudice. For example, women complain that their male colleagues spread rumours that they are lesbians or that they are sexually involved with male prisoners. While male guards routinely go drinking together after work, female staff members who join them are often assumed to be promiscuous. Almost equally unwelcome for many female employees is their male colleagues' assumption that the women will not be tough enough to deal with a real emergency and are therefore compromising everyone's safety. Women can easily feel excluded from the bonding that prison guards believe is important in an environment where staff rely on one another for mutual protection. One of the most disturbing findings of reports on harassment of female staff is that few women feel comfortable about reporting even serious incidents of abuse for fear of being branded "a rat." Women who complain of harassment are also likely to be accused of overreacting in an environment where insult and personal abuse are considered normal.

The mission document requires all employees to respect the basic civil rights of prisoners, but many front-line officers find this very hard to do. A senior administrator described their attitude to me, while explaining the rationale for the policy. "It's hard to act fairly and with integrity to people whose past behaviour may be so abhorrent that to read about it might make one sick," he said. Referring to serial killer Clifford Olson, whose vigilant defence of his own rights has often distressed members of the public and prison officials alike, the administrator commented, "There isn't one thing I like about what Clifford Olson has done, but in order for me to have integrity and follow the mission of the organization, I have to accord him basic human rights. If we say there are some people who shouldn't be enjoying civil rights, where do we draw the line?"

According to Tom Epp, a senior administrator in CSC's Ontario regional headquarters, many of the people hired when the prison system was expanded in the 1970s are now "caught in a time warp" and cannot accept the changes. "The old idea of being hidden behind walls ain't going to cut it any more, but we're dragging a lot of staff who don't see that." The older staff members have seen the correctional service transformed, Epp told me, from a closed and very punitive organization to one that is more accountable to the community, sensitive to victims and respect-ful of the rights and needs of prisoners from a myriad of ethnic and social backgrounds. The work force, which once consisted largely of tough white males, hired to keep prisoners under con-trol, has expanded to include 25 different job functions, mostly carried out by university or community college graduates, recruit-ed under policies that encourage applications from women and visible minorities. Whereas training for correctional officers used to cover weapons, self-defence, penitentiary regulations and little else, new staff are now put through three-month courses that include law, civil rights and sensitivity sessions.

"We are going through a period of profound, inexorable change. Our most common prayer is that we could have a bit of peace and quiet for a few years so we can get on with the changes," said Epp, who conceded, however, that "the public still see us as a parochial, semi-military bunch of thugs. And on a bad day, we're everything you think we are."

People who work in prisons feel as if they are under siege because criticisms tend to come from all directions. They are accused alternately of condoning acts of brutality by guards and of being too soft on prisoners. It is seen as a slow and ponder-ous bureaucracy, yet it has been criticized for failing to collect or pass on enough information about prisoners applying for parole. People get frustrated by a preoccupation with security that can make the service seem uncooperative and secretive, but such complaints pale in comparison with the public uproar when a dangerous prisoner escapes.

The successes of the prison system are often hard to mea-sure, and there is little of interest that one can say about them. Success is when nobody escapes or when a prisoner has been released and has not yet, as far as anyone knows, got into any further trouble. The failures are what catches everyone's attention. As Tom Epp pointed out in his interview with me, "It takes only one incident to label you incompetent."

Like the prison service as a whole, individual employees tend to feel insecure. They can work with the upmost competence for years without being noticed, but one mistake could endanger lives and ruin their careers. Managers and line staff alike are also always conscious that they might end up taking the blame for someone else's mistake or for a systemic problem that was beyond their control. The CSC may be a traditionally militaristic organization, but employees laughed cynically when I asked if the buck ultimately stopped with the most senior officers. A local union president explained with the delicacy of tongue that I had learned to expect from prison staff, "Everyone of us is convinced that shit rolls downhill and ends at your office."

Staff members often have little confidence in their supervisors. "Anybody working here who says they're not afraid hasn't got a grasp. On a daily basis it's scary, because a lot of staff think management don't have a clue what's going on. It's more by good luck than good management that we don't have a riot," said one case management officer. At Millhaven, Nick complained that senior levels of management are completely oblivious to what is really going on within institutions. He described how the CSC commissioner was once taken on a tour of the prison during one of its frequent periods of inmate unrest, but was never shown the cell block inhabited by the most incorrigible prisoners, who had daubed the walls with the slogan "Kill the pigs." Nick said the commissioner congratulated the management on the condition of the prison.

Frequent changes in policy conribute to staff members' feelings of insecurity. While the mission statement set an idealistic policy direction for the correctional service, the policies are continually being updated and changed on a pragmatic basis. New directives and amendments are frequently inserted into the loose-leaf binders that contain the policy manuals and, as one staff member put it, "You only have to read today's headlines to see what tomorrow's policy will be."

Some new procedures are designed to plug holes in the system that have been exposed by investigations of escapes, murders or other serious incidents. But others appear to be public relations exercises that undermine previous policies. For example, public criticisms over a program that funded university courses in prisons led to the program being cut, even though almost everyone in the prison system recognized that helping inmates get a higher education was one of the best proven ways of helping them become law-abiding citizens.

Many people working within the prison system believe that their own efforts and the goals of their organization have been compromised by budget cuts and an ever-increasing workload. CSC Commissioner John Edwards explained in a 1994 article in the CSC publication *Let's Talk*: "In recent years, we have experienced reductions in funding below what our workload would warrant — actual cuts of 4 to 5 per cent. This rises to around 14 per cent when we take into account unsuccessful requests for funding to cover work-load increases, price increases and some new programs. Over the period 1993–4 to 1997–8, further cuts are being required of us, amounting to an additional 9.4 per cent reduction from what our operating budget would have been." Explaining that CSC was hoping to minimize the impact of budgetary cuts by streamlining administrative procedures, Edwards went on to state: "Budget reductions are especially painful to achieve considering that we are dealing, not only with an ever-growing number of offenders, but also with pressures to increase programs offered to offenders."

In the lower echelons of the organization, staff maintain that all this translates into more work, more responsibilities, higher risks and less job security. They complain that management is

continually experimenting with public safety by gradually elim-
inating staff positions or slowly increasing inmate-to-staff ratios.

Prison staff members frequently complain that budget cuts
are jeopordizing prison security systems. In several penitentiaries,
guards drew my attention to the fact that gun towers were mostly unmanned. Most newer penitentiaries do not have walls but
are protected by two rows of chain-link fencing topped by coils
of razor wire. The fences or walls are overlooked by a series of
towers. Most of these towers are now empty, but have cameras
attached to them. There are also motion detectors in the space
between the fences. These devices are operated and monitored
from control rooms, while armed guards patrol the perimeter
in vehicles. Administrators maintain that this system is almost
foolproof. Nevertheless, many correctional officers feel that their
safety is compromised. They feel vulnerable entering an exercise
yard without an armed guard watching from a tower.

Prisons have become reliant on technology for security, but
many employees do not trust the technology. They never feel
completely confident that there is someone watching the mon-
itors in the control rooms or listening for the alarms. A man
who routinely works alone with mentally disturbed prisoners
told me that he was once cornered by an inmate with a homemade knife. He pressed an alarm button in his office, but had
fortunately been able to calm the prisoner down and persuade
him to give up his weapon by the time security staff arrived 40
minutes later.

It is hard, however, for staff to make a case that cutbacks are
endangering security as long as there is no major catastrophe.
That is one reason union officials are continually predicting
riots, escapes or other major disturbances. As one prison guard
explained to me, "We are not paid for what we do, but for what
we might have to do in an emergency."

CSC administrators maintain that order can best be maintained by means of "dynamic security," the term used to denote

the personal relationships that are supposed to be established between staff and prisoners, together with the information-gathering process that should enable staff to anticipate problems and intervene appropriately. But cutbacks in staffing make it more difficult for correctional officers to perform these functions, even if they are willing to do so.

For many overworked staff members, CSC's emphasis on information gathering translates into an intolerable amount of paperwork. As one case management officer put it, "We always have another report to do. We're always filling up forms. We spend 90 per cent of our time on paper and 10 per cent on individuals. We're checking everything up on paper and we can't check the guy." A prominent prison psychologist told me bluntly, "By the time you fill out all their bloody forms, you don't have much time left."

But prison administrators believe that paperwork can protect society. The computerized Offender Management System, which keeps track of all available information pertaining to every offender, is supposed to document all the risks that each prisoner poses, the steps taken to minimize these risks and an assessment of how successful these steps have been. This information can be immediately accessible to officials making decisions about transferring prisoners to lower levels of security and granting them day passes or parole. It can also be used by parole officers and police after the offenders have been released.

Too often in the past, a prisoner's violent and anti-social behaviour would be handled informally by guards without any information being passed on and documented. As a result, the problems and risks that the prisoner posed remained unknown to therapists and case management officers. Guards would, perhaps, roll their eyes knowingly when they heard that the prisoner had been released on parole. But it would never occur to the guards that it might have been their responsibility to warn anyone. Indeed, if they had tried to do so, the chances were that their opinions would have had about as much influence on the final decision as the comments of a security guard in a courthouse corridor might have on legal proceedings inside the court. The forms that many guards hate to fill out now provide a way of ensuring that their valuable insights into prisoners' attitudes and behaviour are communicated and applied.

To some extent, the new bureaucratic approach to prison management is designed to take more account of individual needs and keep better track of each offender's prison career. It is supposed to help prison staff devise a plan to help each prisoner achieve the goal of reintegrating safely with society. Precise information about each prisoner's background can be used in addressing the problems and needs that contribute toward criminal behaviour.

But statistical projections and averages are ultimately more important to the new prison managers than individual outcomes. Decisions about transfer and parole are often made largely on the basis of actuarial tables, similar to those used by insurance companies in assessing rates. The insurance company does not know how well individual policyholders can drive or how careful they are, but it can predict on the basis of statistical information that young drivers are more likely to get into accidents and that those with clean driving records are better risks. The company therefore adjusts its rates according to statistical probabilities. There is virtually nothing that a twenty-year-old with two speeding tickets and a previous charge of careless driving can do to persuade an insurance agent that he should pay less.

The same principles are applied in the risk management process now in place in prisons. Information about individual offenders, gathered on the offender management computer system, is analysed by psychologists and compared with general statistical information about criminal behaviour. In this way, it is possible to come up with the odds in favour of a particular offender committing another crime.

There is no way of telling, for example, whether an individual rapist who has worked on overcoming a problem of drug abuse, will commit another crime or not. But statistics can show that a new offence is committed within two years by 60 per cent of offenders with similar records, backgrounds and problems, who are released from prison after serving sentences for a similar crime. Once this type of information has been obtained, it is up to parole boards or case management teams to assess how the potential risks that each offender poses to society can best be managed. Ultimately, they may still have to take a gamble, but at least they will know the odds.

Since many prison employees oppose the new system, however, it is hard to be sure that accurate or complete information is always provided. Many staff members feel overwhelmed by their workloads and by the magnitude of the problems that they confront on the job. Some of them find that they do not really have time to work with prisoners, as their time is spent recycling second-hand information in forms and reports.

In this context, the bureaucratic process takes on a life of its own. Some prison staff complained to me that their bosses did not seem to worry about what they did with prisoners and whether it worked, providing they filled out a form saying that they had the required number of meetings in any given week. Staff members are often forced to write assessments of prisoners whom they have barely met and can scarcely remember. In such circumstances, offenders might be labelled as cooperative simply because they showed up for classes or appointments. While some staff members cannot be bothered with paperwork, others feel that they need to prove that they are doing a thorough job by recording every detail on files, with the result that files, like the prisons themselves, are becoming overcrowded and confusing.

As the correctional service applies new methods in its attempt to provide protection from crime, it must continue to deal with the old problems that have plagued prisons for generations. CSC is apparently attempting to transform itself, while making changes in the lives of its inmates. In the eyes of many disenchanted employees, however, it is just the image, not the substance, that is changing, and the prison system is only managing to protect itself.

10

PROGRAMS FOR CHANGE

The six men sitting with me represented the collective wisdom, anger and despair of more than 100 years in penitentiaries. They had been talking about the prison environment and what it does to people. Maurice, an aging bank robber summarized their conclusions: "The poor lambs out there on the street are saying they should treat prisoners like dirt, but they don't realize that all they are doing is rattling a cage and slapping a pit bull in the jaw."

The men were all participating in a program for offenders whose aggressive behaviour had created major problems in jail. They were a living testimony both to the prison system's failures and to its potential for success. They told me how the prison environment can make offenders worse, but they also explained what programs can do to help. Their stories and those of many other prisoners whom I met, however, left me wondering whether the positive value of the programs could ever outweigh the negative influence of the prison culture, especially for the depressingly large number of offenders who never had any positive influences in their early lives.

All the six men I met at the Regional Psychiatric Centre in Saskatoon had committed serious crimes on the outside, but it was in prison that their violent propensities had flourished. None of them were psychopaths or sex offenders. Some were impulsive men who continually fought with guards and other prisoners. Others were described as "overcontrolled" individuals, who suppressed their anger and fuelled a simmering rage that would break out in occasional acts of extreme violence. These men had all done hard time in prison and most of them had been released several times, with nothing to show for their prison sentences, but a dangerous combination of rage and helplessness. Their previous prison experiences had rendered them more violent and less able to survive in society. The only skills that they felt they could rely on were their ability to commit more crimes.

All these men had served most of their sentences in maximum security prisons, with frequent spells of punishment in "the hole," the segregation units where prisoners are kept in their cells for 23 hours a day. Half of them had spent periods of time in one of the Special Handling Units, the super-maximum security prisons within the prison system, where furniture is welded to the floor and inmates are constantly watched by armed guards.

Now they were living in a hospital environment. There was still a razor wire fence to keep them in, but inside there were pleasant courtyards, lawns and walk-ways. Instead of maximum security guards, they were dealing with nurses in white uniforms, who called them by their first names. There were carpets on the floor, and when I visited in the second week of December, the lounges were festooned with Christmas decorations.

The program in which these prisoners were enrolled provided them with some hope that they might be able to change their behaviour and learn to live in society. They had all worked hard to get into the program and showed that they had a motivation to change. The therapy was helping them understand why they responded violently to certain situations. It was teaching them ways of controlling their anger and dealing with problems more positively. The prisoners were acquiring skills and attitudes that could help them lead a more socially productive lifestyle.

They were learning how to avoid situations that might get them into trouble.

An intense young man, who remained silent through most of our discussion, told me that he began acting violently in prison when he was forced to defend himself against an attempted gang rape. He said, "I honestly believe that if you're a victim yourself, a victim of system, there are a lot of missing pieces that you can't put together. You can't feel empathy. After you've worked on all that, if you can get into a program like this, you may come to the point where you'll say, 'Jesus Christ, I've hurt a lot of people.'"

Jason, who stabbed several other inmates during a long and turbulent prison career, told me that it was hard at first to get used to seeing the staff as nurses, rather than "pigs." He threatened one of the nurses during the first week that he was there because he wanted to go back to the SHU where everything was predictable and nothing was expected of him. He wanted to return to a place where his violence was simply a problem for other people to control. He said he would have followed through with his threat, but they sent a female nurse to deal with him and he could not bring himself to hit a woman. "To have staff use your first name implies familiarity, emotional responsibility to that person," said Jason. "This was one of the few places that read my file and came to see me as an individual. In most places, you're just a number on a file."

A psychologist told me that Jason had changed his behaviour so much in the program that he was now trusted to work unsupervised in the courtyard. He would handle tools like a hedge trimmer and a chain saw without any problem. Jason explained that the program helped because it encouraged him to examine the reasons for his behaviour and the attitudes that tended to reinforce it, rather than just relying on external controls to keep a lid on his violent tendencies. He said, "If we're given the tools, there're a lot of good people in prison who can do something with their lives. We're not all fucking wash-ups or throwaways."

Acknowledging that he still has dangerous tendencies, Jason said, "I feel that I have enough control of myself never to use them again. I'm not leaving the way I was when I came in. The program has opened up other doors. The only thing I had going for me before was my street smarts. I know I can make it out there. I have the rest of my life to get my shit together."

Another member of the group described what it is like to find oneself on the street after doing time in the SHU. Terry, a heavy-set man, whose elaborate tattoos seemed to cover every inch of his bulging muscles, explained that he was 32 years old and had only spent a year on the street since the age of sixteen. Last time he was out, he lasted only a week. Terry said he managed to get some drugs and a sawed-off shotgun within hours of being released from jail. "You've been in a place where everything is locked up or screwed to the ground. You've been chained up whenever you moved and been watched all the time by guards with rifles. You're big and healthy and you feel that you've been treated like a house dog for ten years. Here you are on the street, but your head's still in the SHU. Your mind is going 1,000 miles an hour. You pass a bank and see money changing hands or you pass a gun store and you see the weapons on display. You say, 'That's not protected. I own all this.'"

The scenario that Terry depicted was disturbing, but it was one with which other members of the violent offenders group easily identified. Prior to the program in which they were currently enrolled, their prison experience had not taught them any control over their own behaviour. It had taught them to be more violent. They had been held in check merely by external controls. They had learned to be resourceful in making weapons out of almost anything. They had spent years watching and being watched, waiting to exploit any minor security slip or oversight. Once they were out on the street, they believed that there was nothing to stop them taking what they want or treating people however they liked. Maurice, the aging bank robber, shook his head and commented, "The public is so naïve."

Ironically, the people whom the public have most reason to fear are least likely to become involved in treatment programs. Some of them may be dangerous offenders sentenced to an indeterminant prison term or murderers on life sentences. In these cases, it may be possible to keep them in jail forever, unless officials are convinced that they are rehabilitated. But most prisoners cannot be kept in jail indefinitely, even though they may be dangerous. It is therefore important that the system attempts to provide effective treatment programs and persuade prisoners to participate.

But in the SHU and in maximum security, where the most violent prisoners spend a large portion of their sentences, the programs tend to be less effective. Educational programs and therapy are provided in a setting that is hardly conducive to learning or growth. At the Quebec SHU, I was shown a schoolroom in which teacher is separated from students by a bulletproof Plexiglas screen. As students sit at their desks, armed guards may watch them through gun ports that open from a catwalk running above and behind the room. When the students want to consult their teacher or hand in exercise books, they do so through a letter-box-sized opening, as in a teller's window at a well-secured bank. I asked a teacher what it was like working in such conditions and he told me, "One gets used to it."

Next door to the schoolroom, there was a small chapel in which a metal grille separates the chaplain from the congregation. When I asked a chaplain how he felt about conducting services in these circumstances, he said, "One comes to regard the bars as a symbol."

The chapel is also used for program groups with prisoners sitting on one side of the bars and their therapist on the other. A program instructor at the Quebec SHU told me that it is difficult to conduct classes in anger management and life skills from behind a screen. He said, "The goal is to change their self view and their world view, but everything else around them ratifies their old view."

At the Saskatchewan SHU, program staff meet with inmates without protective barriers, whenever it seems safe to do so. A program instructor told me, "We're extending trust to them. I sit on a corner of the desk and have a conversation like normal people would. They realize we're making an effort. They feel valued." For the inmates, talking to staff in this way can be scary because it is a violation of the con code, which is still a dominant influence on the inmate culture of the SHU. The instructor told me, "If it is a one-on-one session, they don't have to lose face because other inmates aren't around."

Prisoners cannot be forced to participate in programs, but they have powerful incentives to do so. CSC pays prisoners a daily wage of up to $6.90, providing they do work assignments in the prison and participate in programs. If they refuse to work or do not enrol in a program that they have been asked to take, prisoners' pay can be cut off. Participation in programs is also an important factor when recommendations are made for transfer to lower levels of security or release on parole.

Participation in programs is, therefore, a key for any prisoner who wants to be transferred from the SHUs to a lower level of security. Jason told me that he had to work very hard at programs in the SHU before he was considered for admission to the Regional Psychiatric Centre. He said that about half his fellow inmates participated in programs while the other half refused to take them and seemed quite happy to remain in the SHU "to rot."

For many prisoners, the CSC programs provide a chance to deal with the problems that led them to prison in the first place. The programs include academic upgrading as well as life skills and therapeutic programs to address specific behavioural problems. They were designed to address needs, problems and attitudes that lead people to commit crimes. When an offender enters the federal prison system, the intake assessment process attempts to identify the factors in that person's life that contributed to his or her criminal behaviour. The offender is then encouraged to participate in programs that will address the particular problems that have been identified. The CSC research department believes that this approach can reduce the risk of released prisoners reoffending by as much as 50 per cent.

Data from intake assessments and surveys show that about 65 per cent of prisoners were functionally illiterate when they first arrived in the federal correctional system. Most were high-school drop-outs and chronically unemployed. The percentage of inmates with serious problems of substance abuse has been estimated as high as 70 per cent. The programs provide inmates with educational upgrading and vocational training, as well as help with controlling anger, avoiding family violence and dealing with drug and alcohol abuse.

Many of the people who find their way into the federal prison system have grown up with an extremely limited experience and understanding of human emotions. They tend to respond in a confrontational way to almost any situation because anger and frustration are the only feelings that they have learned to recognize. The cognitive living skills program, which is offered in most institutions, attempts to teach prisoners how to be assertive without being violent and to criticize others or receive criticism without being confrontational.

But many of the people delivering the programs feel that their work is undermined when the prisoners return to their cell blocks. One life skills teacher told me, "Relations between guards and inmates make them not quite sure that what we teach is applicable, because some of the guards don't have life skills."

Some inmates distrust the staff who deliver programs because many of them are former guards. Debbie Taylor, program instructor and former correctional officer at the Saskatchewan Penitentiary, told me that she lost a lot of credibility with her students when she was called in for special guard duty during a crisis. "My cognitive living skills students saw me in uniform, armed to the hilt, and I could see them looking me up and down and shaking their heads," she said. Nevertheless, Taylor felt it an asset to have come though the ranks. She said, "I've seen a lot of guys at their worst. When I used to work the night shift, I would get exposed to a really different side that you would not see in classroom setting. Some of them would be obscene and abusive. They'd maybe stare at you all night. Some guys would sleep and others would be sitting up all night, staring at the wall or doing their hobbies." Taylor told me that she felt her experience as a guard made her more aware of how inmates live on the ranges and less likely to be conned by them. She said she was conscious of the fact that she brought a different attitude to each job. She said, "In programs, you want to impact. In uniform you want to maintain control."

Taylor said she experienced conflicts when she had to charge individual inmates in her class or relay information to security officers. Sometimes, she said, an inmate might disclose information about intimidation while asking for advice about how the skills learned in class can be implemented on the range. She explained that she warns the inmates in her classes that she is bound to report anything they tell her that appears to affect the good order of institution. She said, "If somebody has it in for another staff member — even if he says jokingly, 'I'm going to get him or her,' I'll call the unit manager. Even if I had an argument and he leaves with a lip on, I'll pass it on."

Often distrustful and contemptuous of the instructors, inmates tend to be cynical about the programs and regard them merely as hoops through which they have to jump in order to satisfy the requirements of their case management officers and the parole board. As Willie Gladu at Kingston Penitentiary explained, "Many inmates have a checklist approach. They say, 'I've taken this, this and this. Now let me out.' For some, it's a lot of game playing for parole board purposes. Others refuse to become involved in programs. They say, 'I'm not going anywhere until I do so many years.'"

Case management officers also tend to take a checklist approach to programs. Thèrese Lemieux, a member of the program staff at the Archambault Institution in Ste-Anne-des-Plaines, Quebec, told me, "They need to justify something on paper, so they put the inmate on the list. They're playing with the system. Inmates do it and case management officers do it. It's bad for us because it decreases the credibility of the program."

Lemieux told me that inmates get frustrated because many case management officers do not really believe in the programs and do not take the instructors' evaluations seriously. When they receive positive evaluations, case management officers often assume that program staff have been "taken in" by the inmates. She said, "They don't believe that we can have a good relationship with those guys, that the inmates really revealed themselves in a way that they wouldn't do with the other staff."

Because they do not trust the evaluations and because they are afraid of making mistakes, case management officers often recommend that inmates do further programs. "By the time the guy is in his fifth or sixth program, he's not got much motivation left," said Lemieux. One long-term offender told me that he managed to repeat Grades Five to Ten several times, as records got lost in transfer and prison staff did not really seem to care whether the classes were necessary as long as they could make it look on paper as if they were doing something positive with inmates. Explaining that he just went to class in order to get out of doing work, he said, "You didn't even have to think because you were doing the same grades over."

Prisoners who see the programs as stepping stones to early release often become disillusioned when they find that they are not automatically released. Nevertheless, the programs can help offenders who want to make changes in their lives. One prisoner told me, "The programs saved me. They gave me tools that I had never used in my life, social skills, awareness of where I was coming from. They enable you to work on yourself. I found my freedom in jail. It changed my life around completely." But he echoed Lemieux's concern that the programs are undermined by the prison environment. He said, "They teach us stuff, show us stuff and bring up issues for us. Then they leave. We don't have anywhere to go or anyone to talk to."

Another inmate, reflecting perhaps a more common view, told me, "The programs are a complete waste of time, a joke, a front. Nobody knows what the fuck they're talking about."

One deficiency of the standard CSC programs is that they tend to work best for literate prisoners with good communication skills. Most of them require offenders to read and apply verbal skills that are beyond the capacity of mentally handicapped offenders. At Dorchester Penitentiary in New Brunswick, Gary Jonah, who runs programs for low-functioning offenders, explained that some of them had committed horrendous crimes but had no access to regular programs. Jonah's program teaches basic skills and attempts to address some of the attitudes that might lead the offenders into crime. The program also addresses prisoners' personal hygiene practices and other very basic problems that tend to get "inadequates" into trouble with other prisoners.

CSC provides literacy classes for prisoners who cannot read. Anyone whose skills are measured as being below a Grade Ten level is considered functionally illiterate and asked to attend upgrading classes. The correctional service sets a high standard for literacy because it is hard to compete in the job market without at least a Grade 10 education. Education classes are provided to prisoners up to a high-school-graduation level.

Many prisoners and some staff members told me that they were upset over CSC's July 1993 decision to suspend post-secondary education classes in prisons. The classes, taught by visiting professors and instructors, were popular with prisoners, some of whom were able to earn degrees behind bars. A study in British Columbia showed that prisoners who had taken university courses were more than three times less likely than other offenders to return to prison after their release.

The program was scrapped by CSC, partly to save money, but mainly because it did not seem politically acceptable to provide prisoners with educational opportunities that were not available or were too expensive for many law-abiding citizens. After the courses were cancelled, it remained possible for prisoners to take university correspondence courses providing they could find the money to pay for them, but the number of prisoners enrolled in university fell from 401 to 152.

"University was the best program because CSC didn't run it," one prisoner told me. "When I came into prison, I didn't understand how the institutions in society worked, what they were for, how they developed or how to use them. I learned all that from the university courses. Now they give you these stupid little programs that I learned in Grade Two."

For many prisoners, educational programs provide an escape from the depressing realities of their everyday lives. One prisoner, who maintained that the programs were "bogus," admitted however that they did some good for people who have no other positive values or influences in their lives. He said, "People go to programs for the pleasure of being treated as a normal human being." In several classrooms, I saw students engrossed in their computer terminals or engaged in earnest discussion with their teachers, apparently oblivious, for a moment at least, of the locked doors, armed guards and razor wire fences separating them from world that they were studying.

The programs that generate, perhaps, the greatest enthusiasm among CSC staff and inmates alike are those geared specifically to aboriginal offenders. Native people are present in the prison system in grossly disproportionate numbers, and in the past, none of the rehabilitative programs had much impact.

The programs were culturally inappropriate to aboriginal people and did not address any of the specific problems that Native offenders encounter in their home communities and in the prisons. In recent years, CSC has worked with aboriginal communities and their spiritual leaders to create programs that incorporate Native beliefs and ceremonies.

Some of these Native programs create problems for the prison bureaucracy and the parole board because it is hard to evaluate inmates' participation. The traditions are oral and it is sometimes difficult for outsiders even to comprehend the content of the programs, let alone assess the results. At CSC's Regional Psychiatric Centre in Saskatoon, a Native medicine woman was employed to conduct healing ceremonies, but, when asked to describe the ceremonies for an official report, the healer prefaced a somewhat confusing account of the procedures with the comment "You pretty well have to be here to understand."

Nevertheless, the value of the healing ceremonies is clear from prisoners' accounts of what they experienced. One prisoner said the ceremony enabled him to get rid of "all those ugly feelings, all those angry little feelings that were inside me that I didn't want." Another prisoner said, "It was like all the hate, bitterness, resentments and hurt was hitting me all at once. I cried because it hurt." He went on to describe how he inhaled sacred medicine and was enveloped in a blanket. Then, he said, "I cried because I felt good, like a tremendous weight had been lifted from my body. I felt at peace, a peace that I can't ever remember having existed within me."

The report on the program noted that the Native healer believed that lasting results could be achieved only if a healing lodge were established, where the prisoners could work at changing their lives and rediscovering their culture, away from the negative influences of the penitentiary. She was quoted as saying, "We bring out the inmate, we work on them, but he goes back to that isolation or to that place which makes him very sick. So its very difficult to do the work so it's going to have a lasting impact."

It is a strange and disturbing paradox, however, that healing methods that work best in a natural environment can now be most easily found in prisons. CSC has established a healing lodge for Native women. There are various Native-run community programs for men, and some courts are experimenting with the notion of involving Native communities in finding alternatives to penitentiary sentences, such as banishment to remote islands. But for the vast majority of the Native men who are sentenced to federal prison terms, it is only in the enclosed, violent and unhealthy environment of a penitentiary that they will learn about a culture that is based on balance, respect and harmony with nature.

At Stony Mountain penitentiary, one prisoner talked to me about the sorrow he felt when he heard a visiting elder asking forgiveness from the Creator for using the English language. The prisoner told me, "I was ashamed of coming to jail to learn my culture. For many years I had shame over my head and guilt. But the elder said, 'Maybe it was a blessing in disguise. The Grandfathers wanted it this way for you to understand about life.'"

At hearings of the 1992 Royal Commission on Aboriginal Peoples, Georges Erasmus remarked, "The irony is that it is behind the bars that they are hearing more about their culture than anywhere else and there is a real lack of follow-up." The hearings were told that many small communities no longer have any elders or anyone able to lead ceremonies and teach the traditional culture. Erasmus commented, "It is sounding more and more like unless the outside starts to heal itself and it has the services to heal the average aboriginal person on the street, we are not actually going to be able to help the inmates inside."

The problems associated with Native programs in prison and the difficulty of evaluating their results were both illustrated very clearly for me by a parole hearing that I attended at Stony

Mountain. In recent years, the burgeoning of Native programs within institutions has been accompanied by an effort to make the parole system more accessible to Native offenders. A comprehensive study of parole releases in the 1980s found that Native offenders were less likely to be granted parole than non-Natives. It also concluded that those Native offenders who were released on parole were more likely to return to the penitentiary, either for parole violations or other crimes. Native people have been appointed to sit as members of the parole board, and in the Prairies, Native offenders have the opportunity to have their cases presented in hearings at which an elder is present.

Stan, the prisoner applying for parole at the "elder-assisted" parole hearing that I attended, had been one of the leaders of the Native Brotherhood in the institution. Stan had spent more than seven years in prison for various violent crimes. He was a burly man, whose long black hair was streaked with grey. His big face wore a dour, blank expression as he explained to the parole board members that sometimes he is misunderstood, because people get the mistaken impression that he is mad at them.

Non-Native security staff at Stony Mountain had Stan pegged as a prisoner involved in drugs and intimidation. They described him as the "muscle" behind the leader of the Native Brotherhood. But to the Native liaison workers and the elder at the institution, Stan was an example of the power of Native programs, a prisoner who had successfully turned his life around.

One of the two parole board members was Native and he questioned Stan's commitment to spiritual values by observing, "Sometimes Native inmates burn sweet grass to cover the smell of pot."

"I have spoken out about that. I don't believe in desecrating medicine," replied Stan. He went on to explain that the lifestyle that he used to lead was now over and it was time for him to move on.

Asked about allegations that he had recently been involved in muscling other inmates, Stan explained that he had been placed in minimum security with prisoners who had previously been in protective custody. He said that in such a setting it is easy to be perceived as being violent. He said, "If you give someone a threatening or derogatory look, that's a no no. It was hard for me to understand that, hard to work with people there."

Stan told the board about the insight that he had gained from Native programs. He said he had discovered spirituality and learned about the problems in his own childhood that had made him the way he was. He explained, "I always wanted to be in the limelight. I always wanted to be in charge. Now, I can be a leader in a more constructive and positive way."

Native elders do not give tests at the end of their sweat lodge ceremonies. It is almost impossible to measure spiritual growth and hard to determine whether a prisoner has been seriously committed to the programs or is trying to "con" the parole board. In this case, the elder employed at Stony Mountain told the board that he had seen Stan grow and learn.

The board concluded that Stan was sincere in his commitment to Native spirituality. They decided that his best prospect of rehabilitation lay in releasing him on parole to a rural reserve where he would be supported and encouraged by members of the community.

Before the board made its decision, the elder employed by the parole board to attend such hearings made a speech in broken English. He had opened the proceedings by praying in his own language for honesty, but had remained silent during the hearing. Addressing his comments to Stan, he said, "Ten years back, we never see any Indian people sitting here on the board. I see it here and I like it. People here care about you, want to help you to straighten your life. Face it all your life. Be a man. Not stealing. All Indian people need pipe. If you happen to leave from this building here, be strong. Be good. And never come here again."

I left the hearing wondering whether or not Stan would make it. I did not doubt the sincerity of his spiritual renewal, although

I did not find it hard to believe that many of the allegations of the security staff were also true. I had the feeling that much would depend on the options available to him in the community. While there were grounds for hope that he might achieve his ambition of becoming a Native spiritual leader and make an important contribution to the community, it was also quite possible that the penitentiary would be the only place where he found that he had a role to play.

Six months later, I learned that Stan had indeed returned to the penitentiary after committing a vicious assault. Staff at Stony Mountain were not ready to give up on him, however. Assistant warden Al Maclean told me, "Inmates can be sincere about the ceremonies, but it doesn't mean that they won't do something stupid a few weeks later. Some of them are really struggling with horrific abuse that generates hatred, hostility and anger. Healing is not a short-term, linear process. They continually have to restart the journey."

Many offenders, Native and non-Native alike, enter the prison system with horrendous histories of childhood abuse and neglect and years of negative experiences as young adults, either in the community or in institutions. They may be responsible for the crimes that they have committed, but these crimes must also be understood in relation to the pressures and problems that made the offenders become who they are. Prison programs attempt to bring new influences to bear on these problems and thus give offenders a better chance of finding healthy ways of living in the community. But the problems are often too great and the programs are frequently undermined by the prison environment itself. Even when prisoners do change, they often find that the same problems are awaiting them again in the community. They came to penitentiary partly because they could not find a place for themselves in the world. The community will not be safe unless prisoners can make a life for themselves when they return to society.

11

WORKING IN ISOLATION

I was surprised to find that prisons are usually spotlessly clean. My imagination and the grim exteriors of some of the older buildings had led me to expect that they would be squalid and dilapidated on the inside. I soon realized what a huge misconception that was, as I got used to the sight of prisoners slowly mopping or sweeping corridors whose surfaces were already gleaming and devoid of any particle of dust.

Also unexpected was the quality of the food cooked in prison kitchens. Although I occasionally encountered a dubious sandwich ingredient that prisoners described as "mystery meat," most of the meals that I sampled were wholesome and well-prepared. I later realized that much of the food was produced on prison farms and that it was prisoners who cooked it with great care and served out generous portions.

There is no shortage of labour in prisons, a fact that was underlined for me at one institution where I watched the almost comic routine of a two-man vacuuming crew. One prisoner pushed a normal household-sized vacuum cleaner around a carpeted office area, while another man followed behind him holding the cord. The two men stopped occasionally to confer about how to reach an awkward corner or when to transfer the plug to another outlet.

Make-work programs are a long-established part of prison

culture. Every administrator knows that inmates are liable to create trouble if they spend their days hanging around their cell blocks with nothing to do. At one time "hard labour" was considered a part of prisoners' punishment, and they were put to work at often meaningless, back-breaking tasks, like breaking rocks in quarries. Some jurisdictions in the United States have recently revived the tradition of the chain gang, with the apparent purpose of humiliating prisoners and appearing to be "tough" on crime, even though this may have the effect of making the convicts tougher and more angry. The Alberta and Ontario governments have also expressed an interest in introducing a version of the chain gang to their provinical prison systems.

Rather than use work as a punishment, Canada's federal prison system has the goal of employing prisoners in activities that will help make them productive members of society. Offenders who find a job after their release are far more likely to stay away from crime than those who cannot find work or do not want to. Prison work is therefore regarded as a program to help offenders learn job skills, acquire good work habits and become motivated. When prisoners are released, they should be better equipped to find jobs and keep them.

The problem is, however, that it is hard to create meaningful jobs that teach relevant skills in an extremely isolated and largely dysfunctional environment. Prison employment is often inefficient and unproductive. It may teach prisoners only to be lazy and may reinforce their belief that work is boring and pointless.

All federal prisoners are supposed to be provided with employment within the institution. This provision does not mean that everyone has to have a job because prisoners participating in educational classes or rehabilitative programs are also considered to be employed. Prisoners with less than a Grade Ten education are encouraged to upgrade, and all prisoners are required to participate in the rehabilitative programs specified on their correctional plans. In order to qualify for their daily pay, most inmates end up working part-time, as well as attending programs or school.

Work is regarded as part of the total package of programs designed to help prisoners become law-abiding citizens. CSC research has found that about 80 per cent of offenders lacked adequate job skills, and most had poor work histories prior to being sentenced to prison. Information about prisoners' individual work histories and abilities is gathered during the intake assessment process. This information is subsequently considered at parole hearings, since successful reintegration into the community may depend on an offender being able to find a steady job. Those prisoners who work hard at their jobs within the institution and learn new skills during the course of their sentences improve their chances of being released on parole.

Each institution has a program board made up of staff members, which attempts to place each prisoner in appropriate programs, educational courses or prison jobs. I attended one such board meeting at Springhill Institution, a prison that owes its very existence to a job creation plan, as it was located in an isolated Nova Scotia town following the closure of coal mines that had been plagued by disaster. Prison jobs were in short supply, as were the real jobs in the community outside. As prison staff on the program board deliberated about how to improve individual offenders' skills and work habits, they were no doubt aware of the fact even the most conscientious and well-qualified would have difficulty finding work in the community after their release.

The program board at Springhill used a computer terminal to access information about each prisoner as they considered his case. There were long waiting lists for best jobs in the institution, and the board was anxious to pick the most worthwhile candidates. Their decisions did not involve only the basic considerations that would be present in any job selection process: whether the candidate was well qualified and fitted the needs of the job. They were also concerned about how the particular job would fit with the correctional plan of the inmate, whether it was taking him in a direction that would help make changes in his life. One of the board members was furious when he saw a report from a prison maintenance manager complaining that a certain inmate was not suitable for a cleaning job because he did not have the right attitude. "That's like a mental hospital refusing to treat mentally ill," said the board member, insisting that the maintenance manager be told that it was his job to help prisoners change their attitudes.

Security concerns were also considered. For example, one prisoner seemed well qualified for a job that would require him to work on the prison grounds crew, until the board examined details of the crime that brought him to prison. His conviction was for robbery, a serious enough crime, but not necessarily one that causes alarm bells to ring. When the board members examined details of the crime on the computer, however, they saw that the man had wrapped a telephone cord around his victim's throat, broke two of his fingers and left him almost dying of a heart attack. The job on the work crew involved prisoners sometimes working outside the perimeter fence and the board decided that it was not a good idea to let this man out.

At Springhill, I was told that, officially, only 14 per cent of the 410 inmates were unemployed, but on any given day there were often as many as 200 prisoners idle because of temporary shop closures due to staff absences or lack of work. I discovered a similar situation in most of the prisons that I visited. On paper, there was invariably more than 80 per cent employment, but it soon became apparent at many institutions that staff and prisoners alike were merely going through the motions in order to preserve the illusion that they were all engaged in productive activity.

"We don't create a real work environment," said one prison personnel manager, "It's not helpful to inmates who have bad work habits anyway. Many of them have never been in a real workplace." Some valuable work is done by prisoners employed in the cleaning and maintenance of institutions. It saves money for the taxpayer and can instill a sense of responsibility in some inmates, though it seldom contributes to learning valuable skills that can be applied in the job market. But these jobs can easily become ludicrous when too many people are assigned to them because there is no other work. One older prisoner described working in a tailors' shop in one of the older penitentiaries several years earlier. He said his job involved cutting out fabrics for about two days every few weeks and then sitting around while the other workers slowly put the garments together. He enjoyed the lethargic atmosphere and the feeling that he was getting away with not working, but it hardly prepared him for work in the real world.

Prison work can sometimes become little more than a scam. I saw an example of this as I walked around one prison with a senior administrator. We stopped at an auto-body shop, where prisoners were supposed to be learning a trade and gaining work experience. With four vehicles in various stages of repair, the shop resembled a small commercial enterprise, except in the fact that no one was actually working. The sound of laughter and casual conversation came from an office area where eight prisoners were sitting with their instructor. The administrator fumed as we waited for the instructor to realize that we were there. Eventually he emerged, a little sheepishly, from the office, as the prisoners picked up some tools and wandered over to one of the cars.

The administrator asked whose car they were working on and the instructor explained that it was his. When the administrator asked about each of the other cars in the shop, the instructor admitted that they all belonged to him or a member of his family. He argued that he was doing the inmates a favour by letting them work on his old vehicles.

"He's a crook," the administrator said bluntly, after we had left the shop. He told me he would see to it that the instructor was fired.

Even if there was nothing inherently dishonest in an instructor having prisoners fix his own vehicles, there was little that they could learn in such a shop that was relevant to a real workplace. There was no pressure to work quickly or efficiently. Since the work was generating no income, there was little prospect that the shop would have the revenue to purchase the most up-to-date equipment. Prisoners would learn skills that might have been appropriate for a sleepy small town garage fifteen years ago, but would not impress many employers today.

In order to create more productive prison jobs, CSC has established an agency called CORCAN to establish and run prison industries. CORCAN employs about 1,800 prisoners in manufacturing, farm, forestry and service operations at 32 different federal institutions. The work ranges from the traditional prison industries of farming and sewing mail bags to office furniture manufacturing, data processing and telemarketing. As a federal government Special Operating Agency, CORCAN is a semi-independent entity which has the goal of financing its own operations through the revenues generated from prison industries.

Mike Elkins, director of operations for CORCAN in Ontario, told me that his agency tries to model itself as far as possible on private industry, although its object is not to use prison labour to turn a profit for several reasons. Prisoners tend to be unskilled workers with little experience. They need a lot of training and supervision. The work force is always changing, as prisoners are released or transferred. The CORCAN facilities are relatively small and scattered among various prisons, many of which are in inaccessible locations.

The greatest problem, however, is finding a market for CORCAN goods and services. Ever since the 1880s, when business and labour interests stopped Kingston Penitentiary from hiring out cheap labour, Canadian prison industries have never been allowed to compete with the private sector. CORCAN sells most of its products to CSC itself or other departments of the federal government. It is permitted to sell to private industry, but does not undercut other manufacturers' prices. The consequence of these limitations is warehouses full of unsold office furniture and other products. I visited several institutions where well-equipped workshops were sitting idle, their shelves lined with products that nobody had even thought worth transporting to a warehouse. While I was touring one such shop, an employee told the administrator who was with me that some computer desks appeared to be missing. After ordering a thorough investigation, the administrator told me that one must constantly be on the lookout for theft by inmates. I expressed surprise that prisoners would want to steal computer desks and wondered what they would do with them. "You'd be surprised," said the administrator, whose greatest concern seemed to be that they might be taken apart and converted into weapons.

At the Atlantic Institution in Renous, New Brunswick, administrators were justifiably proud of two initiatives: a salmon hatchery by which inmates were restocking the Miramichi River and a project for building prefabricated "Granny Flats" that were shipped out to be used as accommodation for senior citizens. But these projects employed relatively few inmates in large workshops that were otherwise idle.

Rather than produce more office furniture than the government can use, CORCAN has been attempting to forge partnerships with private industry in circumstances where no one is likely to complain of unfair competition. These operations often produce goods or services that would otherwise be purchased from overseas or produced with offshore labour. They may also involve private industries running operations in prisons and paying CORCAN a fair market value for prisoners' labour.

Paul Urmson, the CORCAN operations manager at Stony

Mountain Penitentiary in Manitoba, told me that it was only as a result of a joint venture with a private industry that he was able to keep his well-equipped carpentry shop in full production. The company was using the prison labour and plant to produce goods that it would then market under its own name. Urmson told me that the shop contained state-of-the-art equipment and cost $946,000 a year to operate, an amount that he had to recover through revenues. He said it was proving particularly difficult to break even, since the recession had reduced government purchasing by about 50 per cent. It was not considered politically expedient to risk antagonizing private industry by selling in the free marketplace, but private companies were competing successfully with CORCAN for the ever-diminishing public-sector market. Unlike some other countries and U.S. jurisdictions, Canada has no regulations requiring that government departments buy from prison industries, if their prices are competitive. CORCAN has built up a huge inventory, Urmson said, "and a lot of plants have almost nothing to produce."

At Springhill, the paper company, Scott Worldwide Inc., runs a tree nursery in a joint venture with CORCAN, employing prisoners to plant and tend seedlings within the prison compound. The supervisor of the operation, Tom Matheson, a Scott employee, told me, "This is a real workplace. We treat inmates as we would workers from the street. Some see it as an opportunity to make money for their family, others to get money for TVs or whatever. They learn what a normal employer would expect of them."

Prisoners are normally paid no more than $6.90 a day for their work, but those working in commercially viable CORCAN shops usually receive additional incentive pay. Sometimes they earn the equivalent of the provincial hourly minimum wage, out of which money is deducted for their room and board.

Some guards complain that the extra pay just gives the inmates more money to spend on drugs, but other staff members told me that the pay is an important aspect of a program designed to give prisoners a sense of self-worth and demonstrate the rewards of hard work. In fact, the demands and discipline of a regular job tend to weed out drug abusers, who often have dif-ficulty showing up for work or doing the job properly. CSC research has found that prisoners involved in work programs are far less likely to be charged for disciplinary offences and breaches of prison regulations.

Prison work sometimes provides offenders with an outlet for skills that they previously used to commit crimes. At one intake assessment unit, a case management officer told me that she provides counselling to drug dealers about the possibility of using their marketing and public relations skills in a legitimate job.

In Kingston, I saw a telemarketing operation, in which pris-oners sat at computer terminals making sales pitches over the phone on behalf of a company that had contracted their services. Elkins declined to tell me who CORCAN's customers were but said it is common to use prisoners for this type of work, adding that in the United States people making reservations for one leading hotel chain are actually talking to prisoners. He said prisoners are often very shy and appreciate a job in which there is no visual contact. Elkins added, "The phone allows them to take on different personalities. Many of them are quite manip-ulative and they can use those skills."

Matheson, the manager of the Springhill tree nursery, told me that prison workers take pride in their jobs and derive great satisfaction from them. He said, "Inmates need something to believe in. Train a guy to drive a tractor, then it's his machine. They don't have anything in here."

Work with animals and plants can foster caring instincts and qualities like patience or gentleness, which have often been almost absent in prisoners' earlier lives and are not normally found in the prison culture. At the minimum security Westmorland Insti-tution in New Brunswick, prisoners work on a farm which supplies food for all the penitentiaries in the Atlantic region.

Prisoners take pride in their tomato plants and exotic flowers that are sold to local florists. I was told that inmates get almost possessive about the animals that are entrusted to their care, getting up early in the morning and staying on the job late in the evening to ensure that they are properly fed and cleaned. The herd of cattle was uncharacteristically friendly, I was told, because prisoners were continually petting the animals. An administrator commented, "Sometimes inmates may not respect human life, but they respect animal life."

Work at the Westmorland farm and the Springhill tree nursery helped prisoners build their self-esteem and learn good work habits, but prison officials were not optimistic that offenders would find similar work after their release. With high unemployment in the Maritime region, there were undoubtedly many more experienced and better qualified farm and forestry workers already looking for work in the community.

Ironically, the jobs that give prisoners most personal satisfaction probably prepare them less satisfactorily for work in the outside world. Prisoners working in CORCAN shops are sometimes frustrated by the fact that they are trained to operate only one or two pieces of machinery, rather than learning a trade. They sometimes suspect that they are being exploited as cheap labour and resent the fact that they are given no credit for their contribution to a product that is marketed under a company brand name. But CORCAN administrators point out that such conditions are not that different from those of work in the real world. They say that learning to work on one or two pieces of equipment in a factory assembly line prepares a prisoner for a real job better than many antiquated vocational training schemes.

More often than not, however, prisons fail to provide enough worthwhile work. The result is that prisoners become demoralized and frustrated. An inmate at Kent Institution in British Columbia said that a CORCAN paint shop and cabinet shop provided little meaningful employment. He said, "We make furniture. We get no training. We're just doing assembly-line work. We learn how to use machines, but we couldn't get a job anywhere based on that. Even the people who do have jobs only work an hour or two a day at most."

Some prison work can be purely therapeutic. At Saskatchewan Penitentiary in Prince Albert, I visited a concrete ornament shop, attached to the prison's mental health unit. I was told that the workshop provided a sanctuary for prisoners who would otherwise be victimized by their fellow inmates. My visit coincided with a tea break and I had an opportunity to meet the prisoners. They were an odd-looking collection of individuals, some grossly overweight, others twitching and talking to themselves. It was easy to see how they might be picked on by other prisoners, even on the basis of their most superficial characteristics. But I was also struck by how proud they all seemed to be of the somewhat grotesque ornamental elephants, deers and bird feeders on which they had been working with painstaking care and deliberation.

A staff member who was supervising the shop introduced me to each of the prisoners in turn and each of them shook my hand warmly. It is rare to encounter warmth and genuine compassion in prison. One of the other places where I encountered such a caring environment was at Dorchester Penitentiary, where a general industrial arts workshop provides low-functioning offenders with opportunities for activities like making toys that can be donated to children's charities. The prisoners I met at this shop were not the actual participants in the program, few of whom would have been capable of holding much of a conversation, but prisoners from the general population who had been brought into the shop to work as tutors.

"If you're a little weak, people try to take advantage of you," said one of the prisoners, who then explained: "I was a different person two or three years ago, one of the rougher guys. I looked at these guys as idiots. This shop learned me to treat them as human beings."

"Here they treat you like a man," another tutor agreed, "They give you responsibilities and make you feel like you're capable of doing things. But go outside of this shop and everybody treats you like a piece of shit."

The perennial problems of prison life are never far away from any penitentiary workshops. Occasionally they intrude on the working environment with murders and other acts of violence. The tools available in workshops can easily be used as weapons and prisoners with a grudge to settle will sometimes take advantage of a workplace, where machinery can block the view of staff and many prisoners are assembled in one place.

Nevertheless, prison work can provide some inmates with a way out of the prison culture, as well as a more positive direction to follow in their own lives. Mike Elkins of CORCAN described a properly run prison industrial shop as "the only place inside an institution where everything is the right way round. The shop becomes a place to escape. There's a boss who knows more than you. The instructions are clear. You pay a price if you don't do it right." When a plant is busy and well managed, he said, "it is a beacon that shows the way out of an inmate culture where might is right, where muscle and intimidation rule."

Since CORCAN shops employ fewer than 15 per cent of penitentiary inmates, however, it is a beacon whose light scarcely penetrates the fog.

12

NO CURE FOR
DEVIANTS

Many people would like to see sex offenders denied parole and
forced to remain in prison until the end of their sentences. One
prisoner, whom I met, did not have any problem with this idea.
In fact, he had chosen to stay in jail until his sentence expired.
His motive was certainly not to protect the public.

I encountered him during a tour of the protective custody
unit of a medium security prison. I had asked to see the inside
of a cell, and a guard suggested one whose inmate would probably not object. The prisoner was an elderly man, who wel-
comed me warmly, saying he was lonely and never had any
visitors. He told me that he was retired from his job and received
a pension from which he was saving money to cover his expenses after release. When he said his cell was quite "cosy," I had
the idea that it might just as well have been a room in a retirement villa, for all the insight he apparently had into his own
predicament.

He told me that he was a sex offender, but did not disclose
any details of his crime. He said he had not taken any programs
because he had his deviant tendencies under control — in his
own way. He said, "It's my choice whether I offend again and I'm
the only one who knows what I'm going to do." He also explained
that he had decided not to take advantage of statutory release
after two-thirds of his sentence, but was staying in prison until

the very last day because he did not want to have parole officers prying into his affairs.

The elderly sex offender told me that he was trying to keep himself busy by doing artwork. He showed me a pastel sketch that he was working on. It depicted a scantily clad young girl, who looked as if she might be thirteen or fourteen years old, with her legs spread in a seductive pose. He had titled the sketch, "Cell mate."

This well-mannered grandfatherly man in his cosy cell disturbed me far more than most of the more menacing and more overtly dangerous offenders whom I met. I do not even know his name and will never know what will happen after he quietly leaves the penitentiary. I wonder whether he will meet the image of his pubescent cell mate and whether she will at first accept him at face value, as a charming, inoffensive old man.

Nothing is more perplexing to prison officials, as it is to the public at large, than the problem of how to deal with sex offenders. They are being sent to prison in unprecedented numbers, and yet society seems to be continually producing more. The correctional system is constantly struggling to provide treatment for them, yet no one really knows whether the treatment works. It is hard to weigh the risks and the benefits of releasing them on parole. There are other risks to be considered when they are kept in prison until their sentences expire and they are free to disappear into the night. Any wrong decision could lead to tragedy and public outrage, but there are no easy answers. Correctional officials, like members of the public, are often nervous and confused.

The number of sex offenders in the federal prison system has increased dramatically since the mid-1980s, when the public and the courts began taking a more serious view of male abuse of women and children. In 1984 sex offenders made up 7 per cent of the penitentiary population. By 1994 the proportion had risen to 17 per cent. In fact, sex offenders probably comprise at least 20 per cent of the inmate population, when one includes prisoners with a previous history of sex offences and those who committed other crimes for sexual motives.

The majority of sex offenders, like most other prisoners, have not committed crimes that warrant locking them away for life. Most of them are serving finite sentences and will be released. People working in the prison system believe that the best way to protect the public is to help these prisoners to reintegrate in the community at the end of their sentences and to provide them with treatment that will decrease their chances of committing further crimes.

Sometimes, circumstances make it impossible to achieve these ends, as psychologist Bruce Malcolm explained to me when I visited the Millhaven Assessment Unit, which receives all newly admitted federal prisoners in Ontario. Malcolm pointed to a file on his desk that suggested that he could be dealing with another Clifford Olson. Yet the inmate had only been sentenced to two and a half years in prison.

The offender, a 60-year-old man named Geoff, told the prison psychologist that he had been framed, falsely accused by his daughters. He said he pleaded guilty to gross indecency and sexual assault because he feared that the court would believe them and impose a longer sentence. But the police report told a very different story.

The evidence that would have been heard in court, if the plea bargaining deal had not been made, disclosed that Geoff had abused his two daughters and son several times a week since they were as young as four years old until each of them in turn was old enough to run away from home. He would hold his daughter's head underwater in a bathtub until she agreed to perform oral sex on him. Sometimes, he would tie his daughters up and sexually assault both of them at the same time. He frequently performed anal sex on his son and once forced the boy to have sex with his mother. The children also witnessed their mother being sexually assaulted by their father and his friends. They said that Geoff would tie his wife to the kitchen table and then take turns with his three friends in raping her. The children remembered their mother screaming and pleading for them to stop. The woman subsequently died in what was ruled to be an accident, but the children believed that Geoff murdered her.

When he arrived in prison, however, Geoff asserted, "I can't be that bad or I wouldn't have got two and a half years. They just made it up."

For the court, the plea bargain may well have made sense. It took a dangerous man off the streets, if only for a short time. It saved his victims the trauma of testifying and avoided a lengthy trial at which the Crown case may not have been proven. But, for Malcolm and his staff, it posed unanswerable questions and created an impossible dilemma. If prison psychologists accepted the court's finding at face value, they would treat Geoff as an incest offender. Incest offenders generally abuse only members of their own family and therefore pose little risk of reoffending when they no longer have children in their homes. The information in the police report, on the other hand, provided a profile of a sadistic rapist and pedophile, who could pose a danger to any woman or child.

The assessment unit, which is responsible for deciding where offenders should be placed and how they should be treated, concluded that Geoff should be regarded as high risk and placed him in Kingston Penitentiary. But Malcolm explained to me that there was no point in putting Geoff in an extensive treatment program, since it would take longer than his sentence allowed. There would be little chance of successful treatment anyway, since admitting one's guilt is a necessary first step in therapy. Geoff was eventually transferred to a medium security prison where he attended some group therapy sessions before being released.

"Shouldn't we be forcing police to collect better evidence and

Crown attorneys not to bargain it away?" asked Malcolm, venting a frustration that I often found among CSC employees, who feel that they are too often held responsible for society's failures. The psychologist explained, "At most, I would be allowed to treat him for five months. At the end, what would I say about him? Can I say that he is not the disgusting individual who came to me? I'm going to say that he will continue to need treatment. He should never be allowed with children. He should probably never be allowed to be alone in a room with a woman. Is he going to be released on parole? Given those recommendations, they will keep him for the rest of his sentence. We will be denied the opportunity to do any community follow-up because a judge and a Crown attorney made some bad errors."

Assessment units, like the one at Millhaven, attempt to determine what risks each prisoner presents and recommend appropriate treatment. Phalometric tests are used to identify pedophiles and others with deviant sexual urges by measuring their arousal to various images and sounds. Their backgrounds, personalities and criminal records are assessed in order to find out what problems and needs underlie their criminal behaviour. Some may be psychopaths who act purely out of self-interest and have no feelings for other people, while others may have varying degrees of insight and motivation for change.

"The public thinks they're all the same — frothing at the mouth and hiding under bushes. They exist. We have them. But the average is a normal-looking, employed businessman, who molested his daughter or step daughter," Malcolm told me.

In the late 1980s, the correctional service was widely criticized for not providing enough treatment to this burgeoning population of feared and reviled prisoners. CSC responded to these criticisms by developing and implementing a comprehensive set of programs, designed to accommodate all sex offenders who need treatment and consent to it. The number of sex offenders in treatment programs rose from 200 in 1988 to 1,800 in 1994. The direct cost of these programs was about $10 million. There is constant debate, however, on whether the money is well spent and resources properly deployed.

Several staff members involved in delivering programs told me that resources are squandered on providing treatment to incest offenders who do not need it and will not benefit. Once it has been determined that an incest offender is not a pedophile and has no propensity to seek out children outside his home, it is safe to say that he will not reoffend. He has been publicly exposed. His family knows about him. Arrangements have been made to ensure that his children are no longer at risk. There are no other victims available. There is no need to provide treatment programs, and studies have found that such programs make no difference whatsoever.

Treatment is particularly pointless in cases of older men convicted of abusing their children many years ago. Bruce Malcolm told me about one case involving an 87-year-old man who was brought to prison on a stretcher, because he was suffering from congestive heart failure. He was repentant and anxious to acknowledge his guilt. The only problem was that he had difficulty remembering what he had done. He had been sentenced to two years for sexually abusing his granddaughters 30 years earlier.

"Why spend hundred of thousands of dollars on incest offenders who committed crimes 30, 40 and 50 years ago?" asked Malcolm, "If they have done nothing in the intervening years, there's no reason to suspect they'll grab another child. What are we treating him for? Because we want to be able to say we treated him to cover our ass."

Prisoners with longer sentences who are classified as high or moderate risk to reoffend often wait for years without receiving treatment, while the system scurries to provide therapy for "low-risk" offenders, whether they need it or not, so that they can be recommended for early parole. It is a "Catch-22" situation for the more serious offenders because the parole board will not look favourably on their cases unless they have made progress in treatment, but they have seldom received enough treatment to satisfy the board by the time they appear to ask for parole or to oppose an order that will result in their being detained until the end of their sentences.

It is common for offenders to wait four years or more before they receive treatment. One rationale for this is that there is no point in treating them too soon if they will merely be sitting in the penitentiary and unable to apply what they have learned in the community. While they are waiting, however, many inmates become bitter and disillusioned. They learn to survive by denying their guilt and either withdrawing more into themselves or becoming more aggressive. "If your leg is broken, you don't want to wait for seven years to get treatment," commented Dan, a sex offender, who told me that he had to work hard to get himself eventually placed in a program at a regional psychiatric centre.

"Rehabilitation is a politician's word. It doesn't have much meaning in prison, except you fight for it," said Dan. He told me that he had written about 50 letters to senior correctional officials, the Correctional Investigator, government ministers, members of Parliament and lawyers in order to get into the psychiatric centre program, which was more intensive than those offered in penitentiaries. Dan said he knew that even after taking this program he would have trouble convincing the parole board to set him free. Many other prisoners get discouraged by this, he said, especially when they have to return from treatment programs to cell blocks where they are "treated like scum." Dan told me that he took the program, not in order to get out on parole, but "because I want to turn my life around. I don't want to rape anybody any more."

Few sex offenders can be "cured" of their deviant desires, and the programs do not attempt to do that. In some cases, offenders may have psychiatric diseases that can be treated in one of the regional psychiatric centres attached to the prison system. In some cases, drugs may be used to reduce sexual desires, a therapy sometimes known as "chemical castration," but this will not work unless the offender is motivated to keep taking the drugs, and even then it may not be effective. Most of the sex offender treatment is like the treatment offered to drug or alcohol abusers. It helps people stay away from crime, as long as they have the motivation to do so.

The programs consist largely of group therapy sessions in which offenders are encouraged to gain insight into the problems that led them to commit crimes, their motivation and the situations in which crimes were likely to occur. They are taught ways of avoid situations or activities that might put them into their "crime cycle," the chain of events that leads them to commit crime. They learn to recognize warning signs in their own moods and behaviours. Therapists help them develop "relapse prevention plans" for staying out of trouble or for bringing themselves under control, if they feel themselves slipping into their crime cycle. These plans usually include lists of places and situations that the offenders will avoid, people they will call for help and "escape hatch" strategies, like throwing away their car keys, breaking their glasses or checking themselves into an emergency clinic, when they feel that their crime cycle has been triggered.

Experts disagree over whether these programs are effective. The CSC programs are widely recognized as representing the cutting edge of current thinking about how to deal with sex offenders, but not enough research has been done so far to prove whether they work or not. The debate is a rather academic one in which both sides end up agreeing that it is worth persevering with the programs anyway.

Queen's University psychologist Vern Quinsey, who does not believe that the programs are effective, told me that he is "looking for a better mousetrap." But he agrees that CSC should persevere with its current program as long as the alternative is "not to do anything and then turn them loose."

William Marshall, also of Queen's University and one of the pioneers of the CSC programs, maintains that the programs help some prisoners, though it is not always possible to predict who will benefit. Therefore, he argues, "We have a moral obligation to offer treatment to as many clients as possible, given the disastrous consequences to innocent women and children of reoffending. Because sex offenders who reoffend typically do so against more than one victim, effectively treating just one avoids considerable human suffering."

Some prison psychiatrists fear, however, that treatment programs can actually make the most dangerous offenders worse. It has been estimated that more than 20 per cent of penitentiary inmates may be psychopaths — highly manipulative, self-centred individuals, who often express great rage and self-pity, but show no capacity to care for other people. They are usually good at detecting weaknesses in others and exploiting them for their own purpose. For some of these people, therapy programs provide an opportunity to acquire skills that can be applied to their own perverse ends. Psychopaths frequently attempt to con and manipulate staff, while playing mind games with other offenders. Often they end up hogging a large proportion of the resources of a program and derailing other offenders' treatment, as well as their own.

Neil Conacher, former head of psychiatric services at the Regional Treatment Centre in Kingston Penitentiary, explained, "Tell psychopaths that people are usually benign and helpful. They will say, 'I can use that.' Tell them that people feel pain and can easily be hurt. They will say, 'I can use that.'" Conacher told me about a sex education class where prisoners were shown a life-like anatomical model of the female body, which opened up to show internal organs. He said, "It's irresponsible to show that to psychopaths. It would give them ideas about cutting up victims next time. Some psychopaths would commit such crimes with the detachment of a boy taking wings off flies to see what happened."

Even many offenders agree that some prisoners are too dangerous ever to walk the streets again and that some sex offenders will never change their ways. In fact, penitentiary inmates are more acutely aware of this reality than most people, since they live at close quarters with some of the most incorrigible criminals and see them with their masks off.

It is possible to keep some violent and troublesome offenders in prison until the end of their sentences. Lifers can be kept in prison until the parole board concludes that it is safe to release them and so can people sentenced to indeterminate prison terms after a court found them to be dangerous offenders. Prisoners on fixed sentences may or may not be granted parole at the discretion of the parole board, but are required by law to be let out on statutory release after two-thirds of their sentences, unless the parole board makes an order that they be detained until their sentences end. CSC must apply to the parole board for a detention order thirteen months before a prisoner's statutory release date. Detention orders can be granted only in cases where the offender has committed a crime involving death or serious harm and is likely to do so again. Since sexual assaults invariably cause serious harm, whether it be physical or emotional, most sex offenders are possible candidates for detention.

At the Regional Treatment Centre, which provides treatment to sex offenders and prisoners with mental health problems, Conacher encountered a number of inmates who had been detained until the end of their sentences, but still appeared to be too dangerous to release. He joined forces with a senior psychiatrist in the Ontario mental health system to have seven such prisoners certified as involuntary psychiatric patients. Some colleagues criticized this move as an abuse of psychiatry and an infringement of the prisoners' civil rights. Five of the seven prisoners were subsequently released or transferred to mental health institutions with a lower level of security.

In a follow-up study, Conacher reported that one of the released prisoners subsequently killed a twelve-year-old girl, while another stabbed a 72-year-old man to death. A third released inmate set fire to a rooming house in a suicide attempt, while another man returned to prison for uttering a threat. A fifth prisoner was transferred to a less secure institution where he sexually assaulted a female inmate. He was returned to prison and subsequently hanged himself.

Conacher's conclusion was that in certain exceptional cases it is possible to predict accurately that a prisoner will be dangerous if released. He told me that treatment does not work for the most vicious psychopaths and that they should remain locked up indefinetely, since an effective treatment has yet to be discovered.

The people who treat sex offenders in the prison system know that making a wrong prediction could have devastating consequences for their future careers and for their own peace of mind. They live in fear of recommending the release of an inmate who may go on to commit vicious or high-profile crimes. Given the public fear of sex offenders and the consequences of making a mistake, most psychologists and case management officers err on the side of safety by recommending that prisoners stay in prison as long as possible. The parole board is also very cautious, often deciding not to release even those for whom correctional staff recommend parole.

Psychologist Sharon Williams, coordinator of sex offender programing for CSC, told me that program staff often illustrate this fact of life to new inmates by means of "the payoff matrix." She said the explanation goes like this: "I say you'll succeed and I am right — who cares? I say you'll succeed and I am wrong — I'm testifying at inquests and being taken apart in the media.

I say you'll fail and you succeed — who cares? I predict failure
and I am right — I am brilliant. The payoff for a positive prediction is neutral or bad. The payoff for a negative prediction
is either neutral or good. Even if there is a 90 per cent chance
that offenders will succeed, we're likely to detain everyone."

On the surface it would appear that prison staff and the
parole board are simply acting prudently in order to protect the
public. But many people who work with sex offenders believe
that keeping them in prison until the last possible moment is
actually contrary to the public interest. Keeping prisoners until
the end of their sentence locked in a cell block — usually in
protective custody, if not segregation — does nothing to rehabilitate them and usually undermines the treatment that they
have already received.

Prisoners living in segregation have no access to programs,
unless a special arrangement is made to run program groups in
their units. Karl Furr, a psychologist running a treatment program for dangerous sex offenders at Kingston Penitentiary, told
me that the more dangerous inmates never participated because
they were locked in their cells. He said that those who did attend
would frequently be harassed by other inmates, even though
the aggressors were often sex offenders themselves, trying to
deflect attention. Furr lamented, "Wherever we move, whenever we try to hide what we are doing, everyone in the institution
knows — except for other staff members."

Dan, who was involved in a treatment program at a psychiatric centre, told me, "When you come to prison, if you're a
known sex offender, you're dead. Before I came here, I kept it
a secret. Now they're going to send me back to the pen and my
life will be in danger because I came here for help." Dan said
he was learning in therapy the importance of telling other people about one's background, as well as disclosing feelings and
fears. That way, he explained, a sex offender can be discouraged
from harbouring secret desires and the people around him can

watch out for any signs of aberrant behaviour. "Secrecy is what keeps us alive in prison, even though, here, they teach us that it's one of the worst things we can do," Dan said.

"In detaining, I don't believe we're serving the public, just protecting ourselves," Bruce Malcolm said bluntly. He went on to explain, "We have too many sex offenders in the prison system. We can't get them out, but we want to get them out because we really believe — and all the science supports us — that it is better to release them gradually into society and help them get into employment. There's no such thing as rehabilitation in a cell block for 23 hours. It doesn't do any good and it gets them angry."

When an offender is released gradually into the community, parole officers can monitor his behaviour and have him returned to prison if he misbehaves. Treatment programs can help the offender apply the lessons he learned in prison. Even Quinsey, the psychologist who does not believe that treatment works, agreed that offenders may benefit from supervision in the community. If the offender is not released until the last day, nobody will know what he is doing or where he is going. He will receive no treatment and get no support.

Dan, the sex offender whom I interviewed at the psychiatric centre, said his therapists had told him that there was little more that he could accomplish in programs within the prison system, but it remained to be seen how he would fare on the street. He said, "It's much more safe to give you gradual release. You have a hook in your mouth and they can pull you back. Sudden release is a scary option."

Wayne, a prisoner who was preparing very carefully for his eventual release, told me, "I'm trying to cover areas of public concern so that I'm either closely monitored or continually assessed." Wayne was a notorious sex offender whose crimes caused widespread fear and public outrage, which will quickly rekindle whenever he is released. He would never avoid being identified as a potential threat to public safety and his life sentence ensured that he would always remain under the supervision of the correctional service, whether in prison or on parole. Nevertheless, I did not feel uneasy about the prospect of Wayne returning to the community, once I had talked with him at length about his many years of therapy and the efforts that he had made to mitigate a small portion of the damage that his crimes had done.

Wayne was a masked rapist who broke into women's homes and terrorized a series of victims over several years. He was a soft-spoken, courteous man, whose predatory crimes seemed all the more shocking because they were committed by some-one who had led an ostensibly respectable life. He told me that he committed his crimes under the thrall of an obsession that dominated his life for years. He said, "It was all I lived for, all I planned, all I wanted to do. It had control over me. There were no emotions tied in with that deviancy, no real emotions. All there was was that excitement, that desire for power." Wayne went on, "I couldn't understand why or what was happening. I tried to understand why I was going out and assaulting women. Once I was arrested, I felt a great sense of relief, because I knew at least it was over."

During the first few years in prison, Wayne did not receive any therapy. He would sit or lie in his cell trying to figure out what had made him the way he was. He did not understand why he had always felt worthless and had never cared for him-self or anyone else. Startling and disturbing memories of abuse that he suffered as a child began to surface. When he was even-tually placed in a treatment program, he began to explore these memories further and came to terms with the fact that he had been sexually assaulted as a five-year-old.

This experience was something that Wayne had in common with many, if not most sex offenders. Therapists involved in sex offender treatment maintain that it is necessary to address offenders' own experiences as victims in order to help them understand their motives and feel empathy for the victims of their crimes. The fact that they were abused does not excuse their crimes, but it is often the source of an unexplained and uncontrollable rage that grips many violent offenders. It can also explains why many sex offenders have learned to disregard other people's feelings. They also know from their own experience that victims are often afraid to fight back or speak out.

Wayne told me that recalling his childhood abuse was "a part of why" he committed his crimes. He said, "It was where my deviance toward sexual activity started. It was why sexual activity had to be deviant and went along with a lot of anger, resentment and frustration. I had spent many years not even recalling the event, but it was a seed planted in me." He had learned how the seed of deviance was nurtured by many other things in his life, some of which he was still struggling to come to terms with after seven years of therapy.

When Wayne first applied for parole, he was told that two of his victims wanted to attend the hearing. At his own request, he became involved in an innovative program known as Victim Offender Mediation. It provides an opportunity for victims and offenders to meet in a secure and supportive setting, after communicating first through a mediator and by means of letters and tapes. It enables offenders to express their remorse and look for ways of making reparation to their victims. For victims, it provides an opportunity to ask questions, voice their pain and perhaps regain some of the emotional security that victims lose through crime.

Both of the victims, whom Wayne eventually met after a long period of preparation, had been sexually assaulted by him. He said he had threatened the life of one of the women in order to gain her submission. One of them had seen him without his mask and subsequently identified him. He had not realized until they met that she lived in terror of him seeking her out to gain revenge after his release from jail. Wayne told me, "I had to reassure her that wasn't even a thought on my mind. I think she needed to hear that."

While the first victim wanted to understand more about why Wayne assaulted her, the second wanted to express the pain and terror that he had caused her. Wayne recalled, "I felt like crawling underneath the rug. Yet I wanted to hear it. I wanted her to know I was listening."

Wayne was forced to confront the reality of the pain and suffering that he had caused. He said, "When I offended, that was the reality I avoided. I didn't want to know. I made efforts to depersonalize everyone. But this was personalizing my victims to the ultimate. You can't get any more real than that."

The meeting was also valuable to the victim, Wayne said, "She said that spending the few hours with me that day meant more to her therapy than three years with a therapist. Her whole nightmare came full circle. It started with me and that day ended with me. Our roles were reversed that day. She was in control. I voluntarily came to put myself in that position. I no longer controlled her life and she was free of me, free of this monster that terrorized her life.

"I thought I really knew what victim empathy was about when I went through the sex offender programs: seeing films and reading books. I thought that was it. I'm not trying to say that the program wasn't good. But it certainly wasn't as powerful as actually sitting across from my own victim. I had met with other victims before and talked. But then I could step back and say 'I didn't do that.' Not so when you meet your own victim. You can't remove yourself."

Wayne told me that his meetings with his victims were not something he would bring up at his parole hearing. He had not participated in the mediation program in order to further his prospects of release. He wanted to be released on his own merits, on the basis of what he had accomplished in therapy and other rehabilitative efforts.

Explaining how his therapy and his meetings with his victims had changed his life, Wayne said, "When I was offending, deviant fantasies were a major part of my day. They were what I lived with. Today, I don't fantasize rape. If things spark thoughts or arousals, they are short-lived. I think right away about hurting a victim. I can't depersonalize. The pain of my own victim is right in there."

Wayne told me that he realized there was no cure for sexual deviancy. Like an alcoholic, he would always have to take one day at a time. He would always be a sexual offender. But he said he believed that he had learned to control his behaviour and meet his needs in appropriate ways. He said he had changed his deviant thinking and got rid of his fantasies of sexual violence and power. His therapy had brought him peace, he said. "Now I have my own inner freedom. I may have been free for 30 years. But, as I now know, I lived in my own prison."

A year after our interview, Wayne was still in prison and still making plans for his eventual release. In the meantime, he told me in a letter, he was continuing with his treatment and trying to make the best of prison life. He wrote, "You know, life carries on whether you're on the inside or outside and it's your choice to make it as quality a life as you can. Personally I choose to enhance mine with good choices. God knows, I've certainly made enough bad choices."

Given the nature of Wayne's crimes, his life sentence and current public attitudes, he may remain in prison for many more years. During the course of my research, I met a large number of sex offenders. Some were otherwise innoffensive men, who had committed crimes of incest and would probably return to the community to live in shame, but without presenting further risks. A few were incorrigible pedophiles, who would, perhaps, start looking for children to molest as soon as they felt that they could get away with it. Others were rapists, whose crimes had been prompted by anger, sadism, hatred of women, perversely distorted beliefs about women and sex, a desire for power, or various combinations of these motives. Of all the rapists I met, Wayne was the one who most impressed me as likely to lead a productive life in the community without putting anyone at risk. Ironically, he is one of the prisoners who is least likely to get that chance.

Society's fear of sex offenders is understandable. Unfortunately, our fear far exceeds our knowledge and understanding of who they are, why they do what they do and how to stop them. Putting them in prison and keeping them there provides society with some temporary protection from certain individuals for as long as they are behind bars. It would be comforting to believe that federal prison staff can treat the thousands of sex offenders sentenced by the courts and return them all to society as more manageable risks. The reality is, however, that the system is forced to muddle through, achieving some progress, while making a series of compromises and choices, some of which may well return to haunt us all.

13

REDESIGNING JAILS

Surrounded by ocean on three sides, the 85-acre William Head peninsula has that striking combination of rugged shoreline and luscious vegetation that has made the warm southern coast of Vancouver Island a popular holiday and retirement resort. It boasts a spectacular view, across the Strait of Juan de Fuca, of the snow-capped mountains of Washington State. Tastefully designed residential buildings, nestled among woods and rocky outcrops, might lead one to believe this was just another one of the many new condominium developments along this stretch of ocean shore, were it not for the security fence, gun tower and gatehouse that barricade the landward side of the peninsula.

William Head Institution, near Victoria, B.C., challenges all one's preconceptions of what a prison should be. It provides prisoners with a serene natural setting and accommodation that would be the envy of many suburban home-owners. When the design concept for William Head's residential units was exported to other, less isolated prisons, the new form of prison accommodation attracted considerable media attention, and many members of the public were outraged. Even prisoners were shocked and one was quoted as saying that the accommodation was "nicer than most of the homes that I've broken into."

A former William Head prisoner told me that he too was in a state of shock when he was brought to the prison, but he soon came to see that he was being offered a valuable opportunity for making changes in his life. He said, "They opened the back of the van, unshackled me and said, 'Here you are. You live in this unit. Have a nice time. Bugger off.' It was a fine sunny day. There was water, wildlife, beautiful houses. It was incredible. At that point, I realized that I was being given a chance."

William Head and other prisons that have copied its concepts are not intended to make inmates more comfortable. In fact, the idea is to provide them with an environment in which they will be forced to look after themselves. These prisons and their programs are designed as an antidote to the poisonous inertia of regular penitentiary life. They also offer prisoners an environment in which they can free themselves of the negative influences of the traditional prison culture.

"Our intention is not to create a country-club atmosphere, but to enable us to approximate a community setting, where offenders are made to feel more responsible for their care," CSC administrator Barrie Friel explained to me. He said, "Life would probably be much easier for us if all we had to do was keep people locked up, fed and clothed. But we would not be doing the community any favours."

As CSC officials were anxious to explain, the site of William Head was not chosen for its natural beauty. It just happened that the federal government owned a peninsula that was previously used as a quarantine station for newly arrived immigrants. William Head has been a federal prison since the 1950s and its setting has always made it an unusually pleasant place for prisoners to serve time and for staff to work. Assistant warden Randie Scott told me that he could not believe how relaxed the prison was when he first arrived there after working in other federal penitentiaries in the late 1980s. "When I first arrived, I was in shock mode. I kept waiting for something to happen," he said.

When Scott arrived, the existing buildings on the property, some of them dating from the days when it was a quarantine station, had become dilapidated to the point where they needed to be replaced. The correctional service had recently formulated its mission statement and was attempting to implement more progressive policies. The warden at William Head initiated a strategic planning process in which prison managers, staff, union and inmate representatives, senior correctional administrators and architects were all asked to help create a concept for a prison that would be most likely to realize the CSC's mission of reintegrating offenders into the community.

The concept that emerged was of a prison that would be, in the words of one CSC official, "a small laboratory in which we can recreate the conditions of the community." The new inmate accommodation consisted of semi-detached houses, divided into two five-bedroom two-storey units. Each unit had a well-equipped kitchen, dining room and living room, with a patio outside. In order to create the atmosphere of a suburban community, the prison's twenty houses were arranged in groups of four to form five separate "neighbourhoods." Each neighbourhood was given a name, like "Orchard Valley," "Swan Beach Heights," and "Olympia Vista." The houses were painted in cool or earthy shades of green, blue, brown, red or grey, with the colour of the buildings helping to create a distinctive character for each neighbourhood.

Houses in each neighbourhood were arranged in slightly different configurations in order to conform to the contours of the land, and to preserve stands of the rare Gerry Oak. House locations also provided occupants with the best possible view. As one prison official observed, "Just because people are in jail, it doesn't mean that they should have an ugly view."

Instead of large institutional buildings for offices, schools and program facilities, each neighbourhood had its own "community centre," where prisoners could attend programs, meet staff and also do their laundry or play pool. The idea that these community centres should be a hive of activity proved to be a little idealistic, however, as inmates — like the middle-class citizens they were learning to emulate — preferred to relax and socialize in their own homes.

The small residential units represented a dramatic saving in construction costs, because they could be built under residential building code standards, which were less stringent than those applied to large institutions. The cost per inmate of the new facilities at William Head was approximately a third that of a more traditional prison building constructed elsewhere at about the same time.

But Scott insisted, "It's not true that we created the design because it was cheaper. We created the design only to find that it was cheaper. The conclusion was unanimous that it should be a residential design. If we were going to prepare inmates for life on the street, we should replicate the community to the greatest extent possible. Everything in here should be a life skills program."

Instead of having their food cooked for them and served on a tray, inmates would be required to purchase ingredients with funds allotted to them and cook their own meals in their living units. They would learn that it was more efficient and more pleasant to cooperate with their house mates than to go their own ways. They would have to do their own laundry and house cleaning. Prisoners would be free to make their own decisions about such matters and have to live with the consequences if, for example, they spent too much on treats and did not buy enough staples. They would learn to live with other people and deal with interpersonal problems or conflicts involving issues like noise, personal hygiene or housekeeping standards.

In order to make inmates accountable for the condition of the buildings, each neighbourhood was allocated a fund for the upkeep of common areas. This fund included an allowance for repairing or replacing broken windows or other incidental damage. If the prisoners had any money left over after meeting these expenses, the surplus could be used for community projects such as buying a picnic table, installing a barbecue or creating a rock garden.

As a result of this policy, damage to property was far less common than in other prisons. Inmates began taking pride in their houses and neighbourhoods. Many of them got interested in gardening and wanted to spend surplus funds on flowers, shrubs and tools. Some prisoners wanted burglar alarms installed in their units, but the administration rejected this proposal because it was too expensive.

William Head has a mellowing influence on prisoners who may have created problems in other jails, Scott said. They do not have staff or other inmates "in their face" continually, although prison overcrowding has required that some rooms be double-bunked and guards do have keys that will permit them to enter the units at any time. All inmates are required to be in their housing units after a 10 p.m curfew, but there is nothing to stop them staying up late to watch television or getting themselves a snack in the kitchen, if they wake up at night.

"Inmates who were a problem in other institutions have the opportunity for venting their frustrations in other ways. It's attractive and peaceful. They can watch deer, racoons, sea otters and killer whales. It's relaxing," Scott said. Some inmates meditate at a Buddhist shrine that they have created on a secluded rocky outcrop. Others can go fishing from a dock for salmon, rock cod and mackerel, providing they first obtain a fishing licence. Prisoners were allowed to swim in the ocean, until staff suspected that an escape was being planned by an inmate who seemed to be building up his strength and resistance to cold water.

Escapes have been a problem at William Head and a source of concern to people in the surrounding community. Many William Head prisoners have succumbed to the temptation to build a raft out of driftwood and paddle their way to freedom.

Before I visited Canada's most unusual prison, a public

relations officer explained: "It's one of the most beautiful pieces of real estate in the province. But it's still a medium security prison and we tell the inmates, 'If you run away, we'll shoot you.'" The public relations man had been exaggerating, however, as CSC staff do not routinely fire their rifles at prisoners fleeing a medium security prison. The law states that they may use lethal force only when they have reasonable and probable grounds to believe that a prisoner on the run poses a threat of death or grievous bodily harm. Guards will be authorized to shoot only when there is an obvious immediate threat to someone's safety or when they know that the inmate in question is dangerous. Many of the William Head prisoners are murderers, but few would be considered a major threat to public safety.

When I visited the institution, staff were hoping that the security problem had been solved by the installation of additional security cameras, together with improvements to the perimeter fence and underwater barriers extending from the ends of the fence. Most of the shoreline is out of bounds to prisoners, and the road that skirts the peninsula shore is constantly patrolled by guards.

"This concept is wonderful, but it's still a prison," said Graham, an inmate serving a life sentence for murder. While readily admitting that he deserved to be punished for his crime, Graham observed that being deprived of one's liberty, even in an idyllic setting, can be a terrible fate to endure. He said, "I hope I will eventually see my children as grown-ups. I haven't seen them growing up. I wasn't there when they first learned to ride a bike. I wasn't there for ball games or graduations. I won't be there for their weddings."

Many of the prisoners at William Head are lifers, like Graham, who are gradually working their way toward parole and trying to live as productively as they can behind bars. "We need this type of setting to learn or relearn social skills. When we hit the street, at least we'll have a fighting chance of making it," said Graham.

In spite of some successful programs that involve prisoners in community and environmental projects, there was a dire shortage of work or vocational training for inmates at the time that I visited William Head. Scott told me that he was frustrated with this situation and blamed the ponderous CORCAN bureaucracy for failing to provide meaningful jobs. Graham said that the lack of work meant that it could be very boring at William Head, in spite of the aesthetically pleasing environment.

Some prisoners use their free time creatively by engaging in activities like the production of a highly respected magazine called *Out of Bounds*. Graham said he devoted his energies to William Head On Stage, an inmate-run theatre group that performs two plays a year in the prison for outside audiences, financing the productions through ticket sales. The group is allowed to hire a director and up to four female actors from the community for each production. The plays run on a budget of approximately $8,000 and attract total audiences of about 1,200 people.

Graham said it is important to ensure that all prisoners involved remain drug free, as a production could be ruined if one of the actors got put in the hole on a drug charge. One production had to be cancelled because one of the women hired to act in the play was accused of possession of contraband, when she left the institution with a letter given to her by an inmate. It is also necessary to make sure that leading actors are not likely to be released on parole before the play has been produced. Throughout the weeks of rehearsals and performances, Graham said, prisoners are transposed into a different environment where everyone is upbeat and supportive. "You forget that you are in jail," he said.

The benefits of the William Head housing units were obvious to people working in the correctional system. The fact that they were cheap to build made them especially appealing. The concept seemed ideally suited for minimum security, open prisons that house low-risk offenders and those considered almost ready for parole.

At the minimum security Ste. Anne-des-Plaines Institution in Quebec, new condo-style units were built and more planned to replace an ugly, aging dormitory building, known as "the ghetto." The new condominium-style units provide a striking contrast to the gun towers, fences and drab buildings of the nearby Archambault penitentiary and the super-maximum security Special Handling Unit. But the contrast that most struck some of the journalists who visited the new facilities was the fact that they appeared nicer and better furnished than the homes that most people living in nearby Laval or Montreal could afford. A popular television show aired an inflammatory report about the new luxury homes for prisoners and its million viewers were furious.

CSC officials struggled to explain that the buildings cost less, that the furniture was all constructed with prison labour and that everything needed to be of good quality in order to stand up to the constant use of the six adult men who would be sharing these houses. Such explanations got short shrift in the media and administrators responded by redesigning the second phase of their redevelopment plan so as to make the buildings look more ugly.

Condominium-style living units also caused a stir when they were first introduced at the Ferndale Institution, a minimum security prison in the scenic Fraser Valley, near Mission, B.C. Warden Ron Wiebe told me, "The public was initially shocked at the good living. We explained that it's cheaper. They keep the units cleaner and take more pride."

J.J. Cote, an official at the Westmorland Institution in New Brunswick, took a firm position when questioned by the media about the apparent luxury of the new accommodation. He told me that his statement to the press was: "Yes, we have something that is this good and this new. Why would we have built something to look old? Naturally it looks good. The taxpayers should know that we've saved millions of dollars by using residential construction standards. And for six men the houses are not that large."

Far from pampering or coddling the inmates with luxurious accommodation, the new housing program requires them to take responsibility for their own lives. They have to get themselves up in morning, make their own breakfast and get to work. Comparing the new social program associated with the housing units with the way things used to be at the prison, Cote said, "For years the bell rang and told them when to get up, go to bed or be fed. All we did was cater to them. When they returned to society, they didn't know how to look after themselves and soon ran out of money." Most Westmorland inmates work long hours on the prison farm. But they also have to find time to maintain their houses, do their own laundry and buy their food.

Most of the prisoners with whom I discussed the subject said they benefited from the condo units and the social programs associated with them. They learned to shop, cook and get along with other people in a less structured environment. "After years of not doing all the daily life things, it seems like a lot to do. If you've never cooked a meal, never had to be responsible for anything, it's hard to cope when you get out on the street, unless you've been through something like this," said one prisoner.

A criticism voiced by one ex-prisoner was that offenders were being given unrealistic expectations, that they were being prepared for a middle-class lifestyle that they could never legitimately attain on the street. He said, "We should be prepared for the reality of the life that we will lead when we get out. We're probably not going to get jobs. We should be told that. We're led to believe that we're going to get out and succeed, but probably what we're going to find is loneliness, isolation and poverty. As long as we know what's going to happen, we can prepare for it."

Nevertheless, these housing programs are a way of addressing some of the problems that plague penitentiary life and ultimately make prisoners more dangerous and unstable. They do not suit every prisoner, however, and other alternatives are also being sought.

Staff at institutions like Westmorland recognize that some inmates cannot handle the responsibilities and physical challenge of maintaining their own living units. More traditional accommodation and food service must be provided for an increasing number of older inmates, together with the many intellectually challenged offenders in the prison system.

Prisons are now being forced to provide accommodation for a variety of people with special needs. In British Columbia, I visited a medium security prison with a population made up entirely of inmates who could not survive in other prisons. Mountain Institution in the Fraser Valley was originally built as a prison for the Sons of Freedom Doukhobors, who engaged in acts of civil disobedience during the 1960s. The institution consists mainly of a collection of metal and concrete huts. These were designed to be fire resistant because arson was one of the forms of protest that the Doukhobors employed.

Like William Head, Mountain is a medium security prison, which means that it is surrounded by security towers and two rows of steel fencing topped with razor wire. Within the fences, it is an open encampment through which one can walk without going in straight lines and passing through security barriers. From everywhere within the prison compound, one can enjoy spectacular views of the Coastal Range mountains, which are only partially visible from the enclosed courtyard or through the barred windows of Kent Institution, the neighbouring maximum security prison.

About 75 per cent of Mountain's 350 inmates are sex offenders. The balance of the population is made up of informants, Crown witnesses and other protective custody inmates. The inmates include some high-profile sex offenders, men who committed murders that had sexual overtones, angry or sadistic rapists and pedophiles. A large number are incest offenders, many of them older men, convicted of crimes committed several decades ago. The population also includes other older offenders and "inadequates" who could not cope with life in most jails.

It is a generally well-behaved population. Like the prisoners at William Head, the Mountain inmates know that they are living in a more pleasant environment than they would encounter elsewhere. They are also motivated by fear. Many of the Mountain inmates, especially those who are considered too high risk to be placed in a minimum security setting, have few options for transfer. Other medium security prisons in British Columbia do accept sex offenders, provided they are prepared to mix with the general population. But most of these institutions are already overcrowded and their staff would not be well-disposed toward taking in an inmate who failed to fit in even at Mountain. Realistically, most inmates realize that their choice is between staying out of trouble at Mountain or finding themselves dealing with the horrors of protective custody at Kent.

"It's a more relaxed atmosphere and the inmates want to keep it that way. That helps keep a lid on a lot of problems," an administrator told me.

Prison officials believe that many penitentiary inmates are too violent and unstable, or too dependant on drugs and alcohol, to be trusted in a setting like William Head or Mountain. More traditional prison designs are still considered as the only option for keeping such prisoners under control and under surveillance. CSC administrators are conscious of the negative impact of such environments and do what they can to make cosmetic changes. Some of the older penitentiaries have undergone extensive renovations which have made dank and dismal cell blocks brighter and more habitable. When new cell blocks have been constructed in recent years, attempts have been made to create a less oppressive environment. In some of the buildings that I visited, cells were arranged in smaller clusters, around bright and airy common areas.

But cosmetic changes can only do so much to make a jail feel less like a jail. Inmates told me that they felt more relaxed, but the problems of overcrowding, drugs, violence and intimidation were still there. Staff said they felt more comfortable working in a more pleasant environment, but they too shared the inmates' perennial concerns.

While it is not possible to make radical transformations in the physical environment of most prisons, CSC staff are continually struggling to bring about changes in the prison culture. Little can be done to improve the atmosphere of a maximum security prison or reduce its damaging effects. The anti-social culture of such places is reinforced by the circumstances in which the most violent and intractable prisoners are held. Physical limitations are imposed by the need for barriers to restrict movement within the institution and by the presence of security posts from which prisoners can be monitored by armed guards. The correctional service therefore attempts to protect the public by maintaining only a few maximum security prisons and keeping as many prisoners as possible at lower levels of security, where there is more chance of influencing them and instilling more humane values.

In medium security prisons, where there are fewer internal barriers, staff and inmates interact more freely. A policy of "zero tolerance" for violence has been imposed in an attempt to reduce the influence of the inmate code. In the past, when a prisoner complained of being the victim of intimidation, threats or physical attack, the victim would be placed in protective custody. That policy is still followed in many maximum security prisons where no other options are available. But, in medium and minimum security, staff now respond to such situations by removing the aggressor from the general population. This usually means sending the guilty party back to maximum security or placing him in segregation.

With a large number of sex offenders in the prison population, many inmates have been forced to change their attitudes. At Dorchester Penitentiary, there used to be a section reserved for inmates in need of protective custody. As the number of sex offenders increased, the protective custody section of the prison grew, until the institution came to be virtually divided in half, with each population receiving equal access to facilities — a situation similar to the one that I encountered at the maximum security Kent Institution.

The population at Dorchester is now "integrated." Sex offenders are not kept separate, and anyone who bothers them is likely to be sent to the maximum security Atlantic Institution at Renous. Although inmates were initially resistant to the idea of joining the two populations, they were eventually persuaded of the advantage of having more freedom of movement within the institution and twice as much time available for seeing visitors, using recreational facilities and attending programs.

The prison administrators whom I interviewed did not claim that they had eliminated violence in an institution where hostage-takings and other incidents claimed the lives of staff in the past. As one administrator explained, "We have a very experienced staff who have developed a rapport with the population. Staff and inmates talk. We're aware of things that are going to happen before they happen. Inmates know that it's difficult to do anything because everyone talks. If the inmate code has been broken anywhere, it's here. But it's not a kindergarten. We're aware that assaults still happen."

The prison population apparently accepted the new reality and had in fact elected a sex offender as chairman of the inmate committee. Paul, the inmate chairman, was a mild-mannered educated man who had committed a high-profile crime for which he was despised in his home community. He told me that his election as inmate chairman followed "a dirty campaign" in which he was personally attacked because of his crime. He told me, "There is a small nucleus of inmates trying to preserve the old inmate code, but it's not surviving here. Rats are probably more scorned than sex offenders. They are given a hard time, though most of it is verbal abuse or being ignored."

Paul told me that sex offenders are still subjected to some harassment, but most of that is verbal. Generally, he said, there was a low level of violence in the institution, although one person had recently been convicted of attempted murder in outside court.

The threat of transferring violent prisoners to maximum security often prompts inmates to change the way they deal with one another. When there are personal conflicts between two inmates, staff bring them together to discuss their differences and try to resolve them. This negotiation often results in both prisoners remaining on the same range and leaving one another alone.

With a more relaxed and less violent atmosphere, staff and prisoners alike are better able to concentrate on rehabilitation and change. The freedom of movement permitted in medium security prisons makes it easier to organize group activities. Volunteers from the community can become more involved in the prison's affairs.

There is a danger, however, that all these efforts will be undermined by the increasing tensions created by overcrowding. When tension rises in medium security prisons, they can become more dangerous than maximum security institutions, because there is less supervision and prisoners have more freedom.

About a week before I visited William Head, staff and prisoners there were given a chilling reminder of the fact that they were not immune from the tensions and dangers of penitentiary life. A prisoner, who had served eighteen years of a life sentence for second-degree murder, was found beaten and stabbed to death in the dining area of his living unit. Two other occupants of his unit were being held as suspects. Although this was the first murder at William Head in more than fourteen years, it was suggested in the local media that it was a sign of the failure of the prison's liberal policies. The main source of these criticisms was a disenchanted ex-employee of William Head, who blamed prison authorities for allowing inmates to have steak knives in their living units and argued that the condominium-style residences were a way of cutting costs at the expense of public safety. He suggested that the prison was now housing more dangerous inmates than had been originally planned when the new facilities were designed.

Prisoners and staff members whom I met rejected these criticisms, pointing out that there were far more murders in maximum security prisons where inmates supposedly had no access to knives. One inmate explained, as we sat in the living room of his well-appointed living unit, "I recognize that I live in a dangerous environment with dangerous people. We have all earned our way here, but I realize that doesn't guarantee anything. In this house there are three guys convicted of murder. They have proven capable of committing that act. It doesn't mean that you have to live in fear, but you must live with a state of awareness."

Innovative architecture and programs cannot eliminate the problems of drugs and violence that are endemic in the prison system, though they can reduce tensions. They give prisoners an opportunity to learn, or relearn, some of the skills that they will need to survive in the community. But it is never possible to create a completely normal environment behind razor wire fences. It is not only the violence that distorts everything behind bars. It is also the lethargy and the state of adolescent dependence that is created in an environment where no one has to take complete responsibility for his or her own life. There are guards and fences to keep everyone from leaving and to protect inmates from the complexity, confusion and temptations of the real world.

14

PRISONS WITHOUT BARS

A prison without fences seems like an absurdity to many people. When inmates walk away from such an institution to commit murder or brutal rape, residents of neighbouring communities are alarmed and enraged. Such tragic incidents leave a confused and nervous public asking, "What security does minimum security provide?"

Yet the purpose of minimum security prisons is to protect the public better by serving as a stepping stone toward release. These open prisons are supposed to give offenders a chance to adjust to the responsibilities that go with freedom. They also let staff test how well offenders will adapt to a life without bars.

Only low-risk offenders are supposed to be in minimum security, so that it should not be a matter for public alarm when an inmate escapes. This was not the case, however, when two men walked away from Ferndale Institution in Mission, B.C. in May 1994 and ended up killing a man in the United States. And there was cause for alarm in southern Ontario's cottage country in 1992 when sex offender Phillipe Clement absconded from Beaver Creek Institution, near Gravenhurst, to rape a woman at knifepoint in her own home, choke her and beat her to unconsciousness.

The investigations that followed these two cases examined how and why these dangerous men were allowed to be in unfenced prisons in the first place. The fundamental question that these cases raised was whether CSC staff were making good judgements about the risk that these prisoners posed to the public. In the Ferndale case especially, the answer left one wondering how many other cases there might be of dangerous and volatile offenders who CSC staff think are safe.

"As long as human beings are making judgements about the future behaviour of other human beings, there is always a possibility that errors will be made," CSC Commissioner John Edwards stated in an August 1994 press release announcing the findings of the Ferndale inquiry. The husband of the woman attacked by Clement made a similar point, but from a starkly different perspective, when he told the CBC's *fifth estate*: "They know that their systems don't work. But maybe it's like this. Maybe it's that the only way that they know whether their efforts have done anything or not is by letting somebody like this loose, and then waiting to see what he does. And if he doesn't do anything, then they say, 'Well, great. We did the right thing.' And if he goes out and butchers somebody, they say, 'Oops.'"

Both these cases prompted many people to demand that fences be erected around minimum security prisons, but that would defeat the purpose of these institutions. Unlike maximum or medium security prisons, where a heavy reliance is placed on "static security" devices like fences, barriers and motion detectors, minimum security prisons rely exclusively on what is known as "dynamic security." It involves staff studying inmates' files, interacting with prisoners, gathering intelligence and watching for any signs of trouble.

If the objective is purely to keep prisoners locked up, static security serves the purpose well. But, even in maximum security, it must be accompanied with a large measure of dynamic security, in order to gain some control over problems like violence among prisoners, extortion, drug abuse and suicide.

The technology of static security has become so sophisticat-
ed that prisoners rarely escape from maximum and medium
security institutions. When they do, it is usually as a result of a
failure in dynamic security: mistakes by guards or ingenuity on
the part of the prisoners. For example, a dangerous offender
escaped from the maximum security Kent Institution in 1995
by hiding in a cardboard box, supposedly containing the personal possessions of an inmate who was being released. A prisoner escaped from medium security Matsqui by hiding among
potato peelings and other kitchen scraps in a refuse container,
after cutting the power supply to the garbage compacter. At the
medium security Bath Institution in Ontario, two prisoners did
manage to get over the security fence, but only because construction workers had left a ladder unattended.

The concept of CSC's three-level security system is that by
the time prisoners have cascaded down to a minimum security
level they will have become responsible enough and well social-
ized to the degree that they no longer need the external controls of static security. There is nothing to stop them from walking
away from the institutions, though staff monitor them carefully
through informal contacts and official counts every few hours.

Putting fences around the institutions would undermine prisoners' sense of responsibility for their own actions. It would also
restrict inmates' interaction with the community and reduce the
value of minimum security as a stage toward returning offenders to everyday life. CSC staff believe that the risks associated
with minimum security are not as great as those of releasing all
prisoners directly onto the street. Minimum security prisons can
make the community safer by letting prisoners have their first
taste of freedom from external restraints while they still have
access to the therapy and support that the institution has to offer.

It is inevitable that some prisoners will be unable to handle
the relative freedom of minimum security after years behind bars.
Staff hope that their dynamic security will be strong enough to

identify many of these individuals before they take off or cause trouble, but everyone is resigned to the fact that a small proportion of the prisoners will go absent without leave. There have been up to 200 walkaways a year in recent years, though the CSC was hoping in 1995 that the 1994–95 total of 92 walkaways was the beginning of a new trend and a sign that new policies were proving effective.

Few of the prisoners who walk away from minimum security present major problems for authorities or any risk to the public. Many are captured within days, if not hours, of their escape. Few commit serious crimes while at large. They should not have been transferred to minimum security if they were dangerous or likely to commit serious crimes. By running away, they usually create more problems for themselves than for the community at large. A study of 95 offenders who escaped from minimum security prison in 1991 found that 88 per cent were recaptured and less than 7 per cent committed serious offences.

These were the kind of statistics that used to provide reassurance to people in the Gravenhurst area, prior to 1992. Located on a former air force base in the heart of Southern Ontario's cottage country, Beaver Creek Institution has a reputation in the province as a "country club" prison for white-collar criminals. People living in the surrounding community were shocked to discover that the minimum security prison housed an inmate as dangerous as 33-year-old Philippe Clement. It was particularly horrifying that they did not make that discovery until after one of their neighbours had been raped and beaten nearly to death in her own home.

Clement was serving a life sentence for the second-degree murder of a Montreal woman, whom he had dragged off the street in February 1977, sexually assaulted, stabbed and choked to death. Traumatic experiences of family violence in early childhood had left Clement with feelings of anger toward women which could explode into sadistic rage whenever he felt that a woman had rejected him. At a prison psychiatric hospital in Quebec, he developed what authorities termed "an inappropriate relationship" with a female nurse. In 1989, a psychiatrist noted that Clement hated women and warned that "any relationship with a female is at risk of awakening any and all of these feelings and a release program is therefore at risk."

Nevertheless, after ten years of treatment in the prison system, therapists believed that Clement had learned to control his behaviour by applying the relapse prevention techniques taught in CSC sex offender programs. He was apparently making steady progress toward gradual release into the community. Clement was transferred to Beaver Creek, in spite of an episode involving his female therapist at the medium security Warkworth Institution. When he disclosed that he had become infatuated with her, she became upset and refused to talk to him. The therapist, who had an honours degree in psychology, subsequently complained that she was not qualified for the job and had not been adequately trained. CSC did not renew her contract.

In August 1991, Clement was sent to Beaver Creek to begin a program of "gradual community re-entry and socialization." At that time, the institution did not have a sex offender relapse prevention program, a deficiency that has since been rectified. Some therapists had warned that Clement needed ongoing treatment, but it was decided it would not be detrimental for him to spend some time in prison without being in a program.

A CSC Board of Inquiry into Clement's escape concluded that the decision to place Clement in minimum security was an appropriate one, in the light of his progress in therapy and behaviour in prison. The judge in a subsequent civil suit did not find any fault in this decision either, although he did determine that CSC was negligent in its handling of Clement's escape.

When Clement arrived at Beaver Creek, staff decided to make a female correctional officer responsible for counselling him. The purpose was to encourage him to establish a normal working relationship with a woman. The CSC inquiry report noted, "In retrospect, had the team more clearly focussed on his offence pattern, they might not have adopted this strategy."

As might have been predicted, Clement felt that he was falling in love with the counsellor and became angry when she rejected his advances. He was due to appear for a parole hearing, and he made a comment to the counsellor that suggested he was thinking about absconding. A male staff member discussed this with him and believed that the situation had been resolved.

At 8:20 a.m. on the day of his parole hearing, Clement failed to respond when he was paged over the public address system by his case management officer. He had been counted as present in his cell three hours earlier. He was paged for a second time and again failed to respond. At about the same time, police were patrolling a nearby road looking for a suspicious-looking man who had been seen in the woods.

It was not until nearly an hour later, however, that the case management officer reported Clement's absence to prison security staff. Correctional officers investigated the inmate's room and discovered "a partial dummy," an inflated plastic bag in a pillow case under the blanket in his bed. They decided to search the prison grounds and do another count of all prisoners before notifying police.

If police had been notified earlier, they would undoubtedly have returned to the spot where a suspicious stranger had been seen. There was a chance that they could have spotted Clement before he entered his victim's home and their presence might have frightened him away. It was not until about twenty minutes after Clement had attacked his victim, however, that police were notified that a dangerous offender was on the run. Clement was eventually captured outside the home of his prison counsellor, whom he had planned to attack next.

In February 1995, a civil court awarded Clement's victim and her family $394,395 in damages to be jointly paid by Clement and CSC. The court found that CSC staff were negligent in failing to conduct an immediate search for Clement when he did not answer his page and for failing to notify police immediately when the dummy was discovered in his bed. The court did not find that CSC was negligent in transferring Clement to Beaver Creek or in monitoring him while he was there.

If CSC learned any lessons from the Clement case and its own internal investigation in 1992, there was little evidence of this in the chain of events that led to Timothy Cronin and Michael Roberts walking away from Ferndale on May 3, 1994. The CSC Board of Inquiry report into their escape noted that various previous studies and investigations of earlier walkaways, including that of Clement, "have not generated any substantial policy review/amendment in relation to minimum security institutions."

The Ferndale report exposed numerous errors of judgement, simple mistakes and oversights which resulted in two violent and unstable men being transferred to minimum security when they should have remained behind bars. When one reviews the background and prison behaviour of these two men, as set out in the CSC report, it is hard to understand how psychologists could have concluded that these men were low-risk offenders. It is perhaps even harder to accept that experienced correctional staff would have believed the psychologists.

Cronin was a 25-year-old man serving a sentence for armed robbery and use of a firearm. During his time in prison, his violence and involvement with drugs earned him a reputation as a "muscle man." He was found in possession of a seven-inch knife on one occasion and also spent time in segregation for possession of a homemade handcuff key. Yet he was described as "a model inmate" when he was transferred to Ferndale, and, the CSC investigative report noted, "there was little or no mention that inmate Cronin had a violent record, previous escape history, drug problems and extensive criminal record."

Michael Roberts was 39 years old at the time of the escape. He was serving a sentence for armed robbery and attempted murder, arising out of a hostage-taking in which he fired at police with a shotgun. During his time in prison, he had been involved in four escape conspiracies. Then, in August 1983, he murdered another prisoner in Collins Bay in what was believed to be a drug-related killing. After three years in a special handling unit, Roberts was transferred to the Regional Psychiatric Centre. A psychologist was impressed with his progress in therapy and recommended that Roberts be transferred to a minimum security prison. After a short period of medium security at Mission, he was indeed transferred to minimum security Elbow Lake Institution. Ten days later, he walked away.

Roberts was at large for 21 months, apparently living in the United States. He was featured once on the TV show "America's Most Wanted." On August 7, 1990, he turned himself in and was admitted to Mission. He was convicted of escaping lawful custody and sentenced to serve four months.

Roberts was sent back to the psychiatric centre for treatment. In March 1992, a consultant psychiatrist evaluating him for a temporary absence and day parole application, found him remorseful and "attempting to rid himself of all his past anti-social values." The psychiatrist concluded, "Certainly, I do not see him as presenting any threat to the community at this time." The psychologist who had recommended that he be transferred to minimum, prior to his previous escape, again concluded that "he would be unlikely to reinvolve himself in a criminal lifestyle in the future."

This recommendation was partly based on errors in interpreting data on Roberts' files. In order to calculate the risk that an offender poses, certain factors in their background are translated into negative or positive numerical values, known as "scores," that are then measured against a "recidivism scale." On the scale that was used in Roberts' case, people with a final score above zero are considered low risk to reoffend, whereas offenders with a negative final tally are assessed as higher risks. In Roberts' case, someone got the score wrong. Roberts should have got a "-4" rating in one category because his last crime was an escape, whereas he got a "+3" on the assumption that murder was his last crime and murderers seldom reoffend. Other mistakes included incorrect entries for how many times he had been in jail and how young he was when he first offended. His final score on the test was a "+4." But, when the CSC investigators had the scale recalculated on the basis of the correct data, the revised score of "-10" placed Roberts in the category of offenders most likely to commit more crimes.

CSC investigators were also astonished by the psychologists' conclusion that Roberts was a low risk in terms of public safety because he did not incur any further charges while he was unlawfully at large. The investigators commented, "We find it difficult to accept that inmate Roberts' unlawful departure from minimum security for a 21-month period and appearance on 'America's Most Wanted' was turned into a positively-weighted factor by the professional consultants and the case management team. We believe that if an inmate with a violent history of the magnitude of inmate Roberts' had ever escaped before, then caution is warranted."

Nevertheless, Roberts was sent to medium security Mission Institution after his treatment was completed at the psychiatric centre and from there transferred to minimum security Ferndale. The CSC investigators concluded that the information provided by the staff recommending the transfer was, as in the case of Cronin, selective and misleading. It contained no mention of Roberts' extremely violent record and his long period of incarceration in special handling units.

Roberts had been at Ferndale for six months when Cronin arrived in April 1994. Roberts had been attending Alcoholics Anonymous meetings and had a job in the institution's barbershop. His productivity as a barber was not very high as other inmates did not seem to want to use his services.

On April 14, 1994 — less than a month before the escape, armed robbery and murder — a psychiatrist examined Roberts at Ferndale and concluded: "There is hardly a trace of his past personality. It could be that the 21 months' 'vacation' from prison did him some good. He is unlikely to return to criminal life, and he definitely would not be able to be violent, after what he experienced, when he has seen a life evaporating in front of him, and which has significantly changed his attitude."

Although Roberts was regarded as a "loner" in jail, he struck up an immediate friendship with Cronin when the younger man arrived. Prison security staff subsequently learned from other inmates that the two men had been seen smoking marijuana together during the days preceding the escape.

The circumstances of their escape exposed lax counting procedures on the part of Ferndale staff, who did not begin looking for Roberts until seven hours after they had realized Cronin was missing. Four days after leaving Ferndale, the two men were arrested in Oregon in connection with the armed robbery of a corner store. The owner of the car that they were driving was subsequently found strangled in his apartment. They were charged in Washington State with aggravated, first-degree murder.

With its nine-hole golf course, comfortable condominium-style housing units and spectacular views of the Coastal Range Mountains, Ferndale Institution is "a very scenic, relaxed and comfortable place," observed a team of CSC investigators, who said they were troubled by staff members' "inattentive performance of correctional duties." But most of the investigators' criticisms were directed at the psychologists and case management staff who believed that it was safe to transfer the two men to a minimum security institution. The report also concluded that the system as a whole had failed, since there were not enough controls on the transfer process. The report stated, "Present CSC policies place too much emphasis on responding to inmate needs while not correspondingly placing adequate emphasis on the Service's responsibility to visibly safeguard the security of the public."

New policies were put in place following the release of this report. The status of all inmates at Ferndale was reviewed after the escape and three prisoners were transferred to higher levels of security. The investigators' fourteen recommendations included measures to monitor the quality of psychological assessments and case managers' transfer recommendations. CSC announced that it was implementing these and other recommended changes. Wardens at minimum security institutions were made personally responsible for approving all proposed transfers.

When I visited Ferndale in December 1994, I was assured that all the problems exposed in the report had been addressed, both within the institution and in the system as a whole. The warden Ron Wiebe, who arrived at Ferndale to assume his duties on the day after the escape, insisted that the public was being well protected. He told me that he personally reviewed each application for transfer with his staff. They all knew exactly who they were receiving into the institution and well understood what kind of offenders they could handle safely. Everyone was making very conservative decisions in the light of the May 1994 walkaways. As a consequence, the institution had twenty empty beds, an extremely unusual situation in a prison system beset with chronic overcrowding.

The warden was evidently worried that a few exceptional, highly publicized tragedies had eroded public confidence in Canada's humane and rational correctional system. He spoke of CSC's "leading edge" practices in risk assessment and sex offender programming. The public is better protected, he told me, by institutions like Ferndale which help offenders practise self-control and exercise responsibility, than by law and order policies that keep more people behind bars. "Security is 90 per cent knowledge," he said. "Yet, if we followed the whims of the people, we would spend money on hardware. We know the guys here. We know their crime cycle. We have relapse prevention for sex offenders. Ask any guy in the institution what his crime cycle is and he'll tell you. Knowledge makes risk acceptable.

"I hope we don't get panicked in Canada into making rash decisions and incarcerate the sons of bitches at risk of public safety," Wiebe said. "We are accused of being wimpy. But our programs require more courage, insight and care, than throwing them behind walls and hoping they get better."

Wiebe went on to discuss the need for prison officials to communicate better with the public. He conceded that he did have some public relations problems, at least initially, over the prison's nine-hole golf course. He explained, "It had nothing to do with making a country club. The property needed a green belt. Inmates were into landscaping and one of them was a golf pro who designed this nine-hole, par-three course. It became a source of embarrassment because nobody used it other than inmates."

Local residents were invited to use the course and a group of seniors accepted the invitation. Close to 40 retired people began playing golf at the prison about three times a week. "At eight in the morning, the parking lot would be packed with old ladies with golf carts," said Wiebe. Inmates provided coaching and organized a tournament for the seniors. The prisoners discovered that some of the older people who used the golf course were lonely and had few social activities during the winter. The inmates therefore initiated an "adopt a senior" program, by which seniors would participate in hobby-craft activities and social events at the prison.

"It was a serendipitous thing. It had a terrific impact on this place," said Wiebe. He said the inmates learned positive values from the seniors and would listen to advice from them that they would not accept from staff. The seniors came to know the prisoners and overcame their fears about such people being released into the community. Wiebe told me that the inmates were very protective of seniors and "won't let the fraud guys talk to them." The institution ended up getting favourable publicity about the golf course when a television network ran a story about inmates coaching the seniors.

A few days after visiting Ferndale, I spoke to a woman whose sister had been murdered, fifteen years earlier, by a man who was now one of Ferndale's inmate golf coaches. I interviewed Nancy in order to learn more about a Victim Offender Mediation program that she had participated in. The prisoner, whom I will identify as Mike, had been married to Nancy's older sister and had murdered her younger sister, his sister-in-law. It was a crime that left a whole family of traumatized victims. Their wounds were reopened when they happened to see Mike on the television news.

"His two children have a father in prison for murdering their aunt. No one in the system bothered to warn us that he was going to be on TV. So the children watched," Nancy told me. A forthright, sensible woman who was obviously not given to displays of emotion, she quivered with indignation as she went on to say, "My anger is so great. I can't help it when it keeps hitting me in the face. It's a nice little resort that he's imprisoned in. If I told the seniors about what he put the kids through and how he murdered my sister, they would run away."

Calming down and resuming the quiet, reasonable tone that she maintained through most of the interview, Nancy said, "I'm not saying that he shouldn't be playing golf. But no one in the system thought about revictimization of the family." Nancy said that she was also bothered by the way in which Mike was lionized by the television news show. "If he's such a good guy, why is he still in jail?" she asked rhetorically.

Nancy told me about the meeting that she had arranged with Mike through the mediation program which puts victims in touch with perpetrators. She explained that she had arranged the meeting after much soul searching because she needed to know whether he had been rehabilitated and whether he might be a threat to other family members after his release. She wanted to know whether he had any intention of trying to see his children, who were still living with his ex-wife, Nancy's sister.

"What was he thinking? How did he really feel? If it was me and I had killed somebody, I don't think I could live with myself," said Nancy, explaining that she wanted to meet him face to face in order to evaluate his mental state.

As a member of society, as well as a member of the victim's family, Nancy felt that she had a vested interest in Mike's rehabilitation. She was worried about how he would be able to cope with life in the community. She said, his crime resulted from drugs and his lack of life skills, his inability to deal with everyday problems. What had he learned in more than ten years of prison and psychotherapy? "For some reason, I felt a sense of personal responsibility that he would not reoffend, that someone else should not die at his hands," Nancy said.

Nancy found her two meetings with Mike very disturbing and dissatisfying. She did not feel that she got the answers that she had wanted to hear. She said, "He walked in wearing a three-piece business suit, wanting to talk about his agenda, his needs and why he was upset about the prison environment. If I had seen any hint of remorse, then I would have felt like there's some hope." Instead, Nancy said, Mike continued to deny responsibility for the crime and blamed the system for his problems. She was particularly alarmed by his apparent lack of empathy for his victims. Nancy said Mike never asked how his kids were or referred to the pain that he must have caused them, though he insisted that he loved them and wanted to see them.

Mike's attitude was deeply troubling to Nancy. She had experienced the constant struggle with grief and pain that marks the lives of surviving victims of violent crime and victims' families. Unlike prisoners, she pointed out, victims do not have the benefit of years of psychotherapy funded by the government. "With all those resources, he messed up every time he was released. It was just good luck that no one was hurt. It makes me angry when prisoners have the gall not to get better," she said.

Although Nancy said she could appreciate the value of victim offender mediation as a way of promoting empathy on the part of prisoners, she felt that she could not deal with Mike any more. She told me, "He wanted to meet again to tell me a few more things that he thought were important. I said, 'I can't do this to myself. I'm expending emotional energy listening to how he feels victimized by prison.'"

Nancy made it clear that she believed in rehabilitating prisoners and returning them to the community. She understood that merely locking them up and treating them like animals will do no good. She said, "I don't expect Mike to become a saint. But him blaming the system for his failures tells me that he has got a long way to go before he's safe in society. I have more confidence about the guys who are admitting that they are not ready, admitting to their fears and asking for more help."

During my interview with Nancy, I recalled a meeting that I had at Ferndale with an offender who had talked to me about teaching seniors to play golf. It was not until I subsequently reviewed my notes that I realized that the golfer had the same first name as the man who murdered Nancy's sister. Other details seemed to fit and I realized that I may well have been talking to the same man.

The Mike whom I met at Ferndale spoke with great enthusiasm about the fact that he had been "clean and sober" for thirteen months. He admitted, "Yes, the public has a concern if I'm using alcohol and drugs. I'm putting the public in danger."

He told me that he had been out on parole four times and returned to the institution each time for taking drugs or alcohol. He emphasized the fact that he had never committed any crimes against the community while on parole. On the last occasion, he stopped in a bar in Abbotsford and found himself taking a taxi into Vancouver to buy cocaine. He said he went to a counsellor for help the next day, but was nevertheless returned to prison. "Why is it people here cannot see a change and have another look at you?" he asked.

"There are points in time when a human being does not realize what he's doing, when he's capable of flinging himself at you like a rat cornered," said Mike. He described life in a maximum security penitentiary, "where doors are banging behind you and guards strip you down or put you in the hole. Even if there wasn't any anger in you to begin with, they would bring some out."

At Ferndale, on the other hand, Mike said prisoners are allowed to take responsibility for their own lives. They are brought into contact with members of the community. The golf games and programs for seniors were examples of activities that made prisoners feel useful and connected with the real world.

Mike talked to me about the value of therapy. He spoke of the sense of release that an offender experiences after disclosing that he has been a victim of sexual abuse. "I always felt more in prison [when I was] outside, because I would hate the world. I'd say, 'Look what you've done to me,'" Mike told me.

I got an uneasy feeling from Mike. The energy with which he spoke about his violent feelings scared me a little. I was not convinced that they had all been resolved and set aside through therapy. It was with relief that I heard him say that he was going to get involved in another, more intensive program.

Most confusing and profoundly disturbing was a comment that Mike made about the CSC therapy programs and the process by which a person like him earns a transfer to a minimum security prison. He said, "We are capable of manipulating the system. We could convince psychiatrists and psychologists."

I do not know whether there was truly anything to fear from this smooth-talking man who charmed old ladies on the prison golf course. Clearly the CSC had assessed him as a "low-risk offender" or he would not be in a minimum security prison. But, in the light of the findings of the investigation into the walkaways, I was left wondering about what other mistakes and naïve judgements CSC staff might have made or might still be making.

Warden Wiebe told me that the local mayor and municipal council of the community had expressed similar fears. He said, "They were demanding a 100 per cent assurance that there would never be another problem. I said, 'We'll do that the day you guarantee your roads.'"

15

THE DILEMMAS
OF PAROLE

A burly young man calmly explained why he pressed a pillow into his rape victim's face.

"My intention was to smother her, so she wouldn't testify," Darren told three members of the National Parole Board at a hearing in a medium security penitentiary.

Perhaps because I shuddered involuntarily at the callous simplicity of his answer, the rapist noticed me for the first time, sitting a few feet away in the corner of the room. He turned and gave me a penetrating look that seemed full of menace but devoid of feeling.

"I noticed that you gave the board-appointed guest a hostile stare," the board chairman told the prisoner sternly.

"I just wanted to see who was sitting there," he replied. Then, with the chilling logic of a psychopathic mind, he continued to explain his actions. He attacked his victim, he said, because "I saw her naked. I thought I was much bigger than her." His reason for putting a towel over her head and tying a cloth around her neck was "to prevent her from struggling too much."

It seemed obvious that Darren was not fit to be turned loose in society. I began to wonder whether the parole board members would have bothered to conduct a hearing if the law did not require them to do so. As I heard further details of this horrendous case, it became even more apparent that this man was a potential threat to any woman he might meet. Yet it also became clear that the parole board had very few options left. Darren was going to be leaving prison soon whatever the parole board decided.

Darren was serving a seven-year term for a prolonged sexual and physical assault that a judge described as "a night of torture and sadism." He had already been denied parole, but he would soon have completed two-thirds of his sentence and therefore be entitled to statutory release. The purpose of this hearing was to consider a detention order that would keep him in prison for the full seven years. Before granting a detention order, the parole board would have to be satisfied that the inmate had committed a crime causing death or serious harm and was likely to do so again.

The parole board would have no trouble deciding that Darren was dangerous. But would keeping him in jail for another two years lessen or increase the risk to the public? Would he benefit from further treatment in jail or would he become even more anti-social? Would it be safer to let him out now and insist that he attend treatment programs in the community? Could probation officers do anything to make sure that he would stay out of trouble if he was released under their supervision?

It is questions like these that the parole board must continually consider, as it determines when and how prisoners should be released. The public expects complete protection and holds the parole board responsible for any crime committed by released offenders. But members of the parole board are frequently faced with impossible dilemmas, as they are asked to weigh imponderable risks.

The National Parole Board is independent of CSC. The board members are citizens, appointed by the federal government. Some past appointments have apparently been made for reasons of patronage rather than ability. In May 1994, the board was criticized in Parliament for what opposition MPs described as a

series of "bone-headed decisions," resulting in dangerous criminals being released on parole. In other circumstances, the board
has been unfairly held responsible for decisions that looked
terrible in hindsight, but made sense on the basis of the information available at the time. Often the board is simply the object
of frustration for people who do not believe that prisoners
should ever be released before their sentences are complete.

During the course of my research, I attended numerous hearings conducted by different board members, mostly in the
Ontario region. As one might expect, I found some members
to be more astute than others, but my general impression was
that they were extremely cautious, conscientious people who
took their responsibilities very seriously. At hearings that I
attended, parole was denied more often than it was granted,
and detention was ordered in most cases where CSC had made
an application.

The federal prison system deals with the most violent and
most dangerous criminals that Canada can produce, together
with thousands of drug abusers, violent alcoholics, people with
severe personality problems, sexual deviants and persistent property offenders. It is inevitable that many of them will keep on
committing crimes after they are released from prison. The
challenge for the parole board and the correctional system is to
try to identify the relatively few offenders who are likely to commit violent crimes in future. In theory, these offenders can then
be held in prison for therapy and programming, until it is determined that they represent a "manageable risk" for release into
the community — or, at least, until their sentences expire. The
problem is that it is hard to tell who they are.

Darren's case was a comparatively easy one for the board.
The savagery of his previous crime suggested that he was dangerous. The only issue was whether treatment programs had
reduced the threat that he posed. If the programs were working, it might make more sense to release him before the end of

his sentence, so that arrangements could be made for ongoing treatment in the community. Prisoners who are kept in jail for their full sentences are likely to give up on treatment and may not be able to obtain help after their release, even if they want it.

Darren was therefore asked what insight he had gained about his motives. He explained, "I had a bad attitude toward women, treating them as objects. It's basically the way I've been all my life, the way society is. It has a lot to do with the people I hang around with."

Asked if he had any understanding of the psychological harm that he had caused his victim, Darren replied, "She's going to be scared of strangers. She'll have relationship problems. She feels that she was responsible because of the way she looked. It had nothing to do with the way she looked." He spoke as if he had learned his lesson by heart and was proud to display how well he could repeat it. He told the board, "I treated her as a sex object. It was deviant thinking."

Darren appeared a little puzzled when he was confronted with a note in his case management officer's report stating that the pornography displayed on the walls of Darren's cell was the worst in the prison. Darren told the board that they were just "basic poses out of Playboy." He said he had taken them down a few months earlier and replaced them with pictures of holiday resorts.

When a board member asked him if he understood the reason for his need for power and control, Darren seemed stumped for a moment. Naïvely, he explained, "I like to be in control." Then, apparently realizing that was not the correct answer, he added, "From what I've learned from group, I don't have to be in control. My attitude to women has changed. I can't view them as sex objects, as property."

"Do you think hitting her on the head was a failure to control violent impulses?" the board member asked.

Perhaps resenting the suggestion that he had lost control and acted irrationally, Darren responded, "The reason I did that was to stun her so she would stop screaming."

One of the board members observed that the attack had shown "almost homicidal intent." He asked Darren what he had learned in therapy that might make him unlikely to behave in that way in future. Darren replied, "I learned thought-stopping techniques. When I start thinking deviant thoughts, I talk myself down. I put myself in somebody else's shoes."

Like many offenders who go through CSC programs, Darren had obviously learned to say the right things and had apparently acquired some understanding of his problems. His therapist had noted that his objective reasoning was good, but commented that Darren "needs to work on his victim empathy."

When the board asked Darren to describe his crime cycle and relapse prevention plan, he again sounded like a student reeling off all he could remember of a half-absorbed lesson. He said, "I'm drinking. I see a woman and I want to have sex. I do everything in my power to get close to her. I try to take her home. If I'm turned down, I would get angry. I'd find out if she lives alone. For relapse prevention I use thought stopping. I say, 'Is that what I want done to me?'"

He apparently remembered that the therapy sessions had also stressed the need for offenders to improve their social skills so that they could establish relationships with women without feeling a need to resort to force. Darren completed his explanation of his plan for rehabilitation by saying, "I will try not to be so shy. I will learn to take criticisms."

None of this gave the board any confidence that Darren really had any feelings for his victims or any real motivation for change. The board members ordered that Darren be detained until the end of his sentence. They advised him to engage in more therapy and offered the carrot that his detention could be lifted at a later date. In any event, he would automatically be released at the expiry of his sentence, early in 1997, after which time authorities would have no knowledge of where he went and no control over what he did. There would be no way of knowing how well he applied what he learned in therapy, unless another victim came forward to prove that his treatment had failed.

The parole board is always extremely cautious about releasing offenders whom CSC has asked it to detain. The board relies to a great degree on the information provided by CSC staff and is therefore reluctant to go against a CSC recommendation, especially where the recommendation is to keep a potentially dangerous offender behind bars.

It is only in rare cases, however, that CSC seeks detention orders or is allowed by law to do so. Only offenders who have committed crimes causing serious injury or death may be detained and then only if there is evidence that they are likely to commit similar crimes in future. Most offenders must be released when they have completed two-thirds of their sentences, even when CSC staff and parole board members are concerned that they are likely to commit serious crimes.

It is hard to see what the parole board could have done, for example, to prevent the January 1995 murder of 23-year-old Melanie Carpenter in Surrey, B.C. Her suspected murderer, Fernand Auger, who subsequently killed himself, was on statutory release after serving two-thirds of a two-year sentence for a gas bar robbery. While in prison, Auger had been diagnosed as having a personality disorder, but so are a huge number of federal offenders. His criminal record included two 1985 convictions for sexual assault and buggery, but an Ontario court had only deemed these serious enough to warrant a provincial jail term of two years less a day.

In November 1993, the parole board had denied Auger release on parole after one-third of his sentence. At that time, the board received a report stating, "Emotional problems related to his dysfunctional youth and his resulting negative attitudes and values, while starting to be addressed, are clearly unresolved."

But authorities had no choice but to release him a year later, when he had served two-thirds of his sentence. He could not be considered for detention under existing legislation because the sentence he was serving was not for a crime causing death or serious harm.

Prior to his statutory release in 1994, a prison report stated that Auger had not involved himself in programming and "close monitoring would be needed following his release." He was released in August 1994, but the monitoring that he received was evidently not close enough. A warrant for his arrest on a charge of failure to report to his parole officers in Alberta was issued on January 9, 1995, three days after Melanie Carpenter's abduction.

When offenders are released on parole or statutory release, it is always quite likely that they will get into further trouble before their period of supervision in the community is over. About a quarter of those released on parole will return to prison, either because they commit new crimes or because they violate their parole conditions. Prisoners held in jail until their statutory release date are more likely to reoffend and past studies have indicated that about 46 per cent of these return to prison before their sentences expire.

Violent crimes by people on parole alarm the public and lead some people to conclude that the system should be scrapped. But such crimes are comparatively rare. There are close to 10,000 offenders on parole or statutory release at any one time and, according to a 1994 report by the federal auditor general, between 110 and 160 of these are charged with committing a violent offence each year. A 1987 study of all parole releases during the previous eleven years revealed that a total of 130 murders were committed by offenders on parole or statutory release. Victims' rights advocates were shocked by this figure, which is often cited as proof that the parole system fails to protect the public. But these 130 murders represented only 2 per cent of the 7,838 homicides committed over that period. About a third of these murders were committed by offenders who had previously been in jail only for non-violent property crimes. Only 15 per cent of the parolees who committed murders had previously been sentenced for violent crimes. These included just two paroled murderers and seven who had previously been convicted of manslaughter. The only way that most of the 130 murders could have been prevented was by denying parole to almost all of the 52,482 offenders released during that period. As a subsequent government report pointed out, even this drastic and expensive measure might have postponed only some of the murders for a short time.

According to statistics, murders are far less likely to reoffend than most other convicted criminals. A study of 457 murderers released on parole between 1975 and 1986 showed that fewer than 9 per cent committed another offence. Only six of these crimes were assaults and just two of them were murders. A similar pattern is revealed by more recent statistics. According to information supplied by the parole board, there were 41 murders committed by people on parole or statutory release from 1990 to 1995. Only one of these was committed by a murderer on parole.

Contrary to public perceptions, parole is not easy to obtain for prisoners who have committed serious crimes. Non-violent property offenders are usually "fast-tracked" for early parole, which is readily granted in most cases. But other offenders go through gruelling hearings at which board members grill them about their past record, their attitude to their victims, their conduct in jail, their participation in programs, their current psychological state and their plans for release into the community. Full parole is denied twice as often as it is granted, while the reverse is true of day parole, which involves offenders living in the more structured and more closely supervised setting of a halfway house. According to a report by the auditor general, the parole board agrees with the recommendations of CSC staff in 85–90 per cent of all cases.

CSC staff believe that they are getting better at predicting the risk that prisoners might pose. The intake assessment process and subsequent participation in programs result in masses of information being gathered about each offender. This information is used to create checklists of all the factors that might lead to someone committing further crimes. These include details of their past crimes, problems such as drug abuse or alcoholism, information about their family background, education and employment record. By calibrating such information and converting it into numerical "scores," psychologists can interpret it with the help of various "risk assessment scales." On the basis of these scales, they can conclude, for example, that an offender has a 60 per cent chance of reoffending. What they really mean when they say this is that 60 per cent of all other offenders with the same score on the scales have gone on to commit other crimes.

Sometimes the parole board and CSC seem to rely too much on this kind of statistical information, which is heavily based on prisoners' past history and their problems. Human behaviour is notoriously difficult to predict and psychologists often cite the maxim that "past behaviour is the best predictor of future behaviour." Many prisoners feel that they are trapped by the information on their files and that nothing they do in therapy and programs can ever make a difference. A prisoner at one parole hearing that I attended complained, "All the things they wrote in my report were things from the past. Doesn't anybody believe in the future any more? Doesn't anyone realize that people can change?"

There is also a danger that the parole board will overlook a crucial piece of information because it gets lost in the mounds of data in each prisoner's file. The auditor general of Canada warned in his 1994 report: "We are concerned that Board members are 'drowning' in information. National Parole Board files are often voluminous and contain some information that does not necessarily help board members to decide whether an offender will be a manageable risk in the community."

Information on the files may also be unreliable. Board members often confront prisoners with hearsay information and unfounded suspicions that have been recorded by police or prison security staff. Prisoners may be assisted at hearings by lawyers but the lawyers have no right to call evidence or cross-examine witnesses. They frequently complain that the process is grossly unfair, but board members are intent on keeping the hearings informal, freewheeling and unhampered by legalistic restrictions.

Ultimately, the parole board members have to make a judgement that draws upon all the files and recommendations, but is also based on their personal assessment of the prisoner. They must evaluate the prisoner's values and attitudes, together with his or her plans for the future. They also have to consider what is practical and realistic in the light of the length of the prisoner's sentence and the options available.

The pressure of public opinion also appears to play a part in parole board decision making, even though board members vehemently deny this. The board is particularly sensitive to fears and concerns voiced by victims of crime and their families. In high-profile cases, where victim's and their political representatives mount a vigorous campaign to keep a prisoner behind bars, the parole board often errs on the side of caution.

When it is reported that convicted murderers may be eligible for parole after so many years — 25 for first-degree murder or from ten to twenty for second-degree — people tend to assume that they will get out of jail that quickly. The reality is, however, that many will apply and reapply for parole several times before being released, in spite of the fact that murderers present a low risk for reoffending.

It is especially difficult for murderers to earn parole when victims' relatives are campaigning against their release. Victims' relatives may not speak at hearings, but they can attend. James, a man who killed an acquaintance in what he described as an act of youthful bravado, told me that his parole hearing was attended by eighteen of his victim's relatives. In these circumstances, James felt, he never had a chance of parole as "it would have been ludicrous for them to recommend my release. Why would they take the risk that I might screw up with all those people breathing down their necks?" A well-educated, articulate man, James insisted that he did feel empathy for his victim's relatives, but believed that they were hounding him. He said, "There is a threshold where you cross the line from empathy to anger. It is high, but it does exist."

Any indication that an offender lacks empathy or has failed to address all his or her problems in therapy is likely to result in additional years behind bars. Prisoners who take responsibility for their own actions and recognize the pain and suffering that they have caused are believed to be less likely to reoffend. Parole board members tend to distrust prisoners who show signs of self-centredness, an inclination to blame other people and a lack of insight into the reasons for their own actions.

All these factors probably weighed against a parole application made by a woman whom I will identify as Marilyn, who was serving a life sentence for first-degree murder in the death of an RCMP officer during a shootout and hostage-taking in 1978. The sentence stipulated that she should not be eligible for parole before 25 years. The only reason that she was able to seek parole in 1994 was that she had benefited from legislation that allows first-degree murderers a judicial review of their parole eligibility after fifteen years of their sentence. This so-called "faint hope" clause in the law gives a jury the right to decide after hearing evidence in court whether to grant permission for the offender to apply for earlier parole. Many victims' advocates and proponents of harsh sentences for criminals characterize this provision as a "loophole" in the law and do not believe that murderers should have the right even to ask for more lenient treatment.

In Marilyn's case, a jury had ruled that she should be allowed to apply for parole, but that did not mean that she would automatically get it. She still had to persuade the parole board that she had earned her freedom and could safely return to society.

Marilyn and members of her family were angry when they realized that I had been given permission to observe her parole hearing. Until new legislation was introduced in 1992, such hearings were closed to the public, but anyone may now apply to attend specific board hearings and will usually be allowed to do so, providing they have a legitimate reason and obtain a security clearance to enter the penitentiaries where the hearings are held.

I was particularly interested in Marilyn's hearing because it was a case in which passions ran high. It was a crime with many victims that had caused lasting pain and grief, but it was also the case of a woman who was the victim of life-long abuse and had apparently become a different person through years of therapy and rehabilitative programs. I was curious to see how the National Parole Board would handle these sensitive issues.

A thick-set, middle-aged woman in a drab grey suit, Marilyn projected the image of an efficient, if somewhat overbearing, office manager as she rattled off a list of the computer programs that she had mastered during her seventeen years in jail. It was hard imagine her as a pill-popping prostitute, involved in sado-masochistic sex and extortion.

"I don't like the person I was seventeen years ago," said Marilyn, as she asked the man and two women sitting across the table to "try to see me as I am today."

If her trial had taken place today, Marilyn probably would not have been found guilty of first-degree murder, since it was her common-law husband who had fired the gun that killed one RCMP officer and injured two others, while the couple attempted to escape from an early morning raid on their motel room. Since then, the law has changed and as a party to the offence she would no longer be found guilty. She may also have had better luck in recent years explaining to a court that she was a victim of abuse, controlled by a vicious man who ordered her to threaten children with a gun while she helped him hold a family hostage in a subsequent stand-off with police.

Marilyn had already been allowed to visit her family on temporary absences. She was now applying either for full parole or day parole. Her case management officer reported that she had successfully completed all the programs specified on her correctional plan and had the support of her family. Police in the community where she intended to reside, had not objected to her release. The case management officer maintained that Marilyn no longer presented any risk to the public and recommended that she be granted full parole.

Before they would begin to consider Marilyn's future, the parole board members wanted to delve into her past. She was asked about her lifestyle at the time of her crimes, but she began her story many years earlier. She had been abused by her brother as a child, but had kept "his dirty little secret" until after she went to prison. When she tried to tell her parents, they beat her for telling stories. Her brother then beat her up for trying to snitch on him and raped her again. As a young adult, she was beaten up regularly by her alcoholic husband and would frequently be forced to leave home with her two young children to stay at her mother's house.

John, her partner in crime, showed up in her life at a particularly vulnerable time. Her mother had just died and her husband had threatened to kill her for the third or fourth time, wrecking their home in a drunken rage. John was "very charming, very debonair. He was all the things I didn't have in my life.

And he had little pills that seemed to solve everything," Marilyn explained to the board.

She ran away with John, who soon persuaded her to put her kids in a foster home and begin working as a prostitute. She said, "He had complete and utter control of my life. He convinced me that nobody else wanted me, that I was utterly stupid and my family wouldn't take me back." For several years, John and Marilyn led a transient lifestyle. He made money by writing fraudulent cheques and put her on the streets, "after he managed to isolate me from my family and everyone I knew." She said he physically abused her and "the bottom line was that he was going to kill me. When it got to the point where I said, 'Death is better than living with you,' he said, 'I know where your kids are.'"

The board members questioned Marilyn on her criminal record and police files. As is usual in such hearings, they wanted her to explain charges that were withdrawn and things that she was suspected of, as well as the crimes for which she was convicted. There was a stay of proceedings in a charge involving fraudulent cheques and a threatening charge, which Marilyn explained as a misunderstanding — she happened to have a knife in her hand from peeling potatoes while she was arguing with a neighbour.

Asked about an extortion charge, Marilyn told the board, "John ordered me to go to one of my clients and demand money." The board had additional information on their files and they wanted to know more about some photographs found in her possession. She explained that John was "part of, for want of a better term, the swingers movement in the 1970s." She said, "John had an extensive porno collection. He ordered me to pose for pictures. This was a client who asked me to take revealing pictures and gave me one."

Marilyn said her memory of the crime that put her in prison
for life was confused because she was injured by a police bullet
during their attempted escape and heavily sedated during her
subsequent hospital treatment. She said they were in a motel
room and the police came to the door. She assumed that it had
something to do with the rented car that they had failed to
return. Marilyn said she remembered going to the bathroom
area to put some clothes on. She said, "The next thing I knew
was that there were bullets all over the place. John was ordering
me to go to the vehicle. He was pointing a gun at me. He said,
'I'm leaving no witnesses.' I was scared and I wasn't ready to die."

Marilyn was shot in the back as they escaped and had very
hazy memories of the next few hours, during which the couple
took a family hostage. She said she remembered John giving
her a gun and instructing her not to let any of their hostages
move. She explained that she was afraid that John would kill the
whole family. "I remember thinking I've got to say something
so frightening to the kids that they won't move."

Board members were uneasy about Marilyn's hazy memories
of the crime and kept probing for more details. In their files,
police had recorded their suspicion that Marilyn had played a
far more active role than she was now prepared to admit. The
police files contained conjectures that would never be accepted as evidence in any court of law, yet they were freely used by
the board members, as they questioned Marilyn relentlessly.
They were especially interested in the fact that John had paid for
the motel room with the credit card of a man who had apparently been murdered. Marilyn explained that the man had been
a client of hers who liked sado-masochistic sex. The last time
she had seen him he was alive. She said she had bound his hands
and feet with a silk scarf during their sexual encounter, but had
not put the scarf around his neck. She had no idea how John
had obtained his credit card.

Explaining that she did not know what John's motives were,

Marilyn said, "He was in control. I did as he told me to do. I would have done what he told me with my last breath." All her life she had been controlled by other men, she said. "But now I can talk about what happened. I realize that I was the victim of some very sick men. My life has to be under my control. I can see warning signs of control or abuse. I can't be positive about what tomorrow will bring, but I know the warning signs. I will have the help of my children and parole officers. I know where help is. I hope to own my own business, but that's a pie in the sky dream. I'll probably find a job and struggle through until my old age pension. I hope along the way to get my own home."

When a board member told her that they had letters on file from victims and their families, Marilyn responded, "I became aware of just how vindictive and how angry they are. I see myself as one of John's victims."

She was reminded of the fact that the wife of the policeman who died was pregnant. She was told that one officer still has psychological problems and another had been forced to take a desk jobs. "Do you feel remorse?" a board member asked.

"I have a great deal of remorse. I still have nightmares about what happened. I feel a great deal of responsibility for having been there. If only I could turn back the clock and give those people their lives."

Marilyn was asked why she had used the word "vindictive" to describe the victims. She explained that one woman had been quoted in the press as saying that she would like to see Marilyn killed.

The surviving victims and their families would have liked to have an opportunity to appear before the board to oppose parole, Marilyn was told. She replied, "I can understand that they would like to express their opinions, but they don't know me today." Asked to explain how she has changed, she said, "I have a personal identity. I am not the shadow of someone else. I have my own views. I have a thought process."

Board member Jane Hackett took up the questioning. She wanted to understand more about why Marilyn had called the policeman's widow vindictive. Hackett suggested that the comment quoted in the newspaper was simply a reference to the fact that capital punishment had recently been abolished at the time of Marilyn's trial. Marilyn replied, "I can understand her feeling of loss. I don't have major resentment. I feel it was a vindictive statement. I can understand her feelings, that there is a great deal of anger and the anger will never go away."

Hackett observed, "There was teariness when you talked about John's abuse, but none of that when you talk about the victims and the terrible consequences of the crime. Do you ever think about the dead policeman?"

"I still have nightmares about him. I have talked about it and cried about it. I have no tears left."

Hackett persisted, "The word victim is sometimes a confusing one. You spend a lot of time talking about your own victimization."

"I have worked extensively with counsellors," Marilyn responded.

"You're very assertive today. Is that your normal way?" Hackett asked.

"It's quite possible that is what came out in therapy," replied Marilyn.

The board member told her that she felt there were other ways of handling emotions besides being assertive. She said that aggression can be unhealthy and observed that Marilyn's prison file noted that she had difficulty with other inmates and sometimes with staff.

"I was very verbally aggressive and demanding to people," Marilyn admitted. "It was probably what I learned, the example being John."

"You are almost constantly bringing the board to the conclusion that you want to come to," said Hackett. "I find it disturbing. I believe you're a tad controlling."

Marilyn conceded, "One of my major faults, I am told, is that I overexplain everything."

The board decided to deny Marilyn's parole application. It was a decision that evidently surprised staff at the Prison for Women, who were impressed with Marilyn's competence and her insight into her own problems. But her apparent lack of empathy toward her victims bothered the board members. They were also concerned that her therapy had concentrated exclusively on Marilyn's own experience as a victim of abuse. They felt that it had not examined her lifestyle during the period leading up to her crime. The possibility that she might have had some responsibility for her own behaviour had not apparently been considered by therapists.

Even though Marilyn's hearing had made her appear self-centred and unsympathetic, it was hard to see how she would present a genuine risk to society, living with her grown-up children and working at some office job. I was left wondering whether the board members' decision was based as much upon a rational appraisal of the risks as upon a feeling that they had about her attitudes and personality, a sense that she was just a little too smug in the face of the enormity of the crime for which society still held her responsible, even if she would not acknowledge her share of the blame.

The parole board also took a hard line with Elizabeth, an Ojibwa woman with a record for violent crimes, who had her statutory release revoked after being charged with theft and break and entry. She had broken into a liquor store and stolen a bottle of booze. Elizabeth said that she had made a mistake by trying to live at home as soon as she was released from jail. She said she would have been better off going to a halfway house where she could have been supervised. Now she was applying for release in order to go to a facility where there were programs for Native offenders.

"I had been incarcerated for two years, with no responsibilities, away from my kids. I went home to live with my mother and my kids. I had all these responsibilities," she explained to the board. "I ran into my daughter's father. He was harassing me. He was just a pest, coming to my mother's house, giving me a hard time, cutting me down and telling me I was an unfit mother. So I left and started drinking. I fell off the wagon. I was very foolish."

Board members told Elizabeth that her violent record associated with drinking and the new charges that had been laid since her release made her a poor risk for a new release. She tried to change their minds by elaborating on her previous explanation, "I feel that if I had been released to a halfway house, it would have been different. I left my daughter when she was two months old. I hadn't seen her since I was incarcerated. She was calling somebody else 'Mommy.' I missed two years out of my children's lives. When my daughter's father came round, bad memories came back. I was scared. I didn't want to be controlled by this man again, so I ran. Memories of beatings came back. He gave me a shove against the wall, so I just left. I drank to get away from him. I guess, I drank to cover the hurt. Even though I knew that if I didn't stop drinking, I was going to die."

A board member reminded Elizabeth that she had run away again, this time from a CSC guard while on an escorted temporary absence. She explained, "I had gone to see my dad at the hospital. I knew I was not going to see him again. I don't know what I was thinking. I just left the guards. I do have a drinking problem. It's a disease I have to live with for the rest of my life."

Elizabeth told the board that she realized that she had hurt someone very badly in the past, the victim of a violent assault committed while intoxicated. She said, "I don't think I could hurt anyone again after what happened."

The board members did not feel that they could take the risk of releasing her to the halfway house, where she had been hoping to benefit from counselling and Native programming.

At another hearing that I attended, the board did decide to give an offender another chance. This was the case of a man in his early 40s, with a long criminal record, mostly for property crimes, but with some assaults. Jim was what is known as "a rounder," a person who has associated with criminals and been in and out of jail most of his life. Like many offenders of his age, he had finally realized that he was wasting his life and had been making a determined effort to go straight.

The board was told that Jim had been doing well on day parole in a halfway house until he received a phone call from his former common-law wife, with whom he was not allowed to have any contact while on parole. She was an inmate at Prison for Women and she told him on the phone that she had just absconded while on a temporary absence.

"I knew the bullshit was going to start all over again as soon as Janet spoke on the phone. But I loved that woman very much," Jim told the board. He ran away with her and they hid for six months in a motel, where Jim did odd jobs for the manager who was a friend of his. Eventually, they were arrested after Janet got into a drunken fight with one of her women friends, who spitefully turned them in to police.

"I'm finished with crime," Jim told the parole board. "When I was on the run, I wanted to get caught. I did not turn myself in because, in a way, I was scared. Last time I was in jail, I testified against some other inmates because I didn't want to do a six-year sentence and then I got piped on the back of the head. And Janet said she wanted to go back on the street, back to prostitution and cocaine. I tried to rescue her from that."

A board member asked, "If you think Janet is in trouble again, can you say no?"

"Next time, I'll rat on her," Jim replied.

One of the board members told me afterward that they had information on their files indicating that Janet would remain in prison for a substantial period of time. This factor influenced their decision, though they did not share that information with Jim. When he was told that he would be granted a new parole, Jim still wanted to apologize for his past behaviour. He said, "I'm very sorry I let you people down."

The board chairperson replied, "No, you let yourself down. If people like you didn't come back every once in a while, we wouldn't have any work."

It is expected that some prisoners will return to jail, while others may have a fighting chance of remaining in the community. Some members of the public would like assurances from the parole board that offenders who pose any risk to society will never be released. But the parole board does not deal with certainties. It is constantly forced to weigh probabilities and degrees of risk. When board members err on the side of caution by not releasing serious offenders on parole, they protect themselves from bad publicity, but society may not, in the long run, be protected. Society is not safe from offenders unless they can get free of the revolving doors of the justice system and succeed in living peacefully in society. To do that, most of the more serious offenders need help. The supervision and support that parole officers can provide to them in the community is often their best and only hope.

16

OFFENDERS ON THE STREET

The entertainment bureau had no idea that the charming young man hired to deliver "gorillagrams" had recently been released from prison, where he had served a sentence for raping women at knifepoint while wearing a balaclava. The masked rapist probably could have kept his job, without anyone being any the wiser, were it not for the fact that he was still under the supervision of parole officers. He had been set free on statutory release, after serving two-thirds of his sentence, instead of being detained until it expired, at which time he could have slipped back into the community and vanished without a trace.

Henry, the parole officer who told me about this case, was one of many I interviewed in various cities across Canada. He explained that his suspicions had not been aroused when he had first been told about the offender's new job, because he had understood that the man would be working in the office, preparing party supplies and novelty items. By the time Henry found out about the gorillagrams, the convicted rapist already had his gorilla suit and mask in the back of his van and was ready to start doing deliveries.

The offender had done well in therapy while in jail and had developed what psychologists describe as "pro-social values." Henry said he found the man a little too smooth and too "pro-social."

When Henry explained that it was not acceptable for a convicted rapist to deliver gorillagrams, the offender argued that there was not any realistic danger of him raping anyone wearing a disguise that would be so easily traceable. He suggested to the parole officer that he was really just "protecting his ass."

Henry readily admitted, "Yes, I was mainly concerned about the media getting hold of it."

The offender was given two choices: either he told his boss that he was not able to deliver the novelty telegrams, or Henry would inform the company of the man's criminal background, with the probable result that he would be fired. In the meantime, Henry warned the man, "If there is any rape perpetrated by a guy in a gorilla suit, the police will know who to look for."

Henry told me that he felt uneasy about the case, though he did not have any basis for suspending his client's statutory release. On the contrary, the offender had been doing what he was supposed to do: look for work and find a job. Finding and keeping steady employment are considered to be key elements in the rehabilitation of offenders. He was also planning to further his education by attending evening classes at a community college. Henry could hardly discourage such a positive initiative, but he was also aware that a college campus could be an ideal stalking ground for a predatory rapist and he was planning to warn the campus police to keep an eye on his client.

In this case, like many of the cases in Henry's files, it seemed that every opportunity for the offender's rehabilitation also entailed a further risk to the public. Yet the risk could be even greater if the offender lost his job and gave up his school plans. He could easily fall into a downward spiral that would probably entail breaking up with a girlfriend who currently appeared to be keeping him in line. Then it would be almost a relief to Henry if the offender started drinking, taking drugs or acting out in other ways that would warrant sending him back to jail. After that he would no longer be Henry's responsibility, but the public would not be any safer, since the prisoner would soon be released and free to do whatever he wanted without any interference from a parole officer.

Parole officers are employed by the Correctional Service of Canada, not the parole board, which is only responsible for conducting parole hearings and making decisions about the release of prisoners. Once prisoners have been let out on parole or statutory release, it is the job of parole officers to monitor their activities in the community. They attempt to ensure that offenders needs are met with whatever programs or services are available. They are continually engaged in a delicate balancing act, as they assess opportunities, anticipate problems and weigh the risks involved.

Supervising offenders in the community is a difficult and risky enterprise, but CSC is trying to do it very cheaply. About 40 per cent of the offenders under the care of the correctional service are usually out in the community on some form of conditional release. But only 13 per cent of the total CSC budget is spent on supervising them.

Overworked parole officers with large case loads struggle to deal with the multiple problems of damaged and sometimes dangerous offenders. The correctional service has limited funds for providing rehabilitative programs to offenders on parole and the communities themselves often have little to offer, particularly at a time when health and social services budgets are being cut. Offenders face an uphill battle in returning to a community that has few resources available to them and little sympathy for their plight.

U.S. author Jonathan Simon, a law professor at the University of Miami, has described the best parole officers as having "something like night vision. They perceive distinctions in the danger posed by different people whose situations look indistinguishably grim to most of us."

As I accompanied Henry and his partner, Elaine, into a

dilapidated downtown rooming house on a visit to a client, it struck me that some prisoners have far less when they return to the community than they had in jail. The impression was confirmed when we entered a small room, lit by a bare light bulb, where Don, a short pudgy man in his mid-thirties, sat on his bed.

"I've got a room," Don said flatly and that was apparently all he had. The fridge was completely empty and the shelves were bare except for a few religious pamphlets. A few shabby clothes were hanging or piled in an open closet. The only bright object in the room was a red woolen scarf, hanging on the back of an upright chair.

"I found a scarf on the street," said Don. He was one of the many mentally challenged people who found their way into the prison system after governments began closing mental health institutions, supposedly returning inmates to the community, but in reality just abandoning them on the street.

As one CSC administrator lamented, "Society is not willing to address problems in the community with programs and policies that negate using the criminal justice system which is the most expensive way of managing problems." Mentally challenged people would be far less likely to end up in prison if the community was able to provide them with adequate housing, supervision and treatment. The cost of such programs would be far less than the $48,000 or more a year that it costs to keep offenders behind bars. But many people like Don seldom have adequate accommodation, unless they are in jail, and only find the community supervision and treatment that they need during the brief periods when they are on parole.

Don's criminal record mostly involved non-violent property crimes and nuisance offences. He was placed in a prison that housed mainly sex offenders, because he was an "inadequate" offender, who would be picked on by other inmates. During his most recent parole, he had acquired a camera and was seen wandering along a city street taking photographs of women. His explanation for this was that being with sex offenders had rubbed off on him. He was subjected to a series of tests that revealed no sexual deviancy, so he was released again on parole, but parole officers were trying to keep a close eye on him.

Don said he was frightened of his welfare worker. He thought she had it in for him. Elaine had arranged for him to see a therapist and get involved in a program group, but he said he was nervous about being probed and analysed. He also wasn't sure that he would be able to find his way to the appointment. Elaine tried to reassure him and said she would give him a ride.

Elaine and Henry were part of a unit that provides intensive supervision to high-risk offenders. Most of their clients were violent or sexual offenders. Some, like Don, needed close supervision more because their needs were so great than because of the risk they posed. CSC views needs and risks as interconnected. Many offenders need counselling or therapy to deal with problems that lead them into crime, while anyone is more likely to survive in society when basic needs for food, shelter, employment or other income are satisfied.

In order to see that clients' needs are met, parole officers are expected to work with offenders, their families, community agencies, employers, health and social services, halfway houses, CSC staff and other available resources. These contacts can also be helpful in managing the risks that offenders present, since parole officers can, for example, check up to see how a client is getting on in therapy or find out from family members if there are any problems at home.

Most parole officers have a case load of 25 to 35 offenders, whom they see, at best, once a week. Their clients are sometimes a random mix of offenders on parole and statutory release. About half of all offenders supervised by parole officers have been convicted of non-violent crimes, another quarter have been serving time for robbery, while the remaining quarter committed violent crimes or sex offences.

In intensive supervision units, the parole officers are usually each responsible for about a dozen clients, whom they contact several times a week, sometimes visiting their homes or their workplaces. I accompanied Elaine and Henry on evening "curfew checks," in which they were dropping in on some of their clients unexpectedly. The reason parole officers conduct their curfew checks in pairs was quite apparent to me when we entered the side door of an old five-storey walk-up apartment building looking for a schizophrenic offender whose crimes had included biting into a dead body after breaking into a funeral parlour. The front door had been locked and there was no paging system. Henry did not know how to get to his client's apartment from the side door and there were no lights in the corridor. The parole officers asked directions from two men who smelled of alcohol and belligerently indicated that they neither knew nor cared. Henry, who was carrying a heavy police flashlight that could easily double as a weapon, wanted to continue the search, but his partner was thoroughly spooked and insisted that they give up.

Many offenders released on parole are placed in halfway houses where staff are on hand to monitor their comings and goings, while providing them with help in dealing with the many problems that newly released offenders face. Ironically, the most high-risk offenders are often the ones who do not end up in halfway houses. These are people who have been held in jail until their statutory release date.

Many halfway houses will not take them, especially if they are not well motivated to stay away from drugs, alcohol and crime. Some offenders on statutory release may be accepted at a halfway house and choose to stay there or be ordered to do so by the parole board. Most of them, however, end up in rooming houses or low-rental apartments, usually in the seedier parts of town. Taverns frequented by prostitutes, drug dealers and other ex-convicts are often the only places where they believe they will find warmth, companionship and friendly advice.

"We could do more with these guys, if we had more resources," said the supervisor of the unit where Henry and Elaine worked. "We need resources in the community. It's a community prob- lem, not just a correctional problem. Even when we have con- tracts with psychologists or psychiatrists, they get booked up quickly. When there's a crisis, the next available appointment may be two or three weeks away. Everybody views this clien- tele as the bottom of the barrel. They don't use community ser- vices well. They don't have the patience to wait in line and don't know where to go. You've got to realize that they're criminals and not the kind of people you want to move into your house."

Nevertheless, Henry told me that he actually liked working with the high-risk offenders better than with residents of a half- way house where he worked previously. They were mostly white- collar criminals. Henry said, "I found them one of the most difficult groups to deal with, especially the disbarred lawyers. They were very litigious, very arrogant and in some instances, didn't think they had done anything wrong. They were person- able and manipulative. They used to con the other convicts, as well as the parole officers. I'd much rather deal with a bank robber or even a drug dealer."

We visited another man who lived in a rooming house much like Don's, but whose surroundings seemed positively luxurious in comparison. Steve had a black-and-white television and books on his shelves. A violent offender whose crimes were all associated with alcohol and drugs, Steve spoke with nervous energy about his busy schedule that included a full-time job, Alcoholics Anonymous meetings, group therapy sessions and activities with a Christian group that he had joined. Henry asked him if he was still taking his medication, and he assured the parole officer that he was doing so.

Steve told me that he felt optimistic about being able to stay away from crime. He said he had "screwed up" on his previous release from jail, because all the programs in which he was involved ended once his sentence was over and he was no longer on parole. This time, he said, he would be able to keep up his involvement with voluntary activities like AA and the Christian group, which was run by another ex-offender.

In a highrise apartment building, we visited a young crack addict who had recently been released from jail and only had a few weeks to go before his warrant expired. At that point he would no longer be the responsibility of parole officers, but it remained to be seen whether he would last that long. He was living with his girlfriend and her children. There were several other young people in the apartment, who left as soon as we arrived. Henry later told me that parole officers are often in more danger from their clients' friends than from the clients themselves, especially if one walks in on a party where people are taking drugs.

Mike, the crack addict, lolled on a sofa, but kept fidgeting continually as he talked non-stop about his success in staying off drugs and in overcoming the impulsiveness that had got him into trouble in the past. When Henry told him that he was going to ask him to come to the office for a drug test in a few days, Mike said that was no problem, but asked "out of interest" how long alcohol takes to pass through one's system.

Mike was awaiting trial on a new charge involving an alleged assault on a police officer and escape from custody. He wanted to discuss his case with the parole officers, explaining that he was merely struggling to take off his jacket and never got far enough away from the officers to escape. He said he had heard the police conspiring to fabricate evidence, and he was planning to call each of them to the witness stand in the hope that one of them would tell the truth. Henry told him he wasn't interested in talking about this case as it would come to trial long after Mike's warrant expiry date, when he would no longer be on statutory release. Elaine later told me that she was planning to warn the police officers about Mike's allegations.

As we were leaving the building, Henry commented that the guy was stupid. Elaine said she once gave him some positive reinforcement, and he had responded well to the suggestion that he did have some hidden talents. Henry said cases like Mike's were always a problem, since he knew the guy was going to get into trouble sooner or later. The only question was whether he could be persuaded to stay out of trouble until he was off Henry's case load. "Even if we're only supervising a guy for two days. If the guy commits a murder, we're going to have to wear it," Henry explained.

Cooperation with police is, of course, crucial for managing offenders risks. Police must become involved if an offender is to be arrested for breach of parole violation or when a parole officer anticipates a risk to public safety. It can also be useful for both police and parole officers to share information and suspicions about individual offenders. In some communities, police have regular meetings with parole officers, while in others, contacts are on a more informal basis.

Some parole officers told me that they do not get as much cooperation from police as they would like. They said police officers tend to regard parole violations as low-priority matters. "We'll call police, but it's sometimes an hour before they can arrest the guy," explained Henry. "I'll have the guy in my office and try to keep him talking till the police show up. But there's only so much I can say. You run out of topics. The guys go home before the police come, and we can't stop them."

Henry told me that outstanding warrants for parole violations are often ignored because police say they do not have the manpower to track people down. He said, "We can have strong suspicions that an offender is up to something. But tell the police and they laugh at you. They say, 'We should be out there watching these guys, but we don't have the resources.'"

Elaine described the next client whom we were due to see

as "a puke." She volunteered to wait in the car, saying that there wouldn't be room for the three of us in Ray's roach-infested one-room apartment. As we were ascending a narrow creaky staircase, Henry explained that Ray had served a prison sentence for sexual assault charges arising from his incestuous relationship with two daughters, who were now in their twenties. He was living with a stripper, crack addict and sometime hooker, who was about the same age as his daughters.

Ray was a robust man with a sallow complexion, greying hair, a mustache and thick stubble on his unshaven chin. He stood assertively in the centre of the small, smoky room, as he told Henry a complicated story about an encounter with police. Ray said police stopped his car after he picked up his girlfriend outside the bar where she was dancing. The police thought she was a "working girl" and Ray had a hard time convincing them that they lived together. He said the police officer gave him a ticket for oil emissions from his car, but he was going to fight it in court.

Ray was presumably worried that Henry would get a different version of the story from police. His manner in telling the story was that of a man who likes to believe that he is in control, a role that probably impressed only his girlfriend. She was a thin, unhealthy-looking woman, who sat twitching and trembling on the bed. She chuckled to herself occasionally, apparently responding to voices within, but took an interest in the conversation when she heard the name of the tavern where she danced. She repeated the name with pride, apparently believing that it was prestigious to be working there.

Henry told me later that Ray seemed to be staying sober and crime free. He said there was no chance of him committing incest again, as his children were all grown up. Henry said, "Undoubtedly, Ray could get nasty with his girlfriend or another woman and get a sexual assault charge in future. But he's not presently a huge concern."

Sex offenders are generally less likely to reoffend than most other inmates, but they are always a worry for parole officers as for the public at large. Henry explained that he was always less concerned about "rounders," the regular criminals involved in robberies and various other offences, even though they might freely admit that they would commit more crimes because it is what they do for a living. He said, "With the rounders, if they go offside, I'm not going to be on the inquest stand. But I tend to have more concern around sex offenders. If red flags go up, I move real quick because if they do reoffend, there's going to be blood flying."

A handful of sex offenders may be sadistic psychopaths too dangerous ever to be safely allowed on the street. Many more are persistent pedophiles or other sexual deviants who either refuse treatment or prove incapable of controlling their problems. But the majority can live in the community and keep their problems under control, given the right kind of treatment and support. There is always a danger, however, that a psychopath has conned the parole board and therapists, that a pedophile is falling away from his treatment plan, or that a personal crisis has sent an angry rapist spiralling into his crime cycle. That is why parole officers must attempt to monitor every aspect of sex offenders' lives.

A parole officer's duties always lie somewhere between those of a cop and a social worker. Parole officers working with the Vancouver sex offender unit act as co-facilitators in group therapy sessions. They become intimately involved in their clients personal problems, but they are still watching them with a wary eye. At regular meetings, attended by police and parole board representatives, parole officers discuss their concerns and observations about every case. For example, a parole officer noticed that one offender seemed to be supportive of others at group therapy sessions, but also sometimes put other offenders down. His home life seemed stable and he was happy in his job. He was possibly going to be promoted to a management position, but that would mean that he would be responsible for hiring and firing others, including women. According to his files, he was once diagnosed as having psychopathic characteristics. Another parole officer happened to notice him having coffee with one of the other offenders after a group session. She said that the two men were looking women up and down in a very deliberate manner, "really checking them out." It was not, yet, a major concern, but something to keep on top of, just in case.

People involved with the Vancouver program explained to me that it works because it combines therapy, social work and control. Clients might fool their therapist or a parole officer individually, but are much less likely to fool a group of people working in consort. Parole officer Marie Resanovic said personal intervention by parole officers is also crucial. All offenders have her pager number and can call her at any time if they need help, she said, explaining that she is prepared to go beyond the call of duty because she does not want to see any more victims: "I have a guy who phones me to say, 'I don't have deviant fantasies any more.' He was one of the most difficult cases we ever had."

She said another client presented such high risks that everyone involved in the program was convinced that he should have been kept in prison until his warrant expired. She said, "Everybody made a bet that he would reoffend, but he hasn't. He has been saying, 'Can I please stay with you?'"

The problem is that the program is no longer available for offenders after they reach their warrant expiry date. Then, if they want to see a therapist, they have to pay for it. Few of them can afford to do that. Without the structure and support of the group and staff, many of them are likely to relapse into crime. Resanovic said, "I would like to see them in a program like this until the day they die."

The federal auditor general's 1994 report cited the British Columbia community sex offender program as an example of effective programming: "Many professionals believe that this type of intervention and supervision is necessary for this group of offenders. In some of the other offices, the management of sex offenders is determined more by available resources than by minimum professional practice requirements."

The report made a similar point about intensive supervision programs for high-risk offenders: "Similarly, many, but not all, regions have team supervision or intensive supervision units designed specifically to manage high-risk offenders. Once assigned to one of those units, an offender can be seen two or three times a week. However, an offender with a similar profile in another area may be seen only once a month."

The federal auditor was concerned that CSC's scarce resources were being distributed unevenly. He warned, "The risk to the public may be greater in those areas with relatively fewer resources." The report observed, "Supervision in the community is the final link in the chain that makes up the Canadian justice system. It is the last point at which the system can directly influence or control offenders. It is also the point at which offenders are the least separated from the public and therefore present the greatest risk to society. For that reason, it is crucial that the supervision of offenders in the community be managed well. We found, however, that Service management is not paying enough attention to this area of corrections."

The auditor general noted that one reason for this lack of attention is that CSC did not take over responsibility for community supervision of offenders until 1977. Before that, parole officers were employed by an independent National Parole Service. Many CSC administrators have "an institutional mindset" and most of the funds available are spent on maintaining the costly prisons.

As more and more people are sent to prison, there is a pressure to spend more on penitentiaries. Public pressure is also making officials more cautious about releasing offenders on parole. While prisons are overcrowded, some community residences are half empty. Community programs are being cut, and many parole officers are finding that their workloads no longer allow them to do what they believe is an adequate job. Like other CSC employees, they also complain about being overwhelmed by the paperwork and the masses of information that they are required to negotiate in order to meet the requirements of CSC's computerized offender management system. As one parole officer put it, "We have to justify every move on paper instead of going out and finding the son of a bitch and seeing whom he's hanging out with today."

Some of the worst cases, those that pose the greatest risk to society, do not even find their way to the parole office. These are prisoners who have been denied full parole and have been forced to remain in jail until their statutory release date. Don Menzies, an administrator with the Vancouver District Parole Office, said that prisoners released on a Friday are likely to go astray immediately. "They want to get a fix, get laid and have a drink. The last place they're going to come is the parole office. You can't expect anybody to survive when they're released from maximum security directly onto the street. They are inevitably the worst cases, who have no resources in the community, have not participated in programming. They're belligerent and isolated. There's no point in trying to set anything up for him. He has a drink, a fix and a screw, then goes right back inside again."

Murderers sentenced to life imprisonment can be kept in jail until they die, if necessary. So can persistent violent criminals who are designated as dangerous offenders at a special sentencing hearing held immediately after they have been convicted. But most offenders have to be let out of jail eventually and these include many violent, dangerous or volatile people. A few high-risk offenders, judged likely to commit further crimes involving serious injury, may be detained in prison until their sentences expire. As a result, when they do get out, it is without the benefit of any help from parole officers or therapy programs. They can go where they choose and do what they like, with no parole officers watching them.

When 50-year-old sex offender Wray Budreo proclaimed in a television interview, "I am not a monster," there was nothing about his appearance that could possibly reassure anyone. His head was completely covered by a woollen mask, with one narrow slit that revealed only his eyes and the bridge of his nose. The mask was patterned in a brown hunting camouflage, appropriate symbolism, perhaps, for a man who had just been released from Kingston Penitentiary, hiding in the trunk of a police car, while protesters swung nooses in the streets. But the hunting camouflage also served as a reminder that Budreo was a predator, a convicted pedophile with a history of seeking out children to satisfy his deviant desires.

Budreo was released from prison on November 18, 1994, the very last day of a six-year sentence for sexually molesting three young boys. A self-described "child diddler," Budreo had been convicted of more than twenty sex crimes over the previous 30 years. He had never used a weapon, threatened children or physically harmed them. His victims were vulnerable kids, aged from seven to seventeen — at least two of them mentally challenged — whom he would pay to act out his sado-masochistic fantasies of torture and death. Apparently unaware of the lifelong psychological harm that he may have caused his victims, he once told a parole board that he did not think he was hurting them, because "to them they were just playing a game."

In 1992, the National Parole Board decided that Budreo was not a high enough risk to the public to warrant his being detained until the end of his sentence. This decision set a process in motion that would have allowed him to leave the prison on statutory release after serving two-thirds of his sentence. The parole board believed at that time that he would benefit from a treatment program at a community residential centre, where he would receive counselling and supervision from CSC staff.

Budreo told the board that he was "a different person," after receiving treatment for pedophilia and alcohol abuse and becoming a "born again" Christian. Continued treatment and good behaviour would be conditions of his release, during the last two years of his sentence, and he could have been returned to the prison if he failed to comply.

Before Budreo could be released, however, an internal CSC document criticizing the board's decision was leaked to the media. The memo stated that his previous offences against young boys occurred while he was on probation, involved with a therapist and taking medication prescribed to reduce his sex drive. It stated that these offences were part of a consistent pattern which began in 1963.

A group representing victims of child abuse mounted a vigorous campaign against Budreo's release. The National Parole Board responded by conducting two further hearings which reversed their earlier decision and ordered that Budreo remain behind bars until the end of his sentence.

The parole board's change of mind was applauded by members of a child advocacy group who were demonstrating outside the prison while the hearing took place. But prison welfare advocates maintained that the decision would merely increase the risk that Budreo would eventually pose. By forcing Budreo to remain in prison until the very last day, the system was losing its opportunity to give him treatment and supervision in the community. When he left, two years later, he would be free to vanish without a trace.

The same protesters were back outside the prison gates when Budreo was due to leave in November 1994. He fled to Peterborough, where he hoped to make his fresh start, but residents soon found out where he was living. "I'm scared, exhausted and striving to the utmost limit of my ability just to make a start," he told a reporter at the small press conference that he convened on the day after his release, "I'm getting sick and tired of running. I just want to become a working, constructive member of society." Budreo explained that he was taking drugs to reduce his sexual desire and showed reporters a letter written by a therapist a few days before his release from prison. The letter stated, "Clinically, Mr. Budreo is alert, rational and very firm in his resolve to avoid future lawbreaking." It remained to be seen how long Budreo's resolve would last and whether it was strong enough to survive in circumstances where he had no support or supervision and was being forced underground by public anger and fear.

For the protestors who opposed Budreo's release, his case was an example of the need for legislation to keep potentially dangerous sexual predators behind bars after their sentences expire. An inquest into the death of eleven-year-old Christopher Stephenson, murdered by pedophile Joseph Fredericks while he was on statutory release, had recently recommended such a law, which could be modelled on one already in place in Washington State. This recommendation was vigorously opposed by civil libertarians since it involved keeping people in jail after they had supposedly paid their dues to society by completing their court-ordered sentences. It also meant keeping people in jail for something they might do in future, rather than what they had already done.

Ironically, the Budreo case could be seen as an argument for not enacting such a law. If there was a sexual predator law in place, authorities may well have succumbed to pressure from the protesters who wanted Budreo locked up forever. Yet this was a man who had never used a weapon or even threatened his victims. Even though Budreo's crimes were disgusting and psychologically damaging to their victims, they were not as serious as those of hundreds of other criminals whose victims have been tortured, raped, mutilated and killed. Henry, the parole officer who introduced me to some of his clients, told me, "I have about twelve guys on my case load that make Wray

Budreo look like Mother Theresa."

Jim Stephenson, Christopher's father, who had been campaigning for a sexual predators law, told the *Toronto Star*, "At the risk of creating hysteria, I believe there are bigger fish to catch. He is not the worst of the bunch. That's small comfort to parents whose children have been sexually assaulted, but Budreo is not a Joseph Fredericks." Then, with a comment that might make anyone concerned about civil liberties a trifle uneasy, Stephenson added, "Let's deal with the most violent predators. Let's get the legislation in place. Then we can widen the net to deal with men like Budreo."

Currently, the correctional system has no right to keep people in custody after their sentences expire, unless they can be declared insane and confined in a psychiatric hospital. CSC does sometimes alert police when a potentially dangerous or troublesome offender is being released. Police forces in various jurisdictions have in turn taken it upon themselves to warn the public.

Often the subject of such warnings has been a pedophile with limited intelligence, who has failed to benefit from treatment in prison, either because of lack of insight into his own problems or because he was not able to understand the programs. Members of the public sometimes respond with panic and rage. In Edmonton, Alberta, a brain-damaged pedophile, released from a five-year sentence for crimes against children under five, attempted to kill himself after he had been named in the local media. Neighbourhood residents picketed his apartment building. A newspaper ran a photograph of someone erecting a sign bearing the slogan: "Apartment #12: The Place of Satan." The sign depicted a man with a noose around his neck and the also bore the inscription: "Go ahead. Hang Yourself. You deserve it."

Pedophiles and other sex offenders are most likely to avoid reoffending if they find some stable situation in the community, where they can get appropriate programs and have a network of people watching out for them. It is counter-productive to force them to run and hide, making them distrust all community agencies and making them think that they are condemned whether they commit a crime or not.

Many of the offenders from whom we have most to fear were themselves victims of childhood violence and abuse. The pain that distorted their desires and feeds their anger may resurface under stress. When they are placed under pressure, they are more likely to regress into their cycle of crime. Some of these people may indeed behave like monsters. But they are monsters that society has created and our own fears may make them worse.

It is obviously important to monitor high-risk ex-offenders where possible, but the public will be better protected if offenders have some incentive and encouragement to stay away from crime. Rather than hound them out of their homes, it would make sense for people to accept offenders into the community with offers of support and practical help, while at the same time remaining wary and vigilant. Society as a whole would be better protected if community treatment programs were available for all who need them. The public would also be far safer if adequate accommodation, employment opportunities and social service support were available, not only to ex-offenders, but to potential future offenders, including children who live in poverty and suffer from abuse. We often demonize offenders and treat them as if they have crawled out of hell to haunt us. But it is hard to recognize our own communal responsibility for crime and criminals.

17

THE ILLUSION
OF SAFETY

My journey through Canada's prison system left me somewhat stunned and deeply distressed. It had been a whistle-stop tour of the most horrific and degrading environments I had ever encountered. Never before had I seen so much anger, cynicism and despair. It was almost equally disturbing to learn about the distorted values and anti-social culture that prisoners adopt in order to survive in jail.

At the same time, I had met many confused, disturbed or remorseful individuals struggling to turn their lives around. Dedicated staff members extolled the virtues of well-designed programs and talked about transforming the negative culture of prisons. Administrators assured me that state-of-the-art assessment procedures and computerized databases were helping to identify prisoners' problems, monitor their treatment and make better decisions regarding release. These efforts often seemed hopeless, however, in a system that is overwhelmed by problems: the enormous personal problems that prisoners bring to jail, the poisonous influences in the prison environment and the overcrowding that compromises every initiative. It is hard to be optimistic about prisoners' prospects of rehabilitation in such circumstances, especially when one considers the lack of resources and programs to help offenders in the community after their release.

My research left me perplexed by many complex issues and seemingly irresolvable dilemmas. No one had been able to tell me what society should do with dangerous offenders who have not yet committed serious enough crimes to keep them in jail for life. Nobody knew how well sex offender treatment programs work. It appeared impossible to say how much non-violent offenders benefited from programs and whether the benefits outweighed the harm caused by prison violence, drugs, intimidation and fear. There often seemed to be no way of knowing whether it was safer to release offenders on parole or keep them in jail until the very last day of their sentences.

"People on the outside have no idea what these places are like," I was told continually, by guards and administrators, as well as prisoners.

Society relies on prisons to provide protection from dangerous criminals. Many people expect prisons to make their communities safe and see tougher sentences as a way of reducing crime. Yet there is little public discussion of what prison sentences are supposed to achieve and whether they work. It is often accepted, almost as an article of faith, that you send criminals to jail when you catch them and that is an end in itself. One seldom hears people even pose the question of whether prisoners will be more or less of a threat to society when they are let out. There can be no doubt that prisons protect the public from a handful of offenders who are judged to be too dangerous ever to release, but we need to discuss what the correctional system does to or for the overwhelming majority of convicted criminals who will return to society sooner or later.

We have to consider why we send people to prison, and examine whether prisons make us safer. Although the prison system has been seen as a failure for more than 150 years, little has changed from the time when Kingston Penitentiary was first built. Judges still impose prison sentences for purposes of punishment, rehabilitation and deterrence. Prison sentences are also supposed to protect the public by keeping criminals off the streets.

The idea that prison sentences act as a deterrent is based on the assumption that criminals make a rational decision, weighing the consequences of their acts, before committing crimes. Violent offenders I met in prison appeared to be governed not by reason, but by alcohol, drugs, inexplicable anger, impulsive aggression, deviant desires and a variety of barely understood mental health problems. Those offenders who were perhaps capable of planning their crimes and exercising self-control told me that they never believed that they would get caught and it was no big deal for them to go to jail anyway.

Research on the effectiveness of deterrents has shown that they have some impact on would-be white-collar criminals and people who might be tempted to drive under the influence of alcohol, but do not impinge upon violent crime rates. International studies have shown, for example, that abolition or reinstatement of the death penalty usually has no significant impact on murder rates. A U.K. study showed that exemplary sentences of twenty years for mugging, handed down by judges in one major city, resulted in no reduction in street crimes, but that a policy of clamping cars did deter people from parking illegally.

In the past, prisons have not been very good at rehabilitating people, but CSC officials believe that their new programs can work. These programs attempt to address the specific problems that have apparently led individual offenders to commit crimes. The programs are targeted to individual needs that are identified during the intake assessment process. But overcrowding in the system makes it difficult for staff to deliver these programs effectively. Their efforts are also undermined by drugs, violence and other negative influences in the prison environment. Prison has the effect of making offenders overly dependent on others, but also anti-social and paranoid, too passive in some respects and too aggressive in others. While some prisoners may benefit from programs, others are less able to fit into society when they leave prison than they were when they arrived.

My discussions with some older offenders and parole officers made me realize that a long prison term can have a debilitating effect on some people, while turning others into walking time bombs. Ex-offenders described how they embarrassed themselves in public as the habit of years in the penitentiary led them to stand in front of doors waiting for a guard to open them by remote control. Others talked about drawing weapons and making death threats when someone jostled them on the street, because in prison, that is what you have to do to stay alive. These are people who have learned how to survive in jail but have forgotten how to live in society. They are not scared of robbing a bank and going back to prison, but they do not know how to buy groceries in a store and are terrified by the choices offered on the menu of the average restaurant.

Prison psychiatrist George Scott's observations, recorded in his 1982 memoirs, are still valid for some offenders today. He wrote: "As I look back over the years, I marvel at the strength and resistance of a person who can handle ten to twenty years in a penitentiary and return to society with even modest motivation and hope of finding a place for himself."

Keeping dangerous or troublesome individuals off the street can be effective for as long as they stay off the street, but it is an extremely expensive option. The fact that it costs up to $80,000 a year to keep an offender in maximum security is sometimes offered as a justification for capital punishment, but studies conducted in the United States have found that the costs of legal processes and appeals can actually make it more expensive to kill offenders than to warehouse them for life. Capital punishment does not offer any solutions to the problems of the Canadian prison system, given that it has been proven not to work as a deterrent and leaves no opportunity to rectify the mistakes that the justice system is prone to make.

There may be no alternative but to keep dangerous offenders in jail for as long as possible when they have been identified as being a clear threat to public safety, and there seems to be no way of treating them or controlling them in the community. But the correctional system and psychiatrists are not very good at predicting who will be dangerous in future. They tend to protect themselves by overestimating the risks that individual offenders might present. It is almost inevitable that many people would be kept in prison unjustly and unnecessarily if prison or parole officials are given the power and responsibility to keep dangerous offenders in prison after their court-imposed sentences expire.

Contrary to popular belief, putting more people in jail and keeping them there longer does very little to reduce crime. There are too many potentially violent people at large in the community and not enough of them can be identified or stopped before it is too late. Dramatic increases in prison populations in the United States have not resulted in any appreciable reduction in crime rates. A U.S. National Research Council report in 1993 found that the average amount of prison time served for each violent crime roughly tripled between 1975 and 1989, but "the increase in severity of punishment had no demonstrable effect on deterring crime." A British government report, also in 1993, estimated that a 25 per cent increase in the prison population would result in only a 1 per cent reduction in crime.

The strongest justification for prison sentences is, perhaps, the most primitive one. People who hurt others and break our community's rules have to be punished. This is a premise that most people would accept. Demands for tougher punishments and harsher conditions in prison are usually justified on the grounds that they would deter criminals. But deterrents are not effective and it is therefore important to recognize that excessive punishments can serve no purpose other than revenge. Harsh conditions and long sentences have the effect of making criminals believe that they are victims of a cruel justice system, instead of reflecting upon their own guilt. Many of them were victims of sexual abuse and family violence during their childhood; aggressive treatment at the hands of authority tends to accentuate their belief in the righteousness of their own rage.

Having spent time with victims of violent crime, I have the upmost respect for their demands that perpetrators be made to pay for the suffering they caused. Nevertheless, my contact with prisoners who have served time in the Special Handling Units, the harshest prisons in Canada, makes me very uneasy about encountering former inmates on the street. Society originally abandoned harsh punishments because they made offenders more incorrigible and more dangerous. Returning to them now would probably increase the risk to public safety. In an article in a British newspaper in January 1995, a prisoner quoted a fellow inmate as saying, "Before you take revenge, dig your own grave," and then went on to warn readers, "Society would do well to take account of this sound advice when deciding what it wants from prisons and prisoners."

It is probably not revenge that most citizens seek from the prison system, but protection. In spite of all evidence to the contrary, people want to believe that prisons can solve the problem of crime. The consensus of correctional officials and criminologists, however, is that prisons cannot make the public safe from crime. Many politicians have also come to realize that building more prisons is not the answer. Former progressive conservative MP and ex-RCMP officer Bob Horner's 1993 Canadian parliamentary committee on crime prevention was convinced that "threats to the safety and security of Canadians will not be abated by hiring more police officers and building more prisons." Federal Justice Minister Allan Rock told the Empire Club of Toronto in March 1995, "If longer sentences and bigger prisons were the answer to community safety, then the United States of America would be nirvana."

Rock and the members of Horner's committee recognized

that Canadians can never be safe from crime as long as communities continue to produce the problems that give rise to crime. As Rock put it, "Crime prevention means recognizing the connection between the crime rate and the unemployment rate, between unsupervised access by young people to movies saturated with violence and the way they behave toward one another, and how a kid behaves in school and whether he has a hot meal."

Horner's committee recommended that up to $25 million, a modest 5 per cent of the annual federal justice budget, be earmarked for crime prevention programs. A year later, the new liberal government followed up on this initiative, but set aside a sum of just $685,000, which would rise to $5 million over five years. It remains to be seen whether this or successive governments in an era of deficit reduction will seriously address the massive social problems like poverty and child abuse that feed the roots of crime. It is more likely that they will follow half of Horner's advice by refraining from building costly prisons, while continuing to crowd more convicts into existing cells.

There are measures that can be taken to reduce prison populations, in the absence of major crime prevention initiatives and fundamental social change. Greater use of parole is one obvious method, but public fears tend to militate against it. The effectiveness of parole programs is also severely limited by the fact that CSC is forced to spend most of its budget on keeping inmates locked up in jail and cannot afford to devote adequate resources to programs that assist and monitor offenders in the community. The communities themselves have few resources available to needy individuals with mental health problems and tend not to welcome former penitentiary inmates. It is easy for ex-offenders to conclude that they were better off in jail and the sad truth is that they are sometimes right.

Some jurisdictions in Canada are making use of alternatives to prison, such as community service orders and house arrest with electronic surveillance. These alternatives are usually applied, however, only in cases involving relatively minor crimes. They may succeed in freeing up some prison space by keeping lesser offenders out of jail. Keeping minor offenders out of jail could eventually have an impact on the penitentiary population, since exposure to the prison culture sometimes results in small-time criminals becoming more serious offenders who end up in the federal prison system. On the other hand, there is a danger that alternatives like house arrest will not be used to reduce prison populations, but will be applied to people who would otherwise have received only a fine or probation.

The ideal of creating a viable alternative to the prison system is enthusiastically endorsed by some prisoners' advocates and a few church and community groups. Many of these endorse the concept of replacing the adversarial and retributive justice system with one that responds to crime by attempting to heal wounds in the community that crimes expose as well as create. They point to the glowing testimonials given by people who have been involved in victim offender mediation, a process by which victims and offenders are brought together to negotiate recompense for crimes. The examples of victim offender mediation that I encountered involved criminals who had already been sentenced to federal penitentiaries for their crimes. It was evidently a healing process for both victims and offenders, but it will obviously be a long time before society sees mediation as an alternative to life imprisonment in the case of a serial rapist.

While politicians talk about crime prevention and a few citizens dream about transforming the justice system, federal penitentiaries are likely to remain society's only method for dealing with serious offenders, especially those who commit crimes of violence. Although the government is promoting lighter sentences and easier parole for non-violent offenders, it is also under pressure to legislate tougher sentences and tighter parole restrictions for more serious offenders.

Caught in the middle of all these pressures, the prison system is now getting unprecedented scrutiny from the outside. It is a system of last resort and is constantly being asked to deal with problems that our society has created and that the rest of our justice system has been unable to resolve. With the public placing more demands on the prison system and becoming more unforgiving of its mistakes, it is a system that feels itself under siege from the outside, while the mounting tensions within are reaching a crisis that threatens to erupt in anarchic violence.

It is a crisis that leaves little room for manoeuvre. No one is advocating building more prisons. It would cost too much and would only encourage judges to sentence more people to federal penitentiaries. A 1994 auditor-general's report on CSC identified some foolish spending and a few misplaced priorities, but did not point the way to any dramatic cost-cutting measures. Privatization of prisons, which has been popular in the United States, is less applicable in the context of the Canadian federal prison service, since our prison system attempts to do far more than merely warehouse prisoners with an eye to the bottom line. Perhaps the pressure of numbers that has already compromised rehabilitative measures will eventually force CSC to give up on them, but that would mean giving up on any hope that prisons can ever make any contribution to public safety.

The tragic irony of the current situation is that the public pressure to put more people in prison is actually making prisons less effective and more dysfunctional. Our fear of crime is therefore making us less safe.

In a society that refuses to come to grips with the problems that give rise to crime, the federal correctional service has been doing its best to grapple with offenders' problems as well as those of the prisons themselves. Prison and parole officials lament that their many successes disappear quietly into the night, while their occasional failures are posted in banner headlines in the daily press. Figures may show that most sex offenders never return to prison or that murderers seldom kill again, but those arguments offer no solace to the parent whose child has been raped and murdered by a man on parole. Even to cite statistics in the face of such agony will raise the righteous ire of victims' groups who maintain that any violent crime is one too many.

Statistics may show that the risk of being victimized is far less than we imagine. They may also indicate that crime rates are levelling off or even declining. We may be far more likely to die on the roads than be murdered, and our jobs may not be any safer than our wallets, but we insist on focussing upon crime as the public enemy that has to be defeated at all costs.

In selecting crime as our number one enemy, we have chosen to ignore the fact that it is inextricably linked to some of the most profound cultural problems and social injustices of our age. In choosing to fight crime by sending more people to prison, we have selected a tactic that provides few solutions to the real problems and may ultimately end up making them worse.

Perhaps, as we arm ourselves for the next campaign in the escalating war on crime, it would be wise to pay attention to the words of a great war hero. In 1911, Winston Churchill wrote: "The mood and temper of the public in regard to the treatment of crime and criminals is one of the most unfailing tests of civilization of any country. A calm dispassionate recognition of the rights of the accused and even of the convicted criminal against the state; a constant heart searching of all charged with the deed of punishment; tireless efforts toward the discovery of regenerative processes; unfailing faith that there is a treasure, if you can find it, in the heart of every man. These are the symbols which in the treatment of crime and criminals make and measure the stored up strength of a nation and are sign and proof of living virtue in it."

Tempered by these words, I am inclined to reflect again on my journey through Canada's prison system and remember that I did meet many good people trying to help and bring about change. Perhaps there is a hope of regeneration even in the depths of Canada's penitentiaries. Perhaps our fruitless quest for false security will not completely destroy that hope.

BIBLIOGRAPHY

Adelberg, Ellen, and Claudia Currie (eds.), *Too Few to Count: Canadian Women in Conflict with the Law*, (Vancouver: Press Gang Publisher), 1987.

Birnie, Lisa Hobbs, *A Rock and a Hard Place: Inside Canada's Parole Board*, (Toronto: Macmillan of Canada), 1990.

Carrigan, D. Owen, *Crime and Punishment in Canada*, (Toronto: McClelland and Stewart Inc.), 1991.

Clear, Todd R., *Harm in American Penology: Offenders, Victims and their Communities*, (Albany, New York: State University of New York Press), 1994.

Culhane, Claire, *No Longer Barred From Prison — Social Injustice in Canada*, (Montreal: Black Rose Books), 1991.

Fleming, Thomas (ed.), *The New Criminologies in Canada: State, Crime and Control*, (Toronto: Oxford University Press), 1985.

Foucault, Michel, *Discipline and Punish: The Birth of the Prison*, (New York: Vintage Books), 1979.

Hudson, Barbara A, *Penal Policy and Social Justice*, (Toronto: University of Toronto Press), 1993.

Jackson, Michael, *Prisoners of Isolation: Solitary Confinement in Canada*, (Toronto: University of Toronto Press), 1983.

McCormick, Kevin, and Livy Visano (eds.), *Canadian Penology: Advanced Perspectives and Research*, (Toronto: Canadian Scholars Press), 1992.

Melnitzer, Julius, *Maximum, Minimum, Medium: A Journey Through Canadian Prisons*, (Toronto: Key Porter Books), 1995.

Morris, Ruth, *Crumbling Walls: Why Prisons Fail*, (Oakville, Ont.: Mosaic Press), 1989.

Reid, Stephen, *Jackrabbit Parole*, (Toronto: Seal Books), 1986.

Scott, George D., *Inmate — The Casebook Revelations of a Canadian Penitentiary Psychiatrist*, (Montreal: Optimum Publishing International Inc.), 1982.

Simon, Jonathan, *Poor Discipline: Parole and the Social Control of the Underclass, 1890–1900*, (Chicago: University of Chicago Press), 1993.

Walker, Nigel, *Why Punish?*, (Oxford: Oxford University Press), 1991.

Yates, J. Michael, *Line Screw: My Twelve Riotous Years Working Behind Bars in Some of Canada's Toughest Jails*, (Toronto: McClelland and Stewart), 1993.

INDEX

behavioural change, 170-1
  of violent offenders, 167-9
Benoit, Gerald, 48, 102
Bernardo, Paul, 8
Big Bear (Cree chief), 114
biker gangs, and prison drug trade, 82
blacks, inmate population, 110-11
bleach, and HIV risk, 99
body piercing equipment, and
  HIV, 99
body searches, and civil rights, 78
Bordeaux jail, prison drug trade, 82
boredom, at William Head, 217
break-ins, within prisons, 80
brew, and riot in P4W, 130
British Columbia, 87
  community sex offender program,
  275-6
  prison for women, 128
  university courses, 175
  See also British Columbia
  Penitentiary; Burnaby Correctional
  Centre for Women; Ferndale
  Institution; Kent Institution;
  Matsqui Institution; Mission
  Institution; Mountain Institution;
  William Head Institution
British Columbia Penitentiary, 33
  and drugs, 78
British government report (1993), 287
brutality, prisoners' complaints about,
  38-9
budget cuts, and prison system, 159
Budreo, Wray, 278
bureaucracy:
  CSC paperwork, 161, 277
  and evaluation of Native program,
  176
  and prison management, 162
Burnaby Correctional Centre for
  Women (British Columbia)
  (BCCW), 128, 140- 3

C
callousness, of prison life, 37
Canadian Forces Base, Chatham, 14
Canadian parliamentary committee
  on crime prevention (1993), 288-9
capital punishment, United States,
  286
carpentry shop, Stony Mountain, 188
case load, of parole officers, 268
case management officers, 152-3
  checklist approach, 173
CBC, *fifth estate*, 227
cells:
  arrangement of new blocks, 221-2
  conditions in, 21-2
  Kingston Penitentiary, 6
  SHU, 64
chain gang, 182
chapel, Quebec SHU, 169
checklist approach, to programs,
  172-3
chemical castration, 200
child advocacy group, 279
child killers, vulnerability of, 48
children:
  at risk, 8
  and conjugal visits, 70, 73
  sexual abuse of, 195-6
Citizen Advisory Committee, 136-7
civil liberties, 280-1
civil rights:
  and dangerous offenders, 203
  and drug smuggling, 78
  of inmates, 151, 156
cleanliness, of prisons, 181
Clement, Philippe, 28, 226, 229-32
cognitive living skills program, CSC,
  29, 171-2
Collins Bay Institution (Kingston),
  90-1, 110
community:
  drug abuse in, 75-6

and Edmonton women's facility,
139-40
and ex-prisoners, 270
minimum security prisons, 228
and new facilities for women, 138
reintegrating offenders into, 213
and William Head, 215
community centre, William Head, 213
community residences, 276-7
community service orders, 289
community supervision, of
offenders, 276
community treatment programs,
need for, 282
computer program, Offender
Management System, 161
con code, 40, 170, 222-4
at the SHU, 62
positive values of, 47
Conacher, Neil, 47, 201
concrete ornament shop, 191
condominium-style units, Ste. Anne-
des-Plaines Institution, 218
condoms, for safer sex, 99
confidentiality, right to, 100-1
conjugal visits, 70
contact visits, 70
contagious diseases, 13
Cooer, Sheelagh, 126
CORCAN, 186-8, 190, 217
correctional officers. *See* guards
correctional plan, for prisoners, 152
Correctional Service of Canada
Board of Inquiry, 230, 232
Correctional Service of Canada
(CSC), 19, 149, 153, 200, 236
AIDS task force (1994), 94
anti-drug strategy, 84, 87-8, 91
cost of, 10-11, 20
employers of parole officers, 266
investigators, 138
Mission Statement, 150

offender management system, 277
and the parole board, 248
and parole service, 11
random drug-testing program, 76-7
riot at P4W, 132-3
staff, 112, 197, 227
therapy programs, 241
Corrections and Conditional Release
Act (1992), 150-1
cost:
of drugs in prison, 76
of maintaining an inmate, 11-12, 28
of maximum security per inmate,
286
of prisons, 10-11, 20
of programs for sex offenders, 198
of residential-style housing for
inmates, 218-19
Cote, J.J., 218-19
country club prison, 229
crack addict, and parole, 271-2
crack cocaine, in prisons, 76
crime cycle, 200
crime prevention, 289
crime and punishment:
changing perception of, 148
on public agenda, 8-9
crime rates, and crime reduction, 287
criminal justice system:
fragmentation of, 9
misuse of for social problems, 267
criminal organizations, 108
criticisms, of prison service, 157
Cronin, Timothy, escape of, 232, 234-5
cruelty, of penitentiary life, 36-7
CSC. *See* Correctional Service of
Canada
Culhane, Clare, 78
cultural problems, and crime, 292
culture, of Native people, 115
curfew checks, by parole officers,
269

H

halfway houses, 269
  and parole, 250-1
  and white-collar criminals, 270
harassment, of women in men's jails,
  155-6
hard labour, 182
harsh punishments, and risk to public
  safety, 288
hashish, 77, 81
healing ceremonies, Regional
  Psychiatric Centre (Saskatoon), 176-7
healing lodges, 118-20, 128, 176-7, 179
health and safety complaints, and
  sweat lodges, 118, 120
health services, 95-7
hepatitis, risk from, 100-1
heroin, 76-7, 82, 87-8, 92
high-profile cases, and the parole
  board, 252
high-risk offenders, 268-9
HIV infected prisoners, 98, 102-3
  and tuberculosis, 94
  See also AIDS
Homolka, Karla, 8, 58-9
homosexual activity, 47-8, 67
Horner, Bob, 288-9
hospital environment, 166
hostage-takings, 61
house arrest, 289
House of Commons standing committee on justice (1988 report), 7-8
housekeeping, by inmates at William
  Head, 214
housing, William Head Institution
  (British Columbia), 213-14, 217-18
"How to be the Warden of Stony
  Mountain" (Majkut), 149
Hudson, Barbara, 105

I

illegal acts, of prisoners, 41-2
illiteracy:

and Native isolation, 116
  and prisoners, 31, 171, 174
incarceration rate, Canada, 23
incest offenders, 196, 198
The Indian Posse gang, 109
industries, in prison, 186
informants:
  CSC use of, 41
  and drug trade, 89
  Mountain Institution, 220-1
information, reliability of in inmates'
  files, 252
inmate code. *See* con code
inmate committees, 83-4
  abolished at Edmonton, 84
  and prison life, 58
inmate population:
  federal prisons, 12-13
  SHUs, 63-4
inmate subculture. *See* subculture
inmates:
  at a high risk of TB, 94
  attitude to guards, 40-2
  attitude to SHU, 64
  confrontation as response of, 171
  and illegal acts, 41-2
  informal rules of, 40
  mail of, 70
  and minimum security, 228-9
Institution Preventive Security
  Officer (IPSO), 77
institutionalization, of guards, 154
intake assessment, 25
  and predicting risk, 251
  and programs for behavioural
  change, 171
intellectually challenged offenders, 49
  in prison system, 220, 267-8
intensive supervision:
  for high-risk offenders, 276
  units, 268-9
international crime, and prison system, 114